Search & Destroy
Why You Can't Trust Google Inc.

Scott Cleland with Ira Brodsky

Telescope Books
St. Louis, Missouri
www.telescopebooks.com

Printed in the USA

Cover art (T-Rex): Miguel De Angel
Dust jacket photo: Dan Smith
Dust jacket design: Triune Communications

ISBN: 978-0-9800383-2-3

Telescope Books
St. Louis, Missouri USA
www.telescopebooks.com

Sales inquiries: sales@telescopebooks.com

To Sara, Adam, and Grace

Table of Contents

Introduction

Information Is Power

This is the other side of the Google story.

Several books chronicle Google's meteoric rise to become the world's most recognized brand. The authors recount how Google was started in a Stanford University dorm room by a pair of exceptionally smart graduate students who invented a better Internet search engine—a search engine that produced more relevant results, delivered the results with lightning speed, and scaled to meet soaring global demand.

Most of the authors marvel at how Google succeeded at precisely the time that many Internet businesses were imploding. They celebrate Google's quirky corporate culture with its myriad perks including free gourmet meals; an in-house masseuse; subsidies for employees buying hybrid cars; and communal bicycles for getting around Google's Mountain View, California campus. The authors are duly impressed by Google's phenomenal growth—both in terms of size (revenue, profits, and number of employees) and power over the digital economy. At times, the awe borders on idol worship; one publication calls books about Google "literary hagiography."[1]

However, some of Google's actions make even its devoted fans uneasy. Google tracks everything you do online, tramples over your privacy, and then gets in bed with a major spy agency. Are Google's leaders—founders Larry Page and Sergey Brin, and hired Chairman Eric Schmidt—straying from their promise to "[make] the world a better place"?[2] Or are they disguising their real goals so effectively that no one has been able to connect the dots?

There is evidence that Google is not all puppy dogs and rainbows. Google's corporate mascot is a replica of a Tyrannosaurus Rex skeleton on display outside the company's headquarters.[3] With its powerful jaws and teeth, T-Rex was a terrifying predator. And check out the B-52 bomber chair in Google Chairman Eric Schmidt's office.[4] The B-52 was a long range bomber designed to deliver nuclear weapons.

Does Google have a hidden agenda?

* * *

One of the 20th century's most important books warned that in the future technology would be used to achieve absolute power. In George Orwell's dystopian novel *Nineteen Eighty-Four*, Big Brother and his ruling clique employ two-way "telescreens" to brainwash, control, and spy on the populace.

Writing in the 1940s, Orwell envisioned the telescreen as a combination television and video camera. The telescreen delivers non-stop propaganda to public places and the homes of the middle and upper classes. And the telescreen permits the Thought Police to monitor individual citizens.

What Orwell did not and could not know is that a potentially more powerful propaganda and surveillance tool would emerge in the 1990s: Internet-connected computers. While telescreens allow operators to watch and listen, the World Wide Web can be used to automatically collect data on millions of search engine, social network, and website users. A camera monitors your movements and conversations; a Web access device provides a direct link to your thoughts and mind.

At first the threat of Web-based surveillance seemed minimal because, it was believed, the information would remain scattered among many competing websites.

Then Google's founders made a momentous discovery: The more information they collect and analyze, the more powerful Google grows.

* * *

Do you really know Google?

Is Google the youthful company that gives you unbiased search results, free email, and useful advertising? Or is Google a virtual T-Rex that crushes your privacy, snatches copyrighted material, and dominates the Web?

Let's start with what Google says about itself. Google has what is probably the most immodest corporate mission in history: "to organize the world's information and make it universally accessible and useful."[5] Most companies talk about being the best in their field; serving their customers, shareholders, and employees; and acting responsibly. Google makes their mission statements seem banal and parochial in comparison. To put it bluntly, Google wants to control all of the world's information.

Google also aspires to be "a different kind of company."[6] Yes, others have said more or less the same thing about their companies. However, there is one big difference: Google's founders have exhibited deep-seated contempt for traditional business practices. It shows in the way they treat investors, other companies, and the public.

When Larry Page and Sergey Brin started Google they had what author David Vise called "an instinctive aversion to advertising."[7] Page and Brin were so averse that they wouldn't even advertise their own company using venture capital funds. Mainly, however, they worried that accepting advertising would corrupt their search service. Flash forward a few years, and Google is making money from advertising hand over fist. The only plausible explanation for this dramatic change of heart is that Google's founders believed their targeted ads and performance-based pricing created a new kind of advertising—the first advertising compatible with their "Don't be evil" motto.[8]

And what precisely does Google mean by "Don't be evil"? Is it a commercial version of the Golden Rule—a quick way to test whether a proposed action is ethical? Or is it Google's way of heaping scorn on the traditional business world? This disarmingly simple motto has launched a thousand debates. And they all lead to the same place: Is Google itself an ethical company? We will return to that question later.

Google's founders demonstrated that they were different in another way. When Page and Brin decided to take Google public, they thumbed their noses at Wall Street and the Securities and Exchange Commission (SEC). In the letter submitted as part of their initial public offering (IPO) filing they bragged that "Google is not a conventional company. We do not intend to become one."[9] They defied decorum by repeatedly referring to the (then) CEO and founders by their first names. They refused to accept the brokerage houses' standard terms and fees.

For a company that looks down on the mainstream corporate world, Google certainly knows how to fashion an image. From its multicolored logo to the brain teasers used to test prospective employees' intelligence, Google has given birth to an elaborate mythology.

Google wants us to believe that its Googleplex corporate headquarters is the digital economy's Emerald City. But who is hiding behind the curtain, and what are they doing?

* * *

In the 1990s, most of us saw the World Wide Web as a liberating technology. Built atop the "network of networks," there is no limit to how much information the Web can hold. And it's incredibly fast: You can jump from one end of the globe to another in a split second just by clicking on a hyperlink. The Web gives consumers access to information on virtually any topic. And anyone can publish on the Web—usually for a fraction of what print media costs.

The Web promised to change everything—and in many ways it has.

Our expectations only seemed to grow as the number of users and websites increased. Many of us believed the Web would perfect the free-market system: all markets would be global in scale; buyers and sellers would always be well informed; and all transactions would occur at the speed of light.

The Web would give everyone yearning for freedom a platform from which to speak, and it would undermine and ultimately defeat anyone engaging in censorship. No government would be able to stem the free exchange of information and ideas.

It was hard to see any downside. The barriers to entry were remarkably low. Anyone with a personal computer and a dial-up modem could get on the Web. High speed access over cable TV networks was rolling out, and telephone companies promised a competing high speed service using phone lines.

We celebrated the fact that the Internet was a self-organized, unregulated, "dumb network." The days when we had to play according to the Phone Company's rules were finally over. No single entity could control the Internet. Most of the intelligence resided at the edges of the network—in the hands of end users and a multitude of small websites.

What could possibly go wrong? The technology was evolving so rapidly that it seemed the moment a threat to competition or choice appeared it was already on the road to obsolescence.

If there was a first mover advantage, we theorized, there was also a second and a third mover advantage. No one worried about the network effect—a large company's ability to extend its market lead by acquiring customers at a faster rate—because online markets were in constant flux. New companies with new solutions emerged daily. Competition was always just one click away.

What we didn't see—what we refused to see—was the Internet's winner-take-all dynamic. I call it the Internet Choice Paradox[10]: The Web offers consumers what looks like infinite variety, but most users eventually select favorite search engines, social networks, and news sites. Information producers trying to reach a large audience soon find that they have very few choices. A relatively small number of sites become the Web's information gatekeepers and e-commerce toll collectors.

That could only mean one thing: the Internet would enter a period of concentration (of information) and consolidation (of companies). The technology might continue to evolve, but only a few business models would thrive. A small group of winners would seize control.

* * *

A search engine is a double-edged sword.

The amount of information online is skyrocketing. Google reported in mid-2008 that it had indexed one trillion Web pages.[11] That's a 1,000-fold increase over the number of Web pages indexed in 2000. And the Web is still growing.

To find specific information on a network as vast as the World Wide Web you need a search engine. Ideally, you tell the search engine what you are looking for and it promptly returns a list of relevant Web pages—with the most relevant pages at the top. A good search engine is your doorway to knowledge.

Some search engines are better than others at delivering relevant results. However, determining what is relevant is as much an art as a science. The method that a search engine employs to rank search results reflects the judgment and biases of the people who own and operate the search engine.

The possibility that one search engine would become most users' preferred doorway to knowledge poses a dilemma. A search engine can promote Web pages, demote Web pages, and even block Web pages. It might do so for good reasons, illegitimate reasons, or by accident. The average user would never even know that it was occurring.

To wit, a popular search engine decides which websites get seen and which websites get lost in the crowd. The operators of a popular search engine will realize sooner or later that they have the power to influence and even manipulate users. If the operators yield to temptation, then their success will depend only on how subtle they are. Blatant deception will eventually be detected. Subtle deception may never set off alarm bells, but it can have a profound impact if practiced on a sufficiently large scale.

Besides, what harm could there possibly be in making sure your own content always shows up at or near the top of the search results?

The flow of information isn't just from the search engine to the user. Each time you use a search engine you disclose something about yourself. And it tends to be more than just passing interests: your searches reveal your wants, needs, desires, and fears. Over time, you may unwittingly divulge your age, sex, religion, ethnic group, profession, political views, and medical concerns.

A large search service with retail and wholesale outlets can follow users around the entire Web. Its retail store is its main website. It can create additional stores by distributing a search tool that can be embedded in other websites and even Web browsers.

A popular search engine that can be accessed from almost anywhere on the Web is a powerful tool for users. But it can also be exploited by its owners to create dossiers on users that would make former FBI director J. Edgar Hoover look like a piker.

* * *

How did Google become the dominant search engine—and arguably the Web's information gatekeeper and e-commerce toll collector rolled into one?

When Google was founded in 1998, most online strategists favored the portal business model over the search engine business model. A search engine dispatches users to external sites almost immediately. A portal, however, contains a search engine plus content and services that keep users hanging around. Most strategists believed that the longer an online business held users' attention, the greater its chances of making money.

Users, however, had ideas of their own. Attracted to the Web by the number and variety of information sources, they weren't looking for do-it-all websites. Most preferred Google's search service because it gave them useful results quickly and otherwise had few distractions. A user could perform a search, follow some of the links on the results pages, and come back to perform another search.

Google's traffic soared. The company had plenty of users but lacked a business model. The founders tried to sell or license their search technology, but they could not find any takers. Larry Page and Sergey Brin disliked the advertising business model so intensely that they wrote: "advertising-funded search engines will be inherently biased towards the advertisers and away from the needs of consumers."[12] Then Google's founders were introduced by a company called GoTo.com to the idea of selling targeted ads using keyword auctions and pay-per-click pricing. Google took the idea and ran with it—and was promptly sued for patent infringement.[13]

By adding paid advertising to its rapidly growing search service, Google quickly became the Internet's top money making machine. The preeminence of paid search advertising over all other Internet business models was now clear.

* * *

Google tracks everything you do online.

By 2006, Google was handling 100 million searches per day.[14] By logging search terms and IP addresses, Google could assemble profiles for millions of individual users. Additional information, such as real names and email addresses, could be collected from users when they registered to use any of Google's free products.

The searches performed by an individual over an extended period of time reveal a great deal about that individual. Details such as the user's profession, hobbies, education, income bracket, age, sex, location, and marital status could have marketing value.

Google's founders understood that this information could be used to sell ads, and the profits from the ads could be ploughed back into the business to gather more information.

For example, they expanded Google's presence to other websites (such as Amazon.com), other types of content (such as video clips), and other hardware platforms (such as mobile phones). By extending Google's reach, they acquired more users and more information about users' online behavior, and they could offer advertisers a larger and more diverse audience. The case for advertising with Google became increasingly compelling.

Google's founders also exploited a network effect: they used their large base of users and advertisers to acquire even more users and advertisers, increasing the distance between themselves and their nearest competitors.

Google's expansion into wholesale search was pivotal. Google offered search services for busy websites such as eBay and America Online— enabling users to search within those sites and over the entire Web. Google's founders understood that by securing more search traffic they could sell more advertising. Consequently, they could pay the most heavily trafficked sites large sums for the exclusive right to handle their search needs. Yet more traffic was acquired by supplying smaller websites with a free search box.

Google also expanded its portfolio of advertising solutions. Ads are served on its retail site with Google AdWords. Ads are syndicated to other websites (such as blogs) with Google AdSense. Google purchased DoubleClick, a company that served banner ads on large websites. With these three distinct solutions, Google's advertisers could reach users almost anywhere on the Web.

Then Google systematically extended search to other types of content: books, human speech, pictures, video, satellite images, and maps. Though Google purchased tools to work with specific types of content, it never hesitated to digitize and organize content without the owners' permission. For example, Google bought YouTube knowing that the company's website was being used illegally to redistribute copyrighted videos.[15] And when Google made digitizing the world's books one of its goals, it just started doing it.

The information gathering implications of expanding into other types of content are greater than first meets the eye. For example, YouTube encourages other websites to embed its videos. To the casual Web surfer, it appears that those websites have downloaded and are hosting copies of YouTube videos. In reality, when you load a Web page with an embedded YouTube video, the Web page contacts YouTube and requests that an image of the video player be sent to your browser. What's embedded on the Web page isn't the actual video but merely code to retrieve the video.[16]

The punch line is this: Google is notified every time you visit a Web page with an embedded YouTube video.

Google has also extended its reach to other types of hardware, including landline telephones, mobile phones, and televisions. Google introduced its free phone service mainly to harvest phonemes, the basic elements of speech as pronounced by individual users, which can be used to develop more reliable speech recognition solutions.[17] Google licenses its Android mobile phone operating system for free. Now, not only can Google track you as you move about the Web, but it can also track you as you roam the streets. And with Google TV, you can watch television and the Web while Google watches you.

With one billion users, Google is the biggest data mining operation in history. It continues to increase the scale and scope of information that it collects. Instead of buying other search engines, Google buys access to information and content, hoping to lock up all of the major information silos before the window of opportunity closes.

Google understands that whoever controls search, video sharing, and location-based services controls the Internet. Search is the index; video is the universal language; and location is the context. And Google already dominates all three.

Google knows when you use its search engine. Google knows when you visit a site featuring Google ads or YouTube videos. If you use Google's Chrome Web browser, then Google can track the sites that you visit and even the links that you click on. Google knows when you visit a website using Google Analytics to measure and analyze its traffic. As Google Chairman Eric Schmidt put it, "We want a little bit of Google in many parts of your life."[18]

Think about what that means. An omnipresent search engine can detect that your marriage is in trouble, your finances are in disarray, or that you or a family member have been diagnosed with a serious illness. Now imagine that information falling into the hands of bad actors.

Other search engines may be just one click away, but a search engine that reaches most websites, most content, and most devices is able to collect and correlate more information about users; offers advertisers more traffic, greater reach, and more precise targeting; and is the one entity on the electronic landscape that approaches omniscience.

Google may know more about you than you know about yourself.

* * *

Google can play with your mind.

As the Internet's information gatekeeper, Google can send Web pages it doesn't like "to the back row of the arena"[19] or even make them invisible.

An information gatekeeper can manipulate public opinion. It can nudge pages promoting a specific viewpoint a little higher in the search results and nudge pages promoting the opposing viewpoint a little lower. It can block search results that undermine the credibility of organizations, people, and ideas supporting its viewpoint, claiming that the pages are spam or that they violate some selectively enforced policy. As you'll see, this has already happened.

Applying these tactics in the days and weeks before an election, an information gatekeeper can boost or hurt the chances of specific candidates and ballot propositions. These days close elections are common; a little nudge here or there may be all that's needed to ensure the desired outcome.

There are many ways that an information gatekeeper engaged in tampering can evade detection—or at least escape responsibility. Isolated incidents can be portrayed as innocent mistakes. An information gatekeeper can block specific pages for short periods or only in certain regions. Or it can block pages and then unblock them after reviewing complaints. (Keep reading: we will encounter a number of cases in which websites were blocked or demoted in search results and then restored—but only after the damage was done.)

Google dismisses these concerns, insisting that its search results are determined by unbiased algorithms. But that's not true. Algorithms are created by humans and embody the biases of their designers. Algorithms do behave consistently—provided that no one tampers with them. Unfortunately, you can't even count on that. Google adjusts its search algorithm almost daily to ensure relevant results and uses filters to block or demote websites that it considers junk.[20] Plus, Google admitted in 2010 that its search engine is not completely automated; human raters are employed to "assess the quality of individual sites."[21]

Refining search algorithms and installing filters may be legitimate search engine maintenance functions, but they do not eliminate bias. If anything, the maintenance functions can be used to camouflage abusive practices. What are needed are not disingenuous claims that the algorithms and filters are unbiased, but clearly defined rules to guide legitimate sites and discourage anyone trying to game the system.

Whenever Google is called on to make its search engine more transparent and accountable, it invokes the spam threat. But most people have no trouble recognizing spam. It's being subtly manipulated that's hard to detect.

* * *

Google knows things that no one else knows.

A dominant search engine can do more than just influence users. It can learn things about individuals, companies, countries, groups of users, and the entire population of Internet users. That knowledge can be used to spot trends, predict events, make money, and intimidate foes.

Google can track and analyze the online behavior of one billion users to identify trends that are not yet visible to others. For example, Google has used search data to detect[22] and characterize[23] flu epidemics. Google's Chairman admitted that the company looked at how search data could be used to spot financial market trends. He hastened to add that Google halted this research when it realized the use of such information might be illegal.[24]

An omnipresent search engine can discover things that the rest of us can only imagine. For example, it could develop detailed profiles of specific groups of people—based on country of residence, ethnic group, religion, age, sex, education, income, and so on. These profiles would be based not on anecdotes but on mountains of data. An omnipresent search engine could learn things about specific groups—such as women, Italians, or Sam's Club members—that even members of those groups do not suspect.

An omnipresent search engine may acquire the critical mass of data needed to detect historic correlations. It may not be possible to predict specific events, but it may be possible to anticipate the interplay of large forces within markets, economies, countries, and the world. Isaac Asimov called this branch of science "psychohistory" and made it the theme of his Foundation science fiction series.

Google may be the first company "to forecast market movements or even revolutions."[25]

* * *

Should we trust Google?

Google's executives like to portray the company as a purveyor of "disruptive technology" and what economist Joseph Schumpeter called "creative destruction." Schumpeter expounded the idea that in a capitalist economy innovation spurs growth even as it undermines established businesses. Though Schumpeter died in 1950, much of what we see happening today—such as the rise of Web publishing and the concomitant decline of printed newspapers—is convincing evidence that he was right.

Google uses Schumpeter's words for its own purposes. Schumpeter was explaining how innovation drives business cycles. Google is dodging responsibility. Google wants us to believe that any harm it causes is the natural and inevitable result of technological progress.

New technologies often create ethical dilemmas. For example, it may be possible to clone human beings. But should we allow it? One line of reasoning provides an easy way out: if technology makes human cloning possible, then it's just a matter of time before someone will do it, so we might as well learn to accept the new reality.

However, we don't accept crimes just because it's inevitable that people will commit them. Likewise, we shouldn't accept every application of a new technology just because it's technically possible. Nor should we let those with financial interests in the outcome be the sole arbiters of society's ethical dilemmas. Yet that's precisely what Google wants us to do.

Google stands Schumpeter's idea on its head, using new technology to cause what is best described as "destructive creation." By harvesting every bit of data it can get its hands on, Google destroys privacy. By copying, distributing, and profiting from others' digital creations without permission, Google destroys property rights. In its mad dash to hoard the world's information, putting speed and openness above safety, Google destroys data security. And by dumping a broad range of "freeware" onto the market, Google destroys competition.

A traditional telephone company makes money by providing reliable service and charging for minutes of use. Google makes money by gathering data and using it to sell targeted advertising. By digitizing voices and sending them over the Internet, Google can provide select telephone services at zero cost (or close to zero cost). From Google's perspective, it makes perfect sense to offer free telephone service and focus on gathering more data and selling more advertising.

Google's decision to offer free telephone service is not the natural and inevitable result of technological progress. It is the result of a business strategy.

It's no wonder, then, that Google tries to draw our attention away from its business strategy. If Google is tracking your every move on the Web, it's only because the technology makes it possible. If Google is undermining existing businesses by offering the same or similar products for free, it's only because the technology is disruptive. If Google is digitizing and/or distributing content that doesn't belong to Google, it's only because the technology makes it inevitable.

And if you worry about what Google might do next, the problem isn't Google's business strategy—the problem is your lack of trust.

Google is like a person you don't really know who asks, "Don't you trust me?" Or as Google Chairman Eric Schmidt asked the *New York Times*, "Do you believe we have good values?"[26] It's a clever way of shifting the burden of proof from the suspected perpetrator to the potential victims.

Trust must be earned. As the gatekeeper for much of the world's public and private information, Google could earn our trust by being transparent and accountable. Instead, Google is extremely secretive, and even Google's customers complain about Google's lack of responsiveness.

* * *

Is Google too powerful?

Google is amassing and centralizing a tremendous amount of information. We don't really know how much information Google has—we can only guess. And we don't really know how much useful knowledge Google is able to derive from the information—we can only imagine.

Google downplays concerns that by centralizing access to information it is amassing too much power by constantly reminding us that "competition is just one click away."[27]

Does it really matter that Google is the dominant search engine when competition is just one click away? Yes, because if you operate an online business and want to make sure that potential customers find you, it's more important to be seen on the search engine with 80% market share than the search engines with the remaining 20% market share. Who can afford to ignore 80% of the market?

Is there really a big advantage to providing both retail and wholesale search? Yes, because a search engine that builds on its retail dominance by providing search for the most popular websites as well as for thousands of smaller websites offers advertisers more traffic and greater reach. A large retail/wholesale search engine is an omnipresent search engine.

How important is access to different types of digital content? If you are selling automobiles, you want your ad to appear whenever someone searches for information on current car models. You probably also want to reach people looking at pictures of current models, watching videos about current models, and mentioning current models in their email. A search engine with tentacles reaching beyond Web pages to other types of content can gather more information about users (for better targeting) and display relevant ads to more potential buyers.

The same applies to different hardware platforms. Worldwide, about twice as many people have mobile phones as Internet PCs. A search engine that serves mobile phones not only reaches more users, but it also has access to more information, which creates additional advertising opportunities. For example, if you install Google Latitude on your mobile phone, then Google can track your location as you travel around town. Businesses such as restaurants can send electronic coupons to your mobile phone whenever you come within striking distance.

As the dominant search service, Google can charge advertisers arbitrarily high fees, impose one-sided terms and conditions, and get away with providing little or no customer service.

There are few checks on Google's ability to collect, store, and use information. Google wants others to be transparent and open—the better for Google to collect information—but Google is opaque and highly secretive. If Google is policing itself today, there is no guarantee that it will continue to do so tomorrow.

When most people worry about someone gaining absolute control over them, they think of the government. However, most governments have some checks on their power (such as an independent judiciary or an elected legislature). By aggressively collecting and centralizing information, a private company may acquire more unchecked power over citizens than anyone in history. Big Brother could turn out to be Big Brother Inc.

Google can legally perform actions that are improper or even illegal in other contexts. For example, it's illegal to eavesdrop on a telephone conversation without a warrant, but there are few if any guidelines about "eavesdropping" on search, email, and other online activities.

In many markets, Google has almost complete information about supply and demand. That is an invitation for wrongdoing. Google could self-deal by using the information that it gathers about companies (including information about their employees, suppliers, and customers) to compete against those same companies. And by being first to detect that startup companies are gaining market traction, Google could make the wisest and most timely acquisitions.

Given Google's search dominance, plus its unprecedented reach and exclusive access, there is a real danger that Google could tip the balance in financial markets, make or break specific companies, sway elections, and influence the public. Google could also use dossiers on individuals and groups to intimidate, harass, or persecute them.

Power tends to corrupt. Absolute power corrupts absolutely.

* * *

Most companies worry about how government regulations and policies might impinge on their businesses. As companies grow, they spend more money lobbying politicians, officials, and government agencies. Ostensibly, their purpose is to ensure that those in positions of authority are aware of how their decisions might affect employees, industries, and the broader economy.

Citizens worry about lobbyists buying votes, favors, and protection. Naturally, these concerns are heightened when the government is busy bailing out some companies while investigating and fining others.

However, what happens when a company such as Google amasses not only money but information about every individual? That could give it unprecedented leverage. While the average corporation tries to influence specific policies, a company with Google's power over individuals might be able to veto some policies and even make others.

Google is becoming an increasingly aggressive lobbyist. For example, Google is leading a broad effort within the online community to change the rules. Digital technology makes it easy to copy and redistribute books, music, and movies. Google and its allies say we need to rethink copyright law.

Google adds another twist to the game: rather than asking for permission to redistribute content such as movie and television clips, Google just goes ahead and does it. When the inevitable complaints stream in, Google promises to review them. By the time infringing content is pulled, irreversible damage has been done. This way of doing things—don't ask for permission, just act, and respond to specific complaints after the fact—has become a Google trademark.

To wit, Google is chipping away at copyright law by making it more difficult and expensive to enforce.

The outcome of this legal drama is far from decided. The Department of Justice's antitrust division has been watching Google for some time. However, Google has close ties to powerful politicians and has received some extraordinary favors.

Some political pundits warn that the United States is drifting toward crony capitalism. A cozy relationship between Google and the U.S. government could be mutually beneficial. Google could nudge public opinion and provide government with information about citizens. Government could enact policies friendly to Google. And Google has demonstrated its willingness to make backroom deals.

As Google's ranking team head Amit Singhal observed, Google is "the biggest kingmaker on this Earth."[28]

* * *

The maxim "information is power" is more relevant today than ever before. Until recently, most information was scattered, disorganized, and hard to get at. Google was among the first to fully appreciate how digital technology changes everything. When information is encoded as 1s and 0s, it is much easier to gather, organize, and use.

That led Google to additional conclusions. If it's easier to manipulate and monetize digital information, then it's worth the effort to digitize existing information (such as in books) and analog information (such as phonemes). Google also realized that the first company to organize a specific type of content (such as video clips) is likely to control access to that content in the future. And the process can be repeated as many times as desired.

Most important, Google understood that the opportunities to centralize control of information would not last forever. Eventually, governments would grasp what was happening and put a stop to it. Google would have to act quickly.

That is why the other side of the Google story urgently needs to be told.

In Part I of this book, I'll show you that Google's business model and your privacy are incompatible. Google's mission is to organize the world's information—including your private information.

I will demonstrate that Google does not respect others' intellectual property rights. For example, federal judge Louis Stanton said that YouTube and Google "not only were generally aware of, but welcomed, copyright-infringing material being placed on their website."[29] And Google dumps free products onto the market, undermining the value of existing products.

Next, I will explain why security is Google's Achilles' heel. Google's mission is to organize information and make it accessible; safeguarding it tends to get in the way. But it's not just Google's problem: the information Google possesses about you is also at risk.

I'll show you that Google is rife with conflicts of interest, has too much unchecked power, and has created a Googleopoly.

In Part II, I'll explain how Google's actions fit together. I'll demonstrate how Google manipulates users and obfuscates its unethical behavior. I'll expose Google's political agenda and the threat it poses to our freedoms. If we aren't careful, Google could become the most powerful crony capitalist in history.

In Part III, I'll show that by centralizing information Google is concentrating the Internet's power in too few hands. I'll present my recommendations for preserving the Web's diversity and choice. It's surprising how little is required. There would be little to worry about if Google respected privacy, property, and the rule of law; if Google acted more responsibly; and if Google were more transparent and accountable. And I'll explain why we must act now to ensure the Internet remains a force for freedom and dissent and not an instrument for tyranny and oppression.

No company becomes as successful as Google without doing many things right. Google is an innovative company that performs to high standards and produces products and services with genuine benefits. The goal is not to stop Google from innovating—it's to get Google to treat others the way Google expects others to treat it.

The stakes are too high to let the first company to collect and organize the world's information gain unchecked power. By centralizing control of information, Google threatens everything from competition to free elections.

Part I

Why You Can't Trust Google Inc.

Chapter Two

Why Google Is a Privacy Disaster

Google's business model is all about destroying your privacy.

Google makes money by selling targeted advertising. The more information Google has about you, and the more intimate the information, the more effectively Google can target ads. The more effectively Google targets ads, the more money it makes. And Google makes a ton of money.

Does Google care about your privacy? It claims it does. But Google's mission, technology, and track record say otherwise. In a study of 23 leading Internet companies, Privacy International (PI) ranked Google last in privacy, awarding Google its black ribbon for "Comprehensive consumer surveillance & entrenched hostility to privacy."[30]

When Google violates your privacy it is unapologetic. Asked if users should trust Google,[31] Chairman Eric Schmidt turned the issue around, implying that if anyone is unethical it's the offended users: "If you have something that you don't want anyone to know, maybe you shouldn't be doing it in the first place." Speaking to fears about omnipresent surveillance, Schmidt suggests that young people can change their names when they become adults to escape past indiscretions.[32] And if you don't like having your house displayed on Google Street View, you "can just move."[33]

It all adds up to this: Eric Schmidt wants us to believe that omnipresent surveillance is simply a modern fact of life. "If you're online all the time, computers are generating a lot of information about you. This is not a Google decision, this is a societal decision."[34]

So why does Google insist that it cares about privacy? The vast majority of consumers care about privacy, and Google understands that it needs to play along even as it expands its tracking capabilities.

Google's Privacy Policy is a masterpiece of prevarication. For example, one of Google's five Privacy Principles is "Make the collection of personal information transparent." But read on:

> We strive to show users the information used to customize our services. Where appropriate, we aim to be transparent about the information we have about individual users and how we use that information to deliver our services.[35]

Google "strives" and "aims" but makes no real promises. The Privacy Notice for Google's Web History product is similarly evasive. It says that you may delete information from your account but Google keeps a copy.[36] When you delete the information you are only denying yourself access to it.

One of the few privacy guarantees Google does make is, "We don't sell users' personal information."[37] As the paid search advertising market leader, Google has no reason to sell users' personal information. Google's user profiles are what keep advertisers coming back for more.

Google wants as much information about you as it can get. What you see as private information, Google sees as data to be harvested, indexed, and monetized. Google doesn't see your privacy as a right to be protected— Google sees your privacy as an obstacle to be circumvented.

The reason is clear: Google makes money off your private information. In Google's business model, you are the product.[38]

*   *   *

Google & Friends want you to believe that privacy is dead.

In an article titled "Why no one cares about privacy anymore,"[39] journalist Declan McCullagh argues that privacy is morally corrosive. In the past, privacy served as an excuse for obstructing freedom of the press. Today, privacy threatens everything from efficient online markets (using behavioral targeting) to healthy online debates (requiring participants to disclose their true identities).

Besides, McCullagh says, Internet users are becoming inured to "informational exhibitionism." McCullagh quotes Facebook CEO Mark Zuckerberg to help drive the point home: "People have really gotten comfortable not only sharing more information and different kinds, but more openly and with more people—and that social norm is just something that has evolved over time."[40]

McCullagh agrees with Google's Eric Schmidt: if you demand privacy, then you are probably trying to conceal something. But he's not relying solely on Schmidt. He also argues that if some people use social networks to tell their friends where they are and what they're doing every hour of the day, then sharing intimate details must be the new behavioral norm.

However, McCullagh is wrong on both counts. The reason most people demand privacy is not to hide embarrassing or incriminating evidence; it's to protect their sovereignty, autonomy, and identity. Without privacy, you can't be who you want, because you are forced to reveal everything. Without privacy, there's little opportunity for independent thought or dissent, because your ideas are immediately subjected to public scrutiny. Without privacy, there can be no human dignity, because others can barge in on you whenever they like.

You cannot establish and maintain your personal identity without privacy. Your account numbers, user IDs, passwords, and phone numbers are your private property. Keeping that information confidential is not only legitimate, it's necessary for your safety. If bad actors can access your private information, then there is no way for you to discern friend from foe. Once inside your circle of trust, con artists may defraud you. If privacy is dead, then so are safety and security.

Google wants us all to be information exhibitionists. I call this state, which is the exact opposite of privacy, *publicacy*.[41]

Under Google's publicacy, people are stores of information to be mined and exploited. There is no need to obtain your permission. However, if others can take and use your private information whenever they want, then you are no longer in charge of yourself. You cease to be a citizen with the right to "life, liberty and the pursuit of happiness." Instead, you are a serf.

McCullagh's claim that no one cares about privacy anymore is simply false. Polls consistently show that most people do care about privacy. It's a remarkable finding given that most people grossly underestimate the amount of their private information that is being harvested.

In 2008, a *Consumer Reports* poll revealed that Americans are "extremely concerned about Internet privacy."[42] Eighty-two percent fear that their credit card numbers may be stolen online. Seventy-two percent worry about their online behavior being tracked and profiled.

Exploding the myth that people demand privacy because they have something embarrassing or incriminating to hide, 68% of respondents reported that they have provided personal information to websites. Still, 93% feel that Internet companies should ask for permission before using their personal information, and 72% feel that Internet companies should give them the opportunity to opt out of having their online behavior tracked.

Contrary to the condescending view that people demand privacy because they have something to hide, polls show that consumers want control over their own information and don't want others deciding what's good for them.

In 2009, a national telephone poll found that "Americans reject tailored advertising and three activities that enable it."[43] Fully 66% of Americans do not want advertisements to be tailored to their interests. When asked about three common ways that Internet companies collect information to personalize ads, the percentage opposing such practices was even higher (86%). The survey also found that Americans want Internet marketers who employ behavioral targeting to operate in an open and transparent manner. Namely, consumers want to know precisely how their information is collected and used, and they want more control over their data.

In 2010, a national poll conducted by Zogby International and commissioned by my company (Precursor LLC) found,[44] among other things, that:

- o "About nine in ten (87%) adults surveyed nationwide are concerned with the security of their personal information on the Internet, while 13% are not."

o   "Eight in ten (80%) are concerned with companies recording their online habits and using the data to generate profit through advertising, and a fifth (19%) are not."

o   "Eight in ten (79%) support a national "Do Not Track List," similar to the current national "Do Not Call List," to prevent tracking where people go on the Internet, and 6% do not."

During the Web's early days you could make the case that online privacy concerns were exaggerated. The threat at that time was that individual websites could identify your computer, track your use of their site, and recognize you when you returned. Website owners countered that tracking enables personalization, and personalization benefits consumers.

Since then, personalization has become a common website feature. However, the dangers posed by personalization have multiplied as more users bank, shop, and even file their taxes online. Identity theft is a big and growing problem.

Several privacy groups—such as the World Privacy Forum—have proposed a "Do Not Track" list for Internet users.[45] These groups believe consumers should have the ability to opt out of the kind of data collection used for behavioral targeting.

Google wants more than just personalization, however. In a briefing at Google's London headquarters in July of 2010, Google search algorithm engineer Amit Singhal talked about efforts to develop a search engine that anticipates users' needs. "I call it searching without searching," he said. He even offered an example: a search engine that reminds you when your spouse's birthday is approaching and recommends a gift in time to ensure on-time arrival. Singhal admits that scenario might shock users who don't realize how much they are revealing and how aggressively Google gathers and analyzes their data.[46]

Eric Schmidt sums it up perfectly: "I actually think most people don't want Google to answer their questions... They want Google to tell them what they should be doing next."[47]

No wonder Google wants us to believe that privacy is dead.

* * *

Google's engineers are constantly developing more powerful tracking tools.

Google wants to know your actual identity, and there are several ways to get it. Many of Google's products require that you set up an account. You may be asked for your real name, email address, or phone number. You may reveal your home address when you use Google Maps to get directions.

If you use Google Checkout, a service that competes with PayPal, then Google may have access to your credit card and/or bank account numbers. Products such as Google Maps, Google Earth, Google Street View, and Google Calendar reveal your home and work addresses, your favorite destinations, and your travel plans.

You can change your name, but you can't fool Google. Google can associate your true identity with (among other things) the sound of your voice (if you used goog-411 before it was discontinued) and the appearance of your face (if you use Google's Picasa software and are tagged in a picture).

Google wants to know where you are at all times. Google can determine your approximate location from your IP address. If you use a wireless LAN, Google may be able to determine your location with greater precision. If you use Google's Latitude mobile phone application or Android operating system, Google tracks your physical location.

Google is digging into your work. Google's personal computer search solution, Google Desktop, scans and indexes all of the files on your PC. If you select the "Improve Google Desktop" option, then the program is automatically updated by Google, and Google collects "a limited amount of non-personal information."[48] Security vulnerabilities in Google Desktop could enable hackers to access your private information.[49] If you use Google

Documents, then Google has access to your business and personal documents, including drafts. Yes, Google is even digging into your wastebasket.

Google's developer partners are also getting in on the fun. Many applications developed for Android mobile phones collect information. Though users are told what information an application collects, they aren't told how it is used.[50] Google puts the onus on the user to police Android applications. A Google spokesperson said in response to complaints, "We consistently advise users to only install apps they trust."[51]

Google tracks your interests with products including iGoogle (a customized start page), Google Alerts (news stories), Google Groups (discussion groups), and Google Reader (website aggregator). If you use Google Buzz, then Google knows who your friends are. If you use Google Health, then Google has access to your medical records.

Consider once again the words of Google Chairman Eric Schmidt. "There is what I call the creepy line... The Google policy on a lot of things is to get right up to the creepy line and not cross it."[52] For example, Google has developed and patented a method for tracking the way you move your mouse pointer.[53]

Google's goal is nothing less than omniscience. "We are very early in the total information we have within Google... we will get better at personalization."[54]

* * *

GoogleWatch deserves kudos for warning that Google is a threat to users' privacy. As far back as 2002, the organization declared that "Google is a privacy time bomb," explaining:

> *With 200 million searches per day, most from outside the U.S., Google amounts to a privacy disaster waiting to happen. Those newly-commissioned data-mining bureaucrats in Washington can*

only dream about the sort of slick efficiency that Google has already achieved.[55]

GoogleWatch continues to raise alarms. From its home page (http://www.google-watch.org/) GoogleWatch links to pages exposing Google's most disturbing practices. For example, the page "Behavioral targeting" explains that Google tracks you whenever you visit a Web page hosting an AdSense or DoubleClick advertisement. You don't need to click on the ad; your presence is detected the moment your browser loads the page.

The page "Google as Big Brother" describes how Google developed innovative ways to circumvent privacy safeguards. For example, Google is credited with introducing the "immortal cookie." A Web cookie is a text string stored on your computer's hard drive. A *session cookie* enables a website to recognize you as you move from page to page. A *persistent cookie* enables a website to recognize you when you return to the site. Websites operated by the U.S. federal government are prohibited from using persistent cookies, so they can't embed YouTube videos. Google got around the restriction by creating cookies that expire in 2038.[56]

While Google claims that it uses its cookie to remember user preferences, GoogleWatch counters that "the real purpose of the cookie is to plant a globally-unique ID on your hard disk for profiling purposes."

The page titled "Rotten cookie" provides an update. Google announced in 2007 that it was issuing new cookies set to expire in two years. According to GoogleWatch this is misleading: Active users' cookies are automatically renewed each time they visit a Google page. In practice, Google's cookie expires two years after you discard or stop using your hard drive.

*   *   *

Google's free email service, Gmail, is one of the most notorious examples of Google's disregard for user privacy.

Google introduced Gmail in the hope of making money the same way it makes money with its search engine: by presenting users with relevant ads.

However, there was one key difference: The ads would not be relevant to search terms voluntarily submitted by users; they would be relevant to the content of users' email messages. Without asking users' permission, Google programmed its computers to automatically scan users' email messages for advertising keywords.

As a Fox News headline put it, "Gmail Selling Access to Key Words in Your Account to the Highest Bidder."[57]

Each Gmail message that you compose becomes part of a three-way conversation between you, the intended recipient, and Google. If you write a friend about the car you plan to buy, you may see an ad for a competing car along with your friend's response. The group Consumer Watchdog likens this to the phone company listening to your conversations and whispering product suggestions in your ear.[58]

The reaction to Gmail was swift—and overwhelmingly negative. Launched on April 1, 2004, many journalists wondered whether Gmail was an April Fools Day joke.[59] Legislation against Gmail was tabled in Massachusetts[60] and California.[61] *The Wall Street Journal*'s influential PC product reviewer, Walt Mossberg, complained.[62] Privacy groups were up in arms.[63]

Google's practice of scanning Gmail messages wasn't the only problem. Exploiting its vast storage capacity, Google offered unlimited email archiving and introduced Gmail without a delete button.[64] By registering Gmail account holders and archiving all of their old messages, Google was acquiring a rich source of information for constructing user profiles.

Most users instinctively understand that deleting old messages is an important way to protect their privacy. If messages are permanently stored on Google's network, then there is a greater risk of them being accessed by hackers or government officials. The U.S. government may subpoena information stored by online service providers. In fact, under the USA PATRIOT Act the government has the right to search your ISP even when it doesn't have a warrant to search you.[65]

How did Google respond to the concerns of consumers and privacy advocates? Google's data mining engineers could not see what the uproar was about. However, almost two years after Gmail was introduced Google finally acquiesced to popular demand, adding a delete button.[66] Instead of recognizing that Gmail had been a public relations debacle, however, the company acted as if its critics now owed Google a quid pro quo.

Google refused to cease robotic scanning of Gmail messages. Instead, Google tried to persuade privacy activists that scanning email messages in order to present users with relevant ads is perfectly reasonable. Most privacy advocates held their ground. Brad Templeton, Chairman of the Electronic Frontier Foundation (EFF) at the time, was a notable exception. Templeton likened the risk posed to users by Google's automated email scanning to the risk posed by online credit card transactions.[67]

Privacy groups normally assume that businesses and government agencies will abuse users' private information if given half a chance, and they rightly put the burden on businesses and government agencies to prove otherwise. Perhaps Templeton was dazzled by Google's grandiose mission and anti-corporate culture.

Gmail's delete button may not be what users expected. Google's privacy policy says that Google reserves the right to retain email messages that the user has "deleted" for a specific period of time in its online systems and for an indeterminate period of time in its offline systems. When you delete a Gmail message, the only thing you can be sure of is that you have denied yourself further access to that message. Like the Hotel California, Gmail lets you check out any time you like, but you can never leave.[68]

One thing is certain: Google never guaranteed Gmail users' privacy. On the contrary, Google maintained all along that it employs computer robots (rather than humans) to scan email messages and, therefore, any privacy concerns are misplaced.[69]

Google's official Privacy Policy contains no verifiable user privacy guarantees.[70] For example, the paragraph that ostensibly limits Google's ability to share information simply says that Google may share your information with any businesses or persons that Google deems appropriate, for any purposes that Google deems appropriate. The only restriction is that the businesses and persons with whom the information is shared are required to comply with Google's Privacy Policy.[71]

It's what we don't know about Gmail that is most worrisome. Is information gleaned from Gmail messages used for other purposes? Does Google forbid recreational reading of users' email by its employees? Has Google ever detected unauthorized Gmail snooping? Would the user be informed if it occurred? These questions remain unanswered.[72]

There are additional Gmail privacy concerns. Gmail scans all of your email—both the email that you compose and send to others and the email that others compose and send to you. By subscribing to Gmail, you are giving Google permission to scan email you receive from people who are not Gmail subscribers, who have not given Google permission to scan and store their email, and who might be horrified if they knew that their messages were being scanned and permanently stored by a third party.[73]

Less well known is the risk posed by a Gmail feature called auto-save. Many desktop programs, including email programs, automatically save draft documents as you compose them. This comes in handy if the program crashes or your PC loses power before you save your most recent work. While desktop applications typically save drafts to your PC, auto-save sends draft messages over the Internet and saves them on Google's servers. If you compose a message out of anger, and later decide to replace it with a calmer message, Google may retain a copy of the embarrassing draft.[74]

The Gmail uproar wasn't really about robotic scanning. It was about the liberties that Google takes in collecting and using private data, how little Google voluntarily discloses, how Google avoids asking users' permission, and how Google refuses to set meaningful limits on data collection and use.

* * *

Until 2004, Google's efforts to "organize the world's information" were limited to indexing the Web, tracking users' searches, and scanning email messages. However, Google understood that Web pages are not the only source of information. Taking its mission quite literally, Google decided to aggressively digitize and index information not yet on the Web—through books, magazines, catalogs, satellite images, street level images, movies, television programs, video clips, voice phonemes, and more.

Google's first major step in this direction was the acquisition of a company called Keyhole. Founded in 2000, Keyhole tried to make money by offering a limited set of satellite images to a select audience on a subscription basis. Google developed a very different plan for Keyhole, viewing the acquisition as the first step toward organizing and making accessible information about the 57 million square miles of the Earth's surface.[75] By linking high resolution images to electronic maps, Google made it easy for users to view the streets, buildings, and terrain at any location.

Google Earth was launched in mid-2005. It was as entertaining as it was informative, giving users a bird's eye view of the world from the comfort of their PCs using images from both aircraft and satellites. But it also raised new and sometimes alarming privacy and security concerns.

Most people don't mind that their neighbors can see the exterior of their house, their backyard, and cars parked on their driveway. But many people find it creepy that Google Earth allows anyone in the world to take a look. As the technology continues to evolve, the images will only become clearer, more detailed, and easier to access. Compounding these concerns, Google introduced a related product in 2008 called Street View that provides 360° horizontal and 290° vertical panoramic views from the street.

Google's publicacy philosophy says that anything that can be seen from a public street or sidewalk is fair game (with a few Google-defined exceptions). The law tends to agree. However, Google Earth and Street View are game changers. We don't mind that our neighbors can see our property because they have a shared interest in protecting the neighborhood. But when the images are readily accessible to anyone, anywhere, we feel more vulnerable. As Robert Halfon, an MP in the United Kingdom, sees it, Google "[is] invading our privacy on an industrial scale."[76]

Some locations are particularly sensitive. Google Earth exposed the roofs of the White House[77] and other government buildings and the layout of military installations. Apparently, there was no meaningful effort within

Google to anticipate the privacy, safety, and national security implications. The ensuing uproar over Google Earth suggested Google had learned nothing from the Gmail debacle. It was another example of Google's launch-now-fix-problems-later approach.

Street View produced even more bad publicity. Google was not just insensitive to privacy concerns; Google's engineers took the scope and scale of voyeurism to new heights. Goodbye privacy, hello publicacy.

Street View showed the faces of people outside abortion clinics, women in bikinis, and men leaving strip clubs. At first, Google defended the images, insisting that people standing in public places (or plainly visible from public places) have no right to privacy. However, Google removed images of domestic violence shelters, began experimenting with face-blurring technology in 2008, and created a process for reviewing complaints and removing (at its discretion) specific images. In 2010, Google removed images of dead bodies on the streets of Brazil after receiving complaints.[78]

Google Earth and Street View revealed what have become two standard Google practices. Google has few if any internal controls and leaves it up to users and others to police its products. And instead of first asking for permission, Google prefers to ask for forgiveness later.

Google doesn't ask permission because doing so would acknowledge that the decision rightfully belongs to someone else. Likewise, Google asks for forgiveness because doing so implies that the issue isn't whether Google acted within its rights but how well Google handled the incident.

Street View called into question Google's claim that it cares about users' privacy. The uproar over Street View became so intense that, in order to protect "spycar" drivers from irate citizens, Google kept secret the details of when and where images were being recorded. Google protected the privacy of its employees to better destroy the privacy of ordinary citizens.

At best, Google doesn't believe average users are smart enough to appreciate the value of products such as Street View until they are presented with the results. Google may also believe that having the images in hand gives it a better bargaining position. Many Google Earth and Street View images are sensitive, and some are embarrassing to specific individuals.

Knowing that a leading Internet company has systematically collected and organized such images may put pressure on those empowered to negotiate with Google to seek compromise rather than risk having their own private information publicly scrutinized.

Google Earth and Street View also call into question Google's attitude that if technology makes something possible then we have no choice but to accept it. For example, Google simply removed images of domestic violence shelters from Street View. But when a user asks that images be removed, Google does not temporarily take them down, nor does it make promises regarding how quickly images will be reviewed. These choices are not imposed on Google by the technology. And Google knows quite well that once an online image has been found it may be copied and redistributed.

For a company that wants us to let it put our homes on public display, Google certainly is secretive about its Street View operations. Google refuses to say how many cars are in its fleet, where they are filming at any given time, or how long the filming will continue. When an article in the *Washington Examiner* displayed a rare photograph of a Google Street View car,[79] Google blamed the company's secrecy on citizens, saying it feared "angered residents might harass the drivers or tamper with the expensive cameras."

Google's double standard was again revealed when CNET reporter Elinor Mills decided to see what information she could find online about Google's Eric Schmidt.[80] When she linked to a public website displaying his home address, Schmidt complained bitterly about the disclosure of private information. Google even retaliated by announcing it would cease cooperating with CNET for one year. Google defends Google Earth by pointing out that the images are either already available or could readily be obtained by others,[81] but condemns CNET for linking to Eric Schmidt's publicly available home address.[82]

The reaction to Street View filming in Europe has been particularly negative. In Britain, Privacy International called Street View "a burglar's charter" and asked Google how information such as car registration numbers would be hidden.[83] Northern Ireland complained that images of British army bases and police stations created security risks. In Switzerland and Germany, officials have said that Street View violates existing privacy laws.[84] In fact, the Swiss government is taking legal action against Google to protect Swiss citizens' privacy.

In Japan, a group of journalists, professors, and lawyers asked Google to take down Street View.[85]

The fears are well founded. Google Earth and Street View images have been used by terrorists to target attacks. For example, the Palestinian al-Aqsa Martyrs' Brigade has used Google Earth to plan attacks on Israel.[86] In early 2007, British intelligence sources claimed Iraqi insurgents were using Google Earth to find soft targets (such as tents and lightly armored vehicles[87]) inside British military bases near the city of Basra.

In 2009, a newspaper reported that Google Earth revealed the location of a British nuclear submarine base in Scotland. A terrorist attack on the Trident base could be devastating to people living within a large radius. Though Google subsequently blotted out the base, it became visible again after an update to Google Earth's database.[88]

Israel's domestic security chief, Shin Bet director Yuval Diskin, observed: "Intelligence once enjoyed only by countries and world powers can now be obtained through Internet systems like Google Earth..."[89]

Google has used Google Earth and Google Maps to referee international disputes, making its own decisions about borders and place names. For example, Google Earth labeled the Temple Mount in Jerusalem's Old City as in "Palestine." In 2007, the Gaza Strip was labeled "occupied" even though Israel withdrew completely in 2005. Abu Nasser, second-in-command of the al-Aqsa Martyrs' Brigade terrorist group, said he was "thrilled" by Google Earth's depictions.[90]

Now it's been revealed that Google's Street View cars have been doing more than taking pictures. The roving cars have been scanning and recording Wi-Fi wireless local area network addresses.[91] This information could enable Google to associate specific networks and computers with specific homes. That, in turn, could enable Google to identify individuals who don't have Google accounts.

The scandal, called Wi-Spy, has only gotten worse over time. Google confessed that while monitoring Wi-Fi networks it "accidentally" recorded user data. Google later admitted that the data included email messages and even user passwords.[92] And it turned out that Google had a motivation for collecting as much Wi-Fi data as possible: it hoped to acquire a competitive advantage over Skyhook Wireless, a pioneer in Wi-Fi-based locating technology.[93] Yet we are asked to believe that equipping the cars with Wi-Fi receivers and storing user data gathered in 33 countries over a period of three years was completely unplanned.

Why did Google ultimately make these disclosures? Google submitted a report in April of 2010 to several governments about its Wi-Fi data collection activities. The company explained that it collects Wi-Fi data for use in location-based services.[94] On May 5, 2010 the Data Protection Authority in Germany asked to see the raw data. Nine days later, Google stated that it had mistakenly collected user payload data from unsecured Wi-Fi networks.[95]

The collection of Wi-Fi data raises another concern. In the report, Google explains that Wi-Fi data can be used to provide location-based services to mobile devices that are "not GPS enabled" or that aren't receiving GPS signals. Since Street View cars record both their GPS coordinates and the addresses of all Wi-Fi networks heard, Google can determine the location of a portable device by cross-referencing any Wi-Fi addresses it receives to the coordinates in its database. In North America, the default setting for GPS-equipped mobile phones permits the phones to report their location only when the user dials an E911 number. In theory, Google could get around this restriction, using Wi-Fi addresses to track phones even when GPS tracking is disabled.

Noting that Street View cars drove past the homes of members of Congress and that some of the homes appear to have vulnerable Wi-Fi networks, the group Consumer Watchdog raised the possibility that Google has been eavesdropping on elected officials. Consumer Watchdog's John Simpson said, "We think the Google Wi-Spy effort is one of the biggest wire tapping scandals in U.S. history."[96]

Google Chairman Eric Schmidt tells a very different story. He says that the Wi-Fi data collection was unauthorized, that very little user data was actually collected, and that Google was the biggest victim because its reputation was sullied. Reacting to the suggestion that Google could be prosecuted, Schmidt said, "No harm, no foul." Yet he insisted that Google will not delete the data unless ordered to do so.[97]

What other information is Google collecting and using without telling us? In the words of CNBC host Maria Bartiromo, "People are treating Google like their most trusted friend. Should they be?"[98]

*   *   *

Google wants to track your physical whereabouts.

In early 2009 Google introduced Latitude, a mobile phone service that lets you see where your friends are and lets your friends see where you are at any time of day.[99]

If you download and activate Latitude, then Google knows when you are at home, when you are at school or work, when you are at the mall or a friend's house, and when you are in transit. It's like having someone shadow you.

It all started in the late 1990s when the Federal Communications Commission (FCC) mandated that mobile phone operators develop the capability to automatically locate mobile phone users calling E911 emergency services. Today, most operators meet the requirement by selling handsets with built-in Global Positioning System (GPS) receivers. Most mobile operators also promise that users will not be tracked unless they go to the phone's setup menu and change location determination from "E911 only" to "Location on."

In order to use Google Latitude, the phone must first be set to "Location on." Latitude displays your current location on a map that friends (designated by you) can see. It indicates not only your last reported location but your current status. Latitude lets you contact friends who are visible on your map via text message, phone call, or instant message.

Google Latitude is a Google Maps application that works on many mobile phones (including Android, iPhone, color BlackBerry, Windows Mobile 5.0, and Symbian S60 models) as well as Apple's iPad.[100]

Google is not the only company that offers a location tracking application for mobile phones. Sprints' Friend Finder lets you track family members and friends, and Verizon's VZ Navigator provides turn-by-turn driving directions. But Google Latitude is unique. Only Google can display ads on your mobile phone that are relevant to both your current location and your likes and interests.

Latitude may be useful and fun, but it enables Google to track you 24/7. You can hide your location from friends or exit the application, but unless you reset your handset to the default mode (Location = "E911 only") you may still be feeding your location to Google. When a friend doesn't see you on his or her map, it tells the friend very little. Google knows where you were when you signed out and can see who you are hiding from. You can limit friends to city-level information, but as long as your handset is set to "Location = On" Google knows exactly where you are.

In an article in the *Wall Street Journal*, reporter Katherine Boehret said: "Usability issues aside, location-based services like Latitude can be just plain creepy, especially when a Big Brother like Google is tracking your whereabouts. So Google incorporated easy-to-change privacy settings so that locations can be automatically detected, manually entered or completely hidden from other people."[101] Ms. Boehret even described Latitude as a form of "stalking."

There is nothing in Google's mobile Privacy Policy that prohibits Google from collecting and using location data. "We use your information to process and personalize your requests. We also use the information for support, to develop new features, and to improve the overall quality of Google's products and services."[102] However, the Electronic Frontier Foundation reported that Google agreed to "overwrite the old data each time you report a new location."[103] The EFF lobbied Google to make the change to prevent law enforcement agencies from accessing Latitude users' location logs.[104] But a few months later, Google announced two new features, Google Location

History and Location Alerts.[105] If you opt in, Google does keep a log of your location, and can add daily routes, favorite locations, and vacation destinations to your profile.

Mobile phone location tracking has not been perfected. The resolution of the location data is not always high: sometimes your location is reported only down to the nearest cell site. And though GPS can be quite accurate, an error of just 100 feet may be the difference between appearing on a street or in a nearby river. Latitude's location updates are sufficiently infrequent that a mobile user may appear quite a distance from his or her current location.

The biggest problem with Google Latitude, as with many of Google's products and services, is that you really don't know how much of your private information is collected, with whom it is shared, and how it is used. Even if you don't enable Google Location History, another application or user could capture and store this data, making it available to advertisers and stalkers.

Having a person shadow you 24/7 would be very creepy—and reminiscent of the old Soviet Union. Having a software robot log your geographic coordinates by time of day may seem less objectionable. But consider this: a human spy may lose your trail or make mistakes due to fatigue. A software robot can track you 24/7 without interruption. It's consistently accurate and reliable, because it's always as fresh as a daisy. While a human spy may be better for short-term assignments, a software robot can track you for years, contributing to what could justifiably be called a log of your life.

* * *

Cloud computing, also known as software as a service (SaaS), is a potential threat to user privacy and security.

The first commercial computers used batch processing. You brought your work (encoded on punch cards) to the computer. Time-sharing was introduced in the 1960s. It enabled information workers equipped with desktop terminals to remotely access applications and data stored in computing centers. The personal computer (PC) became a huge success in the 1980s because it let users install applications and store documents on their own desktop machines. Now cloud computing proposes to turn your PC back into a remote terminal, with most of your applications and documents residing on network servers.

IBM was king of the mainframe era. Microsoft led the PC revolution. Google is driving the switch to cloud computing.

Google's cloud computing service is alluring. Software applications that normally cost hundreds of dollars are offered by Google at little or no cost. In addition to saving money, the service lets you access your applications and data from anywhere in the world, provides automatic upgrades, and makes it easy to share documents (such as calendars) with friends, family, and colleagues.

However, it's a Faustian bargain.

With cloud computing you have less control over your applications and personal documents. Cloud computing applications are often based on insecure open source solutions.[106] And get this: If you use Google Documents, then you must grant Google "a perpetual, irrevocable, worldwide, royalty-free, and non-exclusive license to reproduce, adapt, modify, translate, publish, publicly perform, publicly display and distribute any Content which you submit."[107] Google claims these terms enable it to better serve users and promote its application services.

If you use Google Documents, then there are no guarantees that your private documents will remain confidential.

As the Consumer Reports National Research Center poll described earlier found, many users falsely assume there are strict limits on what information may be collected online and how it may be used. Some incorrectly believe that Internet companies must obtain permission to use the information.[108]

Cloud computing is also offered to enterprises. But as Google product manager Adam Swidler admitted, "We won't let you audit to the degree that you would audit your own infrastructure. ...It's never going to be the same as auditing your own infrastructure. You'll have to extend some level of trust to third-party verification."[109] In other words, let the buyer beware.

Google may not be mining users' documents, but it is definitely acquiring mountains of raw data. Referring specifically to cloud computing, Eric Schmidt stated, "You can get a lot of information about user behavior that you can mine or build interesting products for."[110]

*   *   *

Google can track almost everything you do online.

Google develops software code to spy on you. Normally, when you click on a link on a search results page, the search engine doesn't see which link you clicked on. However, most Web browsers support JavaScript, and JavaScript can be used to provide "click-through tracking." With click-through tracking, when you click on a search results link your browser takes you to the new page and sends Google a copy of the link.[111]

Many Google products serve as Google informants. Google Analytics is a free service that provides websites with visitor statistics. It's estimated that more than 300,000 websites use Google Analytics, including more than 50% of the 10,000 most popular websites.[112] Google Analytics is easy to install; webmasters simply paste Analytics' JavaScript code onto each webpage. Whenever a user visits a webpage containing this code, the user's browser informs Google.[113]

AdSense is Google's advertising syndication service. It enables website owners to host and earn revenue from Google ads. The number of websites hosting AdSense ads has not been disclosed, but it's clearly a large number; Google reported that AdSense accounted for 30% of its revenue during the first quarter of 2010. When a user visits a page with AdSense ads, the user's IP address is automatically reported to Google.[114] The same applies to banner ads served to major websites by DoubleClick, the company acquired by Google for $3.1 billion in 2007.[115]

Using just these tools, Google can track the majority of Internet users over most of the Web. But they are not Google's only tracking tools.

Google's free Web browser, Chrome, takes online tracking to new heights with its combined search and address bar. Google not only sees the search terms you submit, Google sees Web addresses and search terms as you type them. And this feature works with any search engine that supports search suggestions—not just Google.[116] Think of Chrome as a Web browsing information vacuum cleaner.

YouTube is one of Google's most powerful tracking tools. Acquired by Google in 2006 for $1.65 billion (an astounding figure given that YouTube did not have a viable business model at the time), YouTube is the leading video-sharing website. YouTube makes it easy for blogs and other websites to embed YouTube videos in their Web pages. As we've seen, Google is informed every time your browser loads a Web page with an embedded YouTube video.[117]

That's not all. If you right click on the video, you can choose to watch it directly on YouTube where you may rate the video, comment on the video, share the video via email or a social network such as Facebook, or watch related videos. All of these actions are observed and logged by Google.

If you doubt that Google tracks users quite so aggressively, then you should consider this. In an article about the legal battle between Google and Viacom, the Associated Press (AP) reported: "In a statement, Google said it was "disappointed the court granted Viacom's overreaching demand for viewing history. We are asking Viacom to respect users' privacy and allow us to anonymize the logs before producing them under the court's order.""" [118]

In other words, Google not only keeps a log of the YouTube videos you watch, it associates the log with your true identity. Ironically, in seeking to have Viacom's request denied, Google cited a video privacy law (the 1988 Video Privacy Protection Act) passed when legal scholar Robert Bork's video rental records were leaked to the press during his Supreme Court confirmation hearings.[119] The Electronic Privacy Information Center (EPIC) called the Act "one of the strongest protections of consumer privacy against a specific form of data collection."[120]

Other Google products double as tracking tools. Searching Google Books is like permitting a library employee to shadow you while you use the library. The search terms you enter (author, title, ISBN number, or keyword), the books you click on, the searches you conduct within books, the pages you examine, and the time you spend on each page may be logged. It's much easier for Google to keep an accurate log of your book searches than it would be for a library employee. When you look for something specific in a book, a person standing behind you would only see the pages. Google sees your search terms.

Google's book digitization effort preserves old books and makes them more accessible. But it also makes it easier for governments to monitor citizens' reading activity. The American Library Association (ALA) has vigorously opposed the USA PATRIOT Act provision permitting government agencies conducting terrorism investigations to access library patrons' records. Ironically, Google has acquired the ability to log users' book search and reading activity with the help of several large libraries.

Your online search requests reveal more about you than you might think. In his book *Googling Security*, Greg Conti demonstrates that an individual's search queries over an extended period can be used to assemble a detailed profile. In 2006, America Online (AOL) released a dataset containing about 20 million search requests by 658,000 users. Using five people (identified only by their AOL user ID numbers), Conti showed that a user's search activity can reveal his or her location, age, sex, religious affiliation, profession, medical conditions, and hobbies.[121]

Conti notes that Google account holders are allowed to delete their search histories. However, in Google's "Privacy FAQ for Web History," Google admits that it keeps copies of users' search logs for internal use.[122]

Some experts warn that a user's search activity log is a window into the user's mind. Search engine industry watcher John Battelle calls the user's search query log a "database of intentions." Battelle believes the owner of your search query database may eventually be able to predict your behavior, and that search activity patterns could be useful in developing more human-like artificial intelligence.[123]

Few people fully appreciate the power that Google derives from its tracking and profiling capabilities. In March of 2010 it was reported with much fanfare that the social network Facebook surpassed Google in number of users. However, that only compares the number of Facebook users to the number of people who use Google's retail website. Google has developed tentacles that reach most of the Web, most types of content, and most hardware platforms. It's no exaggeration to say that Google is well on the way to becoming the only company that can track nearly all Internet users nearly everywhere they go on the Web.[124]

Not that Google is taking any chances. Google Chairman Eric Schmidt told an audience in late 2010, "The best thing that would happen is for Facebook to open up its data... Failing that, there are other ways to get that information."[125] Schmidt isn't going to let a competitor stand in the way of Google's mission to organize the world's information.

Google is compiling dossiers on Internet users—and perhaps even organizations and companies—that former FBI Director J. Edgar Hoover would have envied.

*   *   *

Google can index and make more accessible the data on your personal computer. Unfortunately, doing so also creates new and frightening surveillance risks.

Google Desktop is a search application for Windows, Macintosh, and Linux PCs. As the data storage capacity of PCs mushrooms, users need more help finding information on their own machines. Today, the average PC's hard drive can store about 500 gigabytes of data. You can find specific files and folders using your operating system's built-in search function, but it is slow and inundates you with irrelevant results.

Google Desktop works not only with folders and files, but with email messages, pictures, songs, videos, and other content. Google Desktop indexes the data already on your machine when it is installed, and it indexes new data as it is stored.

Google Desktop may appear to be just a free PC utility. However, Google is very serious about this product. In 2007, Google filed a complaint with the Department of Justice (DOJ) alleging that Microsoft's Vista operating system was anticompetitive; Microsoft agreed to modify Vista to work with Google Desktop.[126] Google believes it is its right to make Google Desktop available to all PC users.

Could Google Desktop be used to spy on PC users? If you activate the "improve Google Desktop" feature, then Google will collect "non-personal" information from your PC on a regular basis.[127] Another Google Desktop option is "search across computers."[128] Ostensibly for enterprise customers, this feature allows authorized users to search your PC from another computer. When this feature is enabled, your PC's file index is copied and stored on Google's servers. But it gets worse: with Google Desktop V.3 the actual files are copied and stored on Google's servers. Privacy advocates advise users not to activate this feature.[129]

There are more reasons to worry. You can uninstall Google Desktop and close your account, but Google reserves the right to keep your data on its servers for up to ten days.[130] And the Google Desktop user license requires you to agree in advance to any changes made without notice to the Google Pack Privacy Policy.[131]

You might think that as long as "improve Google Desktop" and "search across computers" are not enabled, Google Desktop is an innocuous application. But Google Desktop's acceptance among users is itself valuable information. It gives Google a current indication of the percentage of users that trust Google, are unaware of the dangers, or simply don't care about privacy.

*   *   *

Google wants to know what you look like.

In 2006, Google acquired the face recognition software developed by physicist Hartmut Neven.[132] One possible application involves Google's Picasa photo sharing application: automatically tagging people in digital pictures.

However, Google may have bigger ambitions. Today, Google may know everything about an individual user except his or her true identity. Face recognition software could be used to make that final connection. It can also be used to associate images from drivers' licenses, group photos, Facebook, passport photos, and surveillance cameras.

If that sounds far-fetched, then consider these comments by Google Chairman Eric Schmidt. "We are very early in the total information we have within Google. The algorithms will get better and we will get better at personalization." Talking specifically about Google's progress towards creating the most comprehensive database of information about individuals, Schmidt said, "We cannot even answer the most basic questions because we don't know enough about you. That is the most important aspect of Google's expansion."[133]

It's a safe bet that Google is thinking beyond helping users organize their online photo albums.

*   *   *

Google has turned spying on users into a service.

Google Web History is much more powerful than the "History" function found on leading Web browsers. However, Web History also provides Google with a wealth of information about users' Web surfing preferences and habits.

Google Web History makes it easier to locate previously viewed pages. For example, users can search visited pages for specific words or phrases. Google claims its Web History service also produces more "personalized" search results over time by learning the types of search results that the user finds most valuable.

There is a dark side to Web History. It tells Google which Web pages the user returns to and how often. It gives Google an indication of how satisfied the user is with the search results. Like Google Desktop, it can also be used as a barometer of user trust.[134]

A related feature is included with Google's Toolbar add-on for Web browsers such as Internet Explorer and Firefox. As Danny Sullivan of *Advertising Age* reported, Google Toolbar permits Google to track all of the sites that the user visits. Its "PageRank meter" ranks each site's popularity among Google Toolbar users on a scale of 1 to 10. Unlike Google's famous PageRank algorithm, which ranks Web pages based on the number of links to each page, PageRank meter ranks pages based on the number of viewers. The original default setting for PageRank meter was "off." Then Google began distributing a version of Google Toolbar with the meter enabled by default.[135]

There's more. According to Benjamin Edelman, an assistant professor at Harvard Business School, Google's browser Toolbar continues to collect data even after it has been disabled by the user. After learning about Edelman's research, Google modified its toolbar software, presumably to fix the problem.[136] Still, it's clear that both Google Toolbar and Google Chrome Web browser were designed as information vacuum cleaners, reporting your Web surfing activity back to Google.[137]

With its Web History and Toolbar, Google has tapped a raging river of private information in exchange for a gentle stream of added functionality.

* * *

Television is the final frontier for collecting data on consumer behavior and delivering targeted advertising.

Entrepreneurs have struggled for decades to create a successful interactive TV service. Everyone knows that targeted advertising is interactive TV's killer application. But so far, no one has found the right solution.

Suddenly the answer seems obvious. Most homes have Internet access, and a growing percentage have high definition television (HDTV). To create interactive TV with targeted advertising, you merely tie the two services together.

And guess who is best positioned to make that happen.

Google TV has major advantages over other solutions. Google can deliver powerful new capabilities merely by leveraging its existing products and technologies.[138] For example, using split screen mode Google could permit you to search for information and discussions about programs as you watch them. And Google could let you view YouTube videos and other Google content on your home's biggest screen.

In the future, you will be able to search TV programming not only by titles and other basic information but by different types of content such as closed captions, audio, and video. This is where speech recognition, voiceprints, and face recognition come in handy.

Google TV's business model may be the biggest advantage. While others interested in connecting televisions to the Internet hope to sell more hardware, software, and services, Google stands to benefit the most from the data gathering and targeted advertising opportunities.

Given the number of hours per day that the average person watches TV, the information gathering potential of Google TV is enormous. But its impact on advertising could be even greater. For decades, TV commercials were broadcast to everyone in the same viewing area. Google TV would not only enable commercials to be narrowcast, it would empower consumers to purchase products, download electronic coupons, take surveys, access additional information, and participate in contests via the Web.

By combining television, the Internet, information mining, and targeted ads, Google is creating the ultimate telescreen. Big Brother could turn out to be Big Brother Inc.

*   *   *

If calling Google "Big Brother Inc." seems a stretch, then consider the fact that Google is already collaborating with several government agencies.

It started as an effort to make public data on government websites more accessible—to ensure that government is open and transparent.

It wasn't long, however, before some observers began to see a downside. *New York Times* technology reporter Miguel Helft wrote: "But the increased exposure of government records through Web searches is likely to raise privacy concerns. A search for an individual, like perhaps a corporate executive, a celebrity or even a long-lost friend, may yield links not only to the usual public pages but also to property records, campaign contributions or court filings."[139]

More recently, Google began collaborating with the National Security Agency (NSA) for the ostensible purpose of thwarting cyberattacks.[140] The NSA is chartered to gather intelligence from foreign communications. However, this often involves monitoring communications between people in foreign countries and people in the U.S. While cyberattacks on U.S. information infrastructure are a legitimate national security concern, collaboration between the world's biggest commercial data mining operation and the NSA presents myriad opportunities for abuse.

* * *

Given Google's poor privacy record, you might expect the company to take extra care to avoid further privacy blowups.

Think again.

When Google introduced Buzz, its answer to social networks such as Facebook and Twitter, it wanted to give the service a head start. So Google set up each user with followers and people to follow based on the user's Gmail and Google Chat (instant messaging) history.

Term

That wasn't what upset users, however. The problem was that Google listed the contacts in the user's public profile before the user had a chance to edit the list.[141] The implications were in some cases staggering. For example, one female blogger complained that she was automatically followed by her abusive ex-husband.[142]

Google claims it cares about user privacy. If that's true, it should have anticipated the problems. Not everyone with whom a user exchanges email is a friend. And some users may not want some friends to know about other friends (such as a married person in contact with an old flame). Whether

Google didn't think of the possibilities or chose to ignore them, it's clear that user privacy is not one of Google's priorities.

Nor is Buzz the only example of Google's privacy blind spot.

Goog-411 was a business telephone directory service that used speech recognition technology.[143] Google used the service to harvest phonemes, the basic sounds we speak to form words, to help it improve speech recognition technology. However, recording users' voices can also be used to create voiceprints for identifying individuals.

Goog-411 raised other privacy concerns. When Google launched the service it did not make it clear that callers' voices were being recorded.[144] Later, users were greeted with a synthesized voice that said "calls recorded." Apparently, the disclaimer was added after it was pointed out that recording calls without notifying the other party could be illegal.

Other Google products and services could produce privacy flaps. For example, if you use Google Reader—a Web based news aggregator—you are telling Google the news sources and blogs that you follow. If you use Google Groups, a collection of discussion groups, you are telling Google the topics that interest you and perhaps even the people with whom you are collaborating. It may not occur to most users that this type of information is being collected and used.

Google Health, Google's personal health record (PHR) service, could be a privacy time bomb. Will Google scan your health records for advertising purposes? Will Google claim your PHR content belongs to Google—much as it claims the memos, letters, and reports that you create with Google Documents belongs to Google?[145] Imagine how valuable the information in your PHR would be to insurers, pharmaceutical firms, and others.

Google believes that, over the long term, users will choose functionality over privacy. After all, though many activists and pundits reacted negatively to Google's robotic scanning of Gmail messages, there is no shortage of registered Gmail users today. It's not clear whether that's because most people don't mind having their email scanned, trust Google not to abuse the privilege, or are simply unaware that their messages are being scanned.

It's clear that Google views most user privacy concerns as inflated and many security concerns as bogus.

* * *

Do we have a right to know how much information Google collects and what it does with it?

Kevin Bankston, an attorney with the Electronic Frontier Foundation, puts the question in perspective: "A log of your search history is as close to a printout of your brain as we've ever had."[146]

Much of the world's information is private information. That hasn't stopped Google from organizing it and making it accessible, though. Private information is scarcer than public information and therefore more valuable.

Google assumes that everything its Web crawlers find is public information. However, some webmasters store private information in folders that are not publicly linked, trusting that what isn't linked won't be found. In one case, this led to public disclosure of students' social security numbers.[147]

Users' lack of awareness can also lead to unwanted disclosures. A Ponemon Institute survey of 1,000 Google users found that 89% falsely believed that their searches were private and 77% wrongly believed that their searches could not disclose their personal identities.[148]

Here is just a sample of the information that Google collects:

- o   Your interests, desires, and needs (e.g., Search)
- o   Your search history (e.g., Web History)
- o   The websites you visit (e.g., Chrome)
- o   The videos that you watch (e.g., YouTube)
- o   The news, commentary, and books that you read (e.g., Google Books)
- o   The topics that you discuss (e.g., Google Groups)
- o   The content that you produce (e.g., Gmail)
- o   Your, your family's, and your friends faces (e.g., Picasa)
- o   The sound of your voice and the people you call (e.g., Google Talk)

o   Your medical history and prescriptions (e.g., Google Health)

o   Your purchases (e.g., Google Checkout)

? MapQuest o   Your travel destinations (e.g., Google Maps)

o   Your locations of interest (e.g., Google Street View)

o   Your personal information (e.g., Checkout)

o   Your home, workplace, and hangouts (e.g., Google Latitude)

o   Your activity plans (e.g., Google Calendar)

o   The data stored on your computer (e.g., Google Desktop with "search across computers" enabled)

o   The TV programs you watch (e.g., Google TV)

This is by no means a complete list—there are hundreds of Google products.[149] Google also offers tools that enable application developers to gather information and invests in companies developing new sources of information.

For example, Google has invested in 23andMe, a company that is "helping individuals understand their own genetic information using recent advances in DNA analysis technologies and web-based interactive tools."[150] Personal genomes could be the ultimate tool for targeted advertising, personalization, and even medical fortune telling.

Is there any limit to the information that Google wants to collect, organize, and analyze? With omnipresent surveillance, Google is acquiring unprecedented knowledge for influencing and predicting behavior.

Applying these techniques to the employees, customers, and investors of companies, Google may know more about specific companies than the companies know about themselves. The same could be applied to other organizations such as government agencies.

Information is power. With the information Google is amassing, Google is well on the road to obtaining unprecedented power.

*   *   *

Are there ways for users to fight back?

A program called TrackMeNot (compatible with the Firefox Web browser) generates phantom search queries to obfuscate the user's search history. TrackMeNot, which works with Google and other popular search engines, doesn't hide your searches—it dilutes them.[151]

A site called Scroogle, created by Google critic Daniel Brandt, relays the user's search queries to Google, hiding the user's IP address and intercepting any cookies in the process.[152]

To show that it cares about user privacy, Google introduced Google Dashboard, a product that gives users one place to manage their use of up to 23 Google products. Unfortunately, Google Dashboard is merely a navigation tool. It doesn't increase privacy. As John Simpson of Consumer Watchdog pointed out, that would require adding controls such as "make me anonymous" and "don't track me."[153] Nor does Google Dashboard make Google's collection and use of information more transparent.

Google Dashboard does offer users the ability to delete certain private information. However, when Fox Business anchor Neil Cavuto asked Google Chairman Eric Schmidt "…but how do I know you are deleting it?" Schmidt replied "Because we say so. And because we would be sued."[154] Or as Schmidt explained on another occasion, "… the reason that you should trust us is that if we were to violate that trust people would move immediately to someone else."[155]

What Schmidt doesn't understand, or doesn't want to acknowledge, is that without transparency and accountability user controls are meaningless. The user doesn't know, for example, whether deleted information has actually been erased or is just no longer visible to the user.

*   *   *

Google is against privacy and for publicacy.

Top executives such as Eric Schmidt make that clear. "The only way to manage this is true transparency and no anonymity. In a world of asynchronous threats, it is too dangerous for there not to be some way to identify you. We need a (verified) name service for people. Governments will demand it."[156]

Vint Cerf, Internet pioneer and Google's Internet Evangelist, suggests that we look at bright side. "Privacy is evaporating rapidly, but on the other hand that lack of privacy induces transparency."[157]

This is linguistic chicanery. It's true that when you take away a person's privacy that person becomes "transparent." However, when most people speak about the need for transparency they are not referring to users—they are referring to Internet companies that collect and exploit users' private information.

At times it appears that Google does not even recognize that users' have legitimate privacy concerns. During a panel discussion, Google's Will Devries was asked to speak about the "dark side" of privacy, which he promptly defined as "when people lose faith in us and what we can do."[158] It never occurred to him that there should be limits on the private information that is collected and used.

It's easy to collect data online, because online data consists exclusively of 1s and 0s, and the process can be automated. Google has developed the technology to do this on an unprecedented scale. That's why the founders named their company after the googol—a 1 followed by one-hundred 0s. But none of this makes the destruction of privacy a good thing.

Google's business model, privacy lip service, outrageous privacy violations, and extreme secrecy tell us that Google's attitude is "Privacy for me, radical transparency for thee."

Your privacy is not optional, frivolous, or obsolete. Your privacy is essential to your personal freedom and security. Don't let anyone tell you otherwise.

Chapter Three

What's Yours Is Google's

Google is monetizing information—particularly information that doesn't belong to it.

Google does not respect others' property. Google's founders admit that they picked locks and commandeered personal computers while at Stanford. Google has since been accused of systematically infringing trademarks, copyrights, and patents; aiding and profiting from piracy; and creating new businesses by misappropriating others' property.

Nothing captures Google's attitude better than the popular jest "What's mine is mine, and what's yours is mine." Google repeatedly violates others' intellectual property rights—while zealously guarding its own. Google digitizes and organizes content that does not belong to it—without asking permission. Guided by its radical free business model, Google dumps products, robbing competing products and content of their value. Google makes money advertising on websites trafficking in pirated content. The $30 billion giant even presses freelancers to contribute their artwork for free—as if Google were the starving artist.

Google's founders justify their behavior with extreme unction. In the letter accompanying their stock prospectus, they crowed: "Sergey and I founded Google because we believed we could provide a great service to the world... our goal is to develop services that improve the lives of as many people as possible—to do things that matter."[159]

Google's top executives claim they aren't in it for the money. Yet they employ sophisticated tax avoidance schemes such as the "Double Irish." Of the top five tech firms in the U.S. (in terms of market capitalization), Google paid the lowest foreign tax rate (2.4%).[160]

*   *   *

When Stanford University graduate students Larry Page and Sergey Brin began developing their search engine and Web crawler, they needed as many personal computers as they could lay their hands on. One tactic was to use personal credit cards to purchase the machines. Another tactic was to "borrow" PCs from the Stanford University receiving dock. [161] And the pair hogged so much of Stanford's bandwidth that "We caused the whole Stanford network to go down." [162]

That's not all. The duo's computers—housed in Page's graduate student residence—drew so much power that they constantly tripped the building's circuit breakers. Brin proudly recounted how he mastered the art of lock picking; he broke into the building's basement to reset the circuit breaker whenever needed.[163]

Some observers chalk up these incidents to entrepreneurial zeal. However, it's one thing to do whatever it takes to get the job done and quite another to decide that your needs trump everyone else's.

* * *

No one can deny that Google provides useful products and services. But for the first several years, Google's founders had a great search engine and Web crawler—and no business model. It was only after they began talking to Bill Gross, founder of a company called GoTo.com (later renamed Overture), that Google began making big money.

Gross was first to discover how to monetize search keywords through targeted advertising; that advertisers would compete for the most valuable keywords in online auctions; that a performance-based cost-per-click pricing scheme attracts more advertisers than a cost per one thousand impressions scheme; and how profits from keyword advertising can be used to buy more traffic, generating even more advertising, and creating what businesses call a "virtuous circle."[164]

Bill Gross is the genius of the online economy. He saw the problem and envisioned the solution well before anyone else.

Larry Page and Sergey Brin met Bill Gross at the 2001 TED (Technology, Entertainment, and Design) conference. Gross was looking for a search partner; Page and Brin were adamantly opposed to mixing paid advertising with organic search results. Though Gross's company was making much more money than Google, Page and Brin did not seem interested in working with him. Then in early 2002 Google began offering keyword auctions with pay-per-click pricing—the same ideas Gross had been pitching. Google's revenue skyrocketed, and Gross's company sued Google for patent infringement.[165]

Did Google's founders "borrow" Gross's ideas just as they "borrowed" PCs from the Stanford University receiving dock?

A little more background on Bill Gross: Gross launched GoTo.com in 1998.[166] His first key insight was that the Internet was being overrun by undifferentiated traffic. If he could somehow identify quality traffic, he theorized, he could monetize it.

Gross learned how to make money from arbitrage as a twelve-year-old. When a local store put candy on sale, he bought a quantity and brought it back to his apartment complex, where he sold it by the piece for slightly more than he paid and slightly less than the regular price. He made a little money on each piece, and the other kids saved a little money on each piece. Everybody won.[167]

Years later, Gross realized that if he created a search site and attracted a critical mass of traffic, then he could sell search keywords to advertisers. Gross was a bold thinker: he believed that he could buy traffic from others and make money selling advertising on a performance basis. Instead of charging for the number of people who might have viewed an ad, he only charged when users clicked on it. It was a very attractive proposition for advertisers. Instead of paying upfront for an ad that might not work, they paid only for respondents. To top it off, Gross charged just one cent per click.

When Gross put the concept to work in 1998, search was plagued by spam. Gross's strategy was to first get advertisers addicted to low-cost performance-based advertising, and then to introduce keyword auctions, letting advertisers drive up the price per click. By 1999, GoTo.com had 8,000 advertisers. Gross also conceived the idea of syndicating his search service, offering external sites either a flat fee or a share of the advertising revenue for the right to handle their search requests.

In late 2000, GoTo.com agreed to pay AOL $50 million to handle its search requests. Though it was a risky proposition—paying another site to let you handle its search requests was unheard of at the time—GoTo.com ended up making a nice profit on advertising. A year later, GoTo.com changed its name to Overture, a moniker more suggestive of its business model: making paid introductions.

A successful paid search advertising business requires three things: a quality search engine, plenty of traffic, and a stable of advertisers. Overture managed to acquire traffic from others, and that helped attract advertisers, but the company didn't have an intrinsically valuable search engine. Google, with its popular and fast-growing search engine, was better positioned to acquire traffic and advertisers going forward. Though Overture grew to $668 million in revenue with $78 million in income (2002), Gross knew that competition from Google and Microsoft was inevitable.

Suddenly, Google convinced AOL not to renew its deal with Overture and to instead switch to Google. Gross suspected that Google paid AOL more than it expected to make from the deal just to take the business away from Overture. Fortunately for Gross, he managed to sell Overture to Yahoo! for $1.63 billion in July of 2003.

Meanwhile, Google was scheduled to go public on August 19, 2004. On August 9th, Google announced that it had settled the Overture lawsuit by giving Yahoo! 2.7 million shares of common stock in exchange for a perpetual license to use GoTo.com's patent (US Patent 6269361, "System and method for influencing a position on a search result list generated by a computer network search engine"[168]).

Why did Google's founders offer to settle? Most likely, they didn't want public discussion of the allegations and evidence to cloud their approaching IPO. There were already concerns that the founders had violated SEC rules when their *Playboy* interview was published during the IPO quiet period.[169]

What do IPO investors care about most? It's the inherent value of the company. Google wanted people to believe that its financial success was mainly due to innovations developed in-house such as the PageRank algorithm and the Googlebot Web crawler. The Overture lawsuit suggested that Google's phenomenal revenue growth was driven by someone else's technology. Further public discussion about the GoTo.com patent might have called into question the credibility of Google's founders, putting the IPO's success at risk.

The size of the settlement, 2.7 million shares in Google, was remarkable given the founders' talent for squeezing out every penny of cost. By November of 2004, the 2.7 million shares in Google were worth more than $500 million.

By any measure Google obtained a bargain. Google received a "fully paid, perpetual license" for technology crucial to its search advertising business.[170] No doubt Yahoo! agreed to cease commenting on the merits of its claims. With the lawsuit behind it, Google's business soared.

It's said that the victors write history. Today, when people think of paid search advertising, they think of Google's AdWords service. But the model that proved wildly successful—keyword auctions with performance-based pricing—was invented and patented by Bill Gross's company—not Google Inc.

We may never know how essential Overture's innovations were to Google's success, because by settling out of court Google was able to bury most of the evidence.

◌ ◌ ◌

It wasn't long before Google ran into legal challenges to its AdWords search advertising service. Advertisers began bidding on other firm's trademarks (brand names) as search keywords.

In the days before paid search advertising, businesses mainly worried about competitors misappropriating their brand names to confuse consumers.

By registering their brand names as trademarks, businesses could prevent or at least stop unauthorized use of their brand names.

Paid search advertising introduces a new wrinkle: advertisers using other companies' trademarks as keywords for targeted advertising. It's a great way for a competitor to exploit the market leader's hard-earned name recognition. The competitor gains access to the market leader's customers and potential customers behind the scenes without ever mentioning the market leader's brand name in public.

Google defends the right of advertisers to use competitors' trademarks as search keywords and has won lower court battles in some countries. Consequently, Google's policy regarding the use of trademarks as keywords varies from country to country.

However, there's more to the story. Google's treatment of trademark owners and behavior in court have been very troubling.

In 2003, American Blinds and Wallpaper Factory complained that competitors were using its trademarked name as advertising keywords.[171] Namely, when users searched for "American Blinds" they saw ads for JustBlinds.com and Select Blinds. Google's initial reaction was to stop advertisers from using others' trademarks as search advertising keywords.

In a sudden turnabout, Google took preemptive legal action, attempting to convince a U.S. District court that advertisers should be free to use any keywords they like. In doing so, Google portrayed itself as a champion of free speech. When Google was sued for trademark infringement, however, it invoked a very different argument, pleading that it was merely an intermediary in disputes between trademark owners and advertisers.

In other words, when Google was forced to play defense, it claimed it was just an innocent bystander. But when Google saw an opportunity to launch an offensive, it dropped the innocent bystander pose.

American Blinds sued Google in early 2004. Shortly after, Google announced that it would sell trademarked terms as advertising search terms. Google defended the action as a way to protect free speech and ensure relevant ads. But as American Blinds' attorney David Rammelt pointed out, in other cases Google stopped advertisers from using specific search terms.[172]

Google filed a motion to have American Blinds' case dismissed. The day before the litigants were scheduled to argue for and against the motion in court, one of American Blinds' lawyers did a search for "American Blinds" on Google. Lo and behold, there were no competing ads on the search results page. In fact, American Blinds' advertisement was the only sponsored link. Finding it odd, the lawyer asked colleagues in other parts of the country to perform the same search. They still saw competitors' ads.

Did Google modify its search results in San Jose, California—the trial venue? When American Blinds presented proof that competitors' ads were still running in other cities, Google shrugged it off as a technical glitch, insisting that it never fiddles with search and AdWords algorithms.[173]

American Blinds was not the only company that believed AdWords customers should not be allowed to bid on others' trademarks. GEICO filed a suit against Google for trademark infringement in May of 2004.[174] Google permitted competitors to bid on "GEICO" and "GEICO Direct." GEICO complained that this caused confusion; when users typed in "GEICO" they saw ads from competitors.

Google introduced yet another argument to its legal defense. Drawing an analogy to the "fair use" doctrine for copyrighted material, Google claimed that its trademark policy represented a happy medium between not enough protection and too much protection.[175] However, fair use is designed to ensure free speech; when an AdWords advertiser uses another company's trademark to attract potential customers, the advertiser benefits from the time and money the other company invested in building brand name awareness.

Google continued to claim it was an innocent bystander—despite the fact that it built the platform, offered the service, and defined the rules. Judge Leonie M. Brinkema ruled that GEICO had not established that the use of its trademark as a search term causes confusion and accepted Google's move to terminate the trial.[176]

In March of 2010, the European Court of Justice also ruled[177] that selling trademarks as advertising keywords does not violate trademark law.[178]

Have lower courts forgotten the purpose of trademark protection? Companies use trademarks to build consumer awareness. Over time, a trademark comes to represent the unique value proposition associated with a specific company and/or product. Companies often invest heavily in building brand awareness, and naturally they want to protect those investments. Trademarks are intellectual property just as patents, copyrights, and trade secrets are intellectual property. Legal protection for trademarks should encompass all legitimate business uses—not just display advertising.

There is another dimension to the problem. Letting AdWords customers bid on others' trademarks not only enables competitors to benefit from others' trademarks, it puts pressure on the trademark owners to join the bidding as a way of protecting their investments.

Rosetta Stone, a maker of language learning software, is fighting Google's trademark abuse and has attracted industry support—most notably from the Association for Competitive Technology (ACT) and its 3,000 member firms. ACT's executive director, Morgan Reed, does not mince words:

> *Google is using its search advertising dominance to shakedown trademark holders. It allows counterfeiters to advertise on its networks, forcing companies like Rosetta Stone to outbid pirates to prevent them from selling fraudulent copies of its software. Since Google controls 78% of the search advertising marketplace, Rosetta Stone has no choice but fight the counterfeiters by continually paying Google more money for advertising.*[179]

Google is monetizing others' intellectual property by throwing a dizzying array of arguments at lower courts struggling to understand the digital economy. The defenders of intellectual property rights are likely to win on appeal—but only if they can survive until then.

* * *

Google created Google News by using wire services' copyrighted content without their permission. In the process, Google learned powerful tactics for evading copyright law.

Google News displayed content produced by wire services for their newspapers and other licensees. Agence France Presse (AFP) sued Google in March of 2005, complaining that the firm used its headlines, photos, and stories without permission.[180] AFP also alleged that Google ignored a cease and desist order. Google eventually settled with both AFP and the Associated Press (AP).

Google's response to the Google News copyright infringement complaints became the firm's model for dodging responsibility. Google indicated that it had an opt-out procedure for newswires. In other words, the problem wasn't Google's use of copyrighted material without permission—it was the copyright holders' failure to opt out.

It was a brilliant yet devious strategy. Google made deliberate and blatant copyright infringement look like a minor clerical error. By offering opt-out procedures and review processes Google shifted the burden of policing Google's copyright violations to the victims. Meanwhile, Google benefitted traffic-wise from the unauthorized use of copyrighted material.

Google's strategy boxed in copyright holders, forcing them to choose between endlessly filing complaints, on the one hand, and entering advertising agreements on terms favorable to Google, on the other.

To wit, it's better to make a little money from an advertising revenue-sharing deal with Google than to lose money monitoring and reporting copyright violations as Google monetizes your content.

* * *

By now you get the picture: Google is blazing a trail of new and clever ways to monetize others' intellectual property without their permission.

To sell more advertising, Google needs more information and content to organize and make accessible. Most of the world's information—such as the contents of books, musical recordings, and movies—exists in analog format. To put that material online, it must be converted from analog to digital.

Most of us would like to see more information available online. However, no one stands to gain so much financially as Google, the dominant search and search advertising provider.

But Google has a problem: how can it digitize content created and/or owned by others? Google could request permission, but what if permission were denied? Or Google could go ahead and digitize the content and deal with the legal issues when compelled to later.

Google claims to be a different kind of company—a company with humanitarian goals and extraordinary ethical standards. In the mainstream corporate world, trademark, copyright, and patent infringement are all too common. If Google has higher standards, then shouldn't it be less likely to infringe on others' intellectual property rights?

Specifically, what policies and practices has Google put in place to prevent trademark, copyright, and patent infringement? Let's look at what Google's Code of Conduct has to say.[181]

Chapter VII of Google's Code of Conduct is "Obey the Law." The chapter is divided into four sections: Trade Controls, Competition Laws, Insider Trading Laws, and Anti-Bribery Laws. Tellingly, Google's "Obey the Law" chapter doesn't even address intellectual property rights (IPR).[182]

That omission might be understandable if Google were in a different line of business (such as distributing farm produce). But in Google's business of Internet-based products and services, intellectual property law is of paramount importance.

Google's Code of Conduct, like Google's Privacy Policy, is brimming with platitudes. "Our reputation as a company that our users can trust is our most valuable asset, and it is up to all of us to make sure that we continually earn that trust." How should Google employees earn and maintain users' trust? "All of our communications and other interactions with our users should increase their trust in us."

Google's Code of Conduct does contain a section entitled "Intellectual Property." However, this section is found in Chapter V, "Protect Google's

Assets." Naturally, the chapter's primary concern is protecting Google's intellectual property. Though employees are reminded to "...respect the intellectual property rights of others," that advice is immediately followed by, "Inappropriate use of others' intellectual property may expose Google and you to criminal and civil fines and penalties."[183]

In a section about open source software, the chapter speaks of "our policy of respecting the valid intellectual property rights of others." Clearly, Google is suggesting that others' IPR claims are *not* always valid.

None of the statements in Google's Code of Conduct can be faulted: others' IPR should be respected; not all IPR claims are valid; and infringing on others' IPR could get Google in hot water.

However, the overall impression given by Google's Code of Conduct is that safeguarding Google's IPR is every employee's duty, while respecting others' IPR claims is merely prudent.

* * *

Google's founders appointed themselves, in blatant disregard of copyright law, to digitize and make searchable all of the world's books.

The goal of the Google Books Library Project is to scan 32 million books over ten years at an estimated cost of $800 million. Three-quarters of the targeted books are out of print but still under copyright protection. Google started copying them by redefining the "fair use" exemption to copyright law to suit Google's purposes.[184]

The Fair Use Doctrine permits using brief excerpts from books for purposes such as discussing or teaching. An excerpt could be a sentence, a paragraph, or even a page—but certainly not a complete chapter or an entire book.

Google's founders have, in effect, exempted themselves from copyright law. They argue that it is acceptable for them to digitize entire books because they are doing so only to make the books searchable. However, copyright owners have the exclusive right to prepare derivative works such as foreign language versions of their books, and the same should apply to digital versions.

Google's argument that it is digitizing entire books for the limited purpose of making them searchable is not a convincing defense. It's easy and inexpensive to redistribute books once they've been converted to digital form. If Google's network is hacked, then the content of any books stored on Google's servers may fall into the hands of content thieves or pirates. By digitizing entire books and storing them on Internet servers, Google exposes the copyright owners to serious risks. In terms of its potential harm to authors and publishers, the Google Books Library Project looks more like piracy than fair use.

Libraries have legitimate reasons for wanting to digitize their collections. Physical books deteriorate with age and wear, and digitization is a way to preserve their content. While many libraries wish to offer their patrons faster and more convenient access to books, it is in the libraries' best interests to uphold copyright law.

Google is partnering with libraries because—to paraphrase bank robber Willie Sutton—that's where the books are. Google began by working with libraries at Stanford University, the University of Michigan, the University of Oxford, and Harvard University, as well as the New York City Public Library. Subsequently, another fifteen libraries signed on. Google has also enticed some publishers to provide digital files of newer books.

Make no mistake about it: the Google Books Library Project is an intentional and audacious effort to copy all of the world's books without permission. Instead of seeking copyright owners' permission, Google sought to create a fait accompli. Google understands that the more digital books it possesses, the stronger its bargaining position.

It's one thing to negotiate the sale of property before it changes hands. It's another to negotiate the sale of property to someone who has already taken possession. The former is a legitimate business transaction; the latter is a kind of extortion.

As commentator Jonathan Last observed:

Google's corporate philosophy is based on the model which brought them success: organizing and giving away other people's content, creating space for advertisements in the process. ...In the Google worldview, content is individually valueless. No one page is more important than the next; the value lies in the page view. And a page view is a page view, regardless of whether the page in question has a picture of a cat, a single link to another site, or the full text of Freakonomics. When all you're selling is ad space, the value shifts from the content to the viewer. And ultimately the content is valued at nothing ...In the world of books, it is the ideas and the authors that matter most, not the readers. That is why the copyright exists in the first place, to protect the value of these created works, a value which Google is trying mightily to deny.[185]

Google began digitizing books in 2002. Two years later, Google introduced Book Search, an online service that gave users a "full view" of books in the public domain and a "snippet view" of books still under copyright protection. Later, a "limited preview" mode was introduced as a potential sales tool for publishers.

The Authors Guild filed a class action lawsuit against Google in September of 2005. Less than a month later, the Association of American Publishers (APA) also filed suit, naming McGraw-Hill, Pearson Education, Penguin Group USA, Simon & Schuster, and John Wiley & Sons as plaintiffs. Google responded by creating a mechanism for copyright owners to opt out of the program (as it did for newswires earlier), but Google also insisted that "snippet view" qualifies as fair use under copyright law. Patricia Schroeder, president and CEO of the APA, disagreed: "...the whole principle of copyright law is that you get to decide if it's good for you."[186]

There was a further complication. The plaintiffs claimed to speak for all U.S. copyright holders. Small publishers complained that momentous decisions about the future of the industry were being made without giving them a say. In 2006 the parties commenced settlement negotiations, and in 2008 a proposed settlement agreement was announced under which Google would pay a paltry $125 million upfront plus a share of revenue going forward.

Though the proposed settlement went too easy on Google, it also represented a tacit admission by Google that it was guilty of copyright infringement. The U.S. Department of Justice (DOJ) protested that the proposed settlement violated U.S. antitrust law. The settlement was amended in early 2009 to require Google to pay rights holders a small fee per book plus 63% of revenue generated through subscriptions, advertising, and other means.

The DOJ also opposes the amended settlement agreement (ASA) on the grounds that it violates class action, copyright, and antitrust law. In comments submitted to the court, the DOJ warned that the ASA would "grant Google sweeping control over digital commercialization of millions and millions of books."[187] The DOJ characterized the ASA as a price-fixing scheme.[188]

Most telling, the DOJ described the ASA as an effort to "carve out an exception to the Copyright Act."[189] Consequently, the DOJ "...believes that the Court lacks authority to approve the ASA."[190]

Not all libraries are enthusiastic about the Google Books Library Project. Some public libraries are troubled by the prospect of one corporate entity—whether Google or another company—digitizing all of the world's books. They worry that a single entity might respond to pressure by censoring or banning specific books or authors.[191] Many libraries also fear that digitizing all of the world's books could spell the demise of physical books, putting traditional libraries out of business.

Others worry that Google Books (Google's online book search service) creates a log of each individual user's book search activity, and that Google could be required to surrender the logs to governments spying on dissidents and political opponents. Jean Noel Jeanneney, former President of the National Library of France, also complains that Google Books favors English language and American books.[192]

And what about foreign authors and publishers—where do they fit in the settlement? The Open Book Alliance released a study that warns:

The settlement would (1) grant Google automatic rights to exploit digitally millions of books without requiring Google to obtain any authorization from any foreign copyright owner or author; and (2) require these foreign rights holders to jump through burdensome hoops.[193]

There is, in fact, no excuse for digitizing books without permission. Projects such as Europeana, Gallica, and HathiTrust have proved that permission-based digitization is quite viable.

Google isn't just working to digitize and make searchable all of the world's books. Google is leading an effort to chip away at and ultimately gut copyright law.

* * *

Google acquired YouTube, the leading video sharing site, for $1.65 billion in late 2006. YouTube did not have a viable business model at the time. What it did have was heavy traffic, a great video sharing platform, and trouble brewing over copyright infringement.

Many YouTube users routinely upload copyrighted video clips. They do so despite being warned not to upload copyrighted material without permission. Certainly fair use applies to videos as well as books. Just as you can quote from a book to make a point, you can show a video clip to make a point. However, copyright protection becomes meaningless if users are allowed to upload an entire movie or TV program as a series of five-minute clips.

Before it was acquired by Google, YouTube clearly understood that what it was doing was illegal. There is undeniable evidence of this (from YouTube emails and other sources) presented in the Statement of Undisputed Facts filed by Viacom et al. in their legal battle with Google.[194]

YouTube's strategy was to quickly build as much traffic as possible and then sell the company. YouTube cofounder Steve Chen told product manager Maryrose Dunton to "…concentrate all our efforts in building up our numbers as aggressively as we can through whatever tactics, however evil."[195] Cofounder Jawed Karim asked his partners, as captured on video, "At what point do we tell them our dirty little secret, which is that we actually just want to sell out quickly…"[196]

YouTube understood that it would have to violate copyright law to achieve its goals. For example, in a September 7, 2005 email, Chen said: "You can find truckloads of adult and copyrighted content…"[197] He knew that the founders couldn't rely solely on user-created videos: "Steal it! .... We have to keep in mind that we need to attract traffic. How much traffic will we get from personal videos?"[198]

Chen worried about the consequences of encouraging copyright infringement: "We're going to have a tough time defending the fact that we're not liable for the copyrighted material on the site… when one of the co-founders is blatantly stealing content from other sites and trying to get everyone to see it."[199] But he also worried about what would happen if they didn't do it: "If you remove the potential copyright infringements… site traffic and virality will drop to maybe 20% of what it is."[200]

Ultimately, Chen concluded that there are ways to skirt copyright law: "But we should just keep that stuff on the site. I really don't see what will happen. What? Someone from CNN sees it? He happens to be someone with power? He happens to want to take it down right away. He get [sic] in touch with CNN legal. 2 weeks later, we get a cease and desist letter. We take the video down."[201]

Chen's partners were more guarded. Jawed Karim suggested in an email: "Let's just leave copyrighted stuff there if it's news clips." Cofounder Chad Hurley was less optimistic: "Save your meal money for some lawsuits!"[202]

Google must have known what YouTube was doing when it bought the company. You don't pay $1.65 billion for a company without checking and double-checking every aspect of its operations.

Viacom's Statement of Undisputed Facts once again provides crucial evidence. Google's VP of content partnerships David Eun told Eric Schmidt in a pre-acquisition email: "I think we should beat YouTube—but not at all costs. One senior media executive told me they are monitoring YouTube very closely and referred to them as a 'Video Grokster.'"[203] Grokster facilitated the redistribution of copyrighted music without permission and was forced to cease operations by the U.S. Supreme Court.

Eun reported that Sergey Brin said during a meeting, "Is changing policy to profit from illegal downloads how we want to conduct business? Is this Googley?"[204] An email from Google video business product manager Ethan Anderson gave the top ten reasons "why we shouldn't stop screening for copyright violations." The number one reason was, "It crosses the threshold of Don't be Evil to facilitate distribution of other people's intellectual property…"[205]

After YouTube was acquired by Google, it continued to violate copyright law. For example, Julie Havens wrote in an email: "a trend we see is that people upload copyrighted videos to their private videos… and then invite large numbers of people to view the video which bypasses our copyright restrictions."[206]

In early 2007, media conglomerate Viacom sued Google for $1 billion claiming that:

> *YouTube is a significant, for-profit organization that has built a lucrative business out of exploiting the devotion of fans to others' creative works in order to enrich itself and its corporate parent Google. Their business model, which is based on building traffic and selling advertising off of unlicensed content, is clearly illegal and is in obvious conflict with copyright laws.*[207]

Viacom specifically complained that more than 100,000 clips from its programs were hosted on YouTube without permission, that the clips were viewed more than 1.5 billion times, and that as a result Viacom lost revenue while Google gained revenue.

Google promised to remove any copyrighted video upon the copyright owner's request. However, that would only be after the video became available for viewing, the copyright owner complained, and Google reviewed the complaint. Viacom argues that Google has the ability to screen uploaded video clips before they are released for viewing but chooses not to do so. By putting the onus of enforcement on the copyright holder, Google ensures that infringing videos get posted. Even if a video is removed, another user may subsequently upload the same video, sending the copyright owner back to square one.

In addition to arguing that YouTube should be permitted to host short clips of copyrighted videos under the fair use doctrine, Google claimed exemption under the Digital Millennium Copyright Act (DMCA). The DMCA says that a service provider can't be held responsible for copyrighted content uploaded by users without permission, as long as the service provider promptly blocks or removes the content when notified. However, the DMCA's safe harbor was originally intended to exempt Internet service providers (ISPs) and others who serve mainly as conduits. YouTube more closely resembles a publisher.

Just as search engines can be gamed to achieve higher placement in search results, laws can be gamed to secure more favorable business deals. Could Google be exploiting a loophole in the DMCA to pressure copyright holders into signing advertising agreements?

Google argued strenuously against unsealing documents unearthed in the discovery phase of its legal battle with Viacom. Viacom agreed that some documents should be excluded as business confidential—but not all. The evidence that Viacom wanted made public, and that Google wanted kept sealed, included:

- o "YouTube's pre-acquisition intent, policies, and practices..."
- o "Google's intent, policies and practices..."
- o "Issues regarding valuation and financial benefit realized by defendants..."
- o "Right and ability to control issues..." and
- o "Storage and direct liability issues."[208]

The evidence was eventually made public, and much of it proved embarrassing to Google. Two disclosures were particularly stunning. Google understood early on that YouTube was a video version of the peer-to-peer file sharing company forced to cease operations by the decision of the U.S. Supreme Court in *MGM Studios, Inc. v. Grokster, Ltd.*[209]

An even more stunning disclosure, however, concerned Google's strategy. Google Senior VP Jonathan Rosenberg discussed selectively policing copyrights—intercepting infringing videos for the company's business partners while making others submit complaints: "Pressure premium content providers to change their model towards free... Threaten a change in copyright policy" and "use threat to get deal sign-up."[210]

When Viacom attempted to negotiate a deal with Google, David Eun told Viacom that Google's tools included an "audio fingerprinting system whereby the content partner can send 'reference fingerprints' to Audible Magic's database" and added that the fingerprints "are now live as well and are only offered to partners who enter into a revenue deal with us."[211] Apparently, Eun was applying pressure just as Rosenberg had suggested.

Other media companies have already succumbed to Google's pressure tactics. For example, CBS (ironically, Viacom's sister company) agreed to add advertisements to video clips that appear on YouTube and share the revenue with Google. The deal was struck after YouTube introduced technology to help media companies flag their copyrighted content. YouTube suggested using the technology to monetize the videos rather than remove them.[212]

YouTube is the leading online video streaming site with approximately 43% market share,[213] ten times that of its nearest competitor. YouTube also enjoys the advantages of being owned and promoted by the dominant search engine. It's not surprising that some media companies would cut a deal rather than continue to incur costs fighting Google, the world's most powerful information gatekeeper.

However, it's not just big corporations that are complaining about YouTube copyright infringement. German composer Frank Peterson says his business is being hurt by free music videos on YouTube. "I feel extremely bullied, ripped off and threatened by Google YouTube... The ongoing expropriation of artists and the exploitation of copyrights without owners' consent or even against their will by companies like Google and YouTube should also be considered as a crime against arts and culture."[214]

Google won a court victory in mid-2010 when federal judge Louis Stanton ruled that Google had followed the DMCA's take-down procedures. However, in his written decision he admitted that YouTube and Google "not only were generally aware of, but welcomed, copyright-infringing material being placed on their website."[215] Viacom plans to appeal, knowing that the Supreme Court overturned a lower court in the seminal and analogous Grokster case.

The Supreme Court understood that in the digital online era, if the burden of policing copyrights is placed mainly on copyright holders, then the intellectual property rights guaranteed by the U.S. Constitution become useless.

*   *   *

Google has even been accused of aiding and abetting online piracy.

Google sold ads to Easy Download Center and Download Place—websites trafficking in copyrighted content. Was Google unaware of what the sites were doing? People familiar with the affidavits say that Google supplied the sites with keywords such as 'pirated' and 'bootleg movie download.'[216]

As we've seen, the movie industry believes that Google has the technology to flag potentially infringing videos and hold them for review. What Google lacks is the motivation to do so. Google invites abuse, and pirates respond by posting samples at YouTube that lead viewers to sites selling pirated movies.

There are also complaints from the music industry that Google is facilitating illegal downloads of copyrighted music for Android mobile phones. An Android application called Tunee boasts "...download any MP3 music you want for free." One music blogger wonders if Google's strategy is "to turn a blind eye to illegal music downloading until they launch their own music store."[217]

Another music blogger contends that Google sells advertising to sites that are themselves "selling illegal copies of the very works that Google wants to license for its 'legit' business."[218] If this is true, then it is reminiscent of Google Vice President Jonathan Rosenberg's words "use threat to get deal sign-up."

Independent filmmaker Ellen Seidler was disturbed to find that her film *And Then Came Lola* was being redistributed by hundreds of websites without permission. She was doubly disturbed to see that supposedly legitimate businesses such as Google are advertising on the sites and making money from her stolen content. Seidler said, "From my point of view, Google fences stolen goods."[219]

Seidler complained to the Motion Picture Association of America (MPAA); the MPAA told her it was working on the problem. When she complained to Google, Google told her that she had to file a DMCA complaint with AdSense. Seidler eventually learned that the moment one complaint was resolved, other sites appeared with her film and Google advertising. That inspired her to coin the phrase "Google-Go-Round."[220]

*   *   *

If any company can afford to pay freelance artists for their creations, then surely it is the mammoth cash machine known as Google. Yet when Google invited artists to provide themes (background art) for its Chrome Web browser in 2009, the company told artists that they would be paid not in dollars but in "exposure" to Google's global market.[221]

This is a classic technique that unscrupulous businesses use to exploit artists, consultants, and other self-employed people. For individuals just starting out on their own, "exposure" may sound like just the ticket. But most quickly learn that what they really need are paying customers.

When a company of Google's size and stature embraces this tactic it is particularly outrageous. At first glance, it appears that Google offered freelance artists an opportunity to gain visibility and that the artists were free to decline. However, it's not that simple. The market for freelance commercial art is limited, and there are many artists struggling to establish a foothold. If one major corporation succeeds in persuading dozens of artists to work for free, then other corporations will question why they are paying. By paying artists in "exposure" rather than legal tender, Google not only obtained a disgraceful bargain, Google undermined the broader market for freelance commercial art.

Freelance artists, like everyone else, need to earn a living. By getting artists to contribute their valuable designs at no cost, Google shifted the cost of producing the designs to the artists' other customers.

In addition to undermining the value of the freelance artists' work, Google's approach is exceptionally hypocritical. Google expects to be paid in dollars when users click on advertisements. When asked about its dishonorable practice of soliciting free artwork, Google responded "While we don't typically offer monetary compensation for these projects, through the positive feedback that we have heard thus far we believe these projects provide a unique and exciting opportunity for artists to display their work in front of millions of people."[222]

In other words, Google justifies not paying artists for their work by the fact that it is getting away with it.

* * *

Google's approach to property rights is based on double standards. Google employees are instructed to protect Google's intellectual property. But others' intellectual property should be respected only when it is valid—and mainly to avoid trouble.

However, it's an attitude that could blow up in Google's face.

Dozens of companies have sued Google for patent infringement.[223] While some of the cases may be nuisance suits, there is compelling evidence that Google shows the same lack of respect for patents and confidentiality agreements that it shows for copyrights.

Many recent complaints concern Google's Android operating system for consumer devices. For example, Android mobile phones replicate Apple's iPhone user interface right down to the pinch and zoom gesture. Google may have miscalculated: companies such as Apple play for high stakes.

Google Chairman Eric Schmidt was a member of Apple Inc.'s board of directors for three years. He resigned in August of 2009 under pressure from the Federal Trade Commission (FTC). While Schmidt was a member of Apple's board, he insisted that Apple was not one of Google's primary competitors.[224] However, since that time Google has made several moves that directly pit the company against Apple: Google launched its Nexus One phone (Android devices compete with Apple's iPhone and iPad); Google disclosed plans for Google TV (which competes with Apple TV); Google disclosed plans for a Web-based Google music store[225] (which would compete with Apple iTunes); and Google outbid Apple to acquire mobile advertising company AdMob, paying more than ten times AdMob's sales.[226]

Apple sued Taiwanese manufacturer HTC, maker of mobile phones using Google's Android operating system, for infringing 20 Apple patents.[227] The patents cover hardware and software elements as well as the iPhone's graphical user interface.

Google is also being sued for infringing seven of Oracle America's Java patents.[228] Oracle America, formerly Sun Microsystems, filed suit because Google is using Java in its Android mobile operating system despite not having procured a mobile Java license (several years ago Microsoft paid dearly for the same offense) and not participating in the Java Community Process.[229] Oracle charges that Google must have known about the patents (having hired engineers from Sun) and, consequently, that the infringement is willful.[230] If Oracle can prove willful infringement, the penalties are by law tripled.

Commenting on the case, business journalist Dana Blankenhorn said, "I'm as big a fan of Google as anyone. I like their stuff and I like their style. But there's an old legal saying that when you don't have the law on your side you argue the facts, and when you don't have the facts you argue the law, but when you don't have either you pound the table. Google is doing a lot of table pounding."[231]

When asked to comment on Oracle's lawsuit, a Google spokesperson said, "We are disappointed Oracle has chosen to attack both Google and the open-source Java community with this baseless lawsuit. The open-source Java community goes beyond any one corporation and works every day to make the Web a better place. We will strongly defend open-source standards and will continue to work with the industry to develop the Android platform."

That's a breathtaking response. Oracle accuses Google of patent infringement; Google characterizes it as an attack on the entire "Java community." Oracle accuses Google of willfully violating patent law; Google claims it is working for the benefit of everyone who uses the Web. Oracle accuses Google of using its technology without the required license; Google insists it is defending the entire industry.[232]

Not long after Oracle filed suit, another complaint against Google surfaced. Skyhook Wireless, a company specializing in location-based services, sued Google for patent infringement and unfair trade practices.

Skyhook's allegations, if proved in court, could have devastating consequences. Skyhook Wireless began mapping Wi-Fi networks years ago and has amassed a database of over 250 million Wi-Fi access points in tens of thousands of cities. Google tested Skyhook's technology from 2005 to 2007. Skyhook complains that Google is infringing four of its patents.[233] Furthermore, Skyhook alleges that Google is using strong-arm tactics to stop Skyhook's partners from shipping handsets with Skyhook's XPS technology installed.[234]

There's more to the story. Google began mapping Wi-Fi networks using its Street View cars. Then Google got into trouble for recording private user data such as emails and passwords. According to one of Skyhook's complaints, "Google tracks phones when the user is unaware and in a way and to an extent that is never clearly disclosed to the end customer."[235] The implication is that Google is surreptitiously using Android mobile phones to map Wi-Fi networks.

It gets even worse. Skyhook says that it landed a deal to put its XPS technology in Motorola's Android handsets. However, in April of 2010,

Google Vice President Andy Rubin called Motorola co-CEO Sanjay Jha and demanded that Motorola stop shipping XPS-equipped phones immediately. Rubin claimed that Skyhook's XPS technology is not compatible with Android; Skyhook insists that XPS was tested for Android compliance and passed. [236]

This case is particularly egregious because if the allegations are true, Google used information obtained from Skyhook Wireless under a non-disclosure agreement (NDA) to develop a competing solution and later pressured two handset makers to stop shipping units containing Skyhook's software.

The pattern is clear. When Google decides to enter a business that requires developing a new product or service, it simply ignores others' intellectual property. Google apparently believes it can take what doesn't belong to it, stonewall any legal actions, and make so much money off others' intellectual property that in the end it will be able to offer the IP owners more than they could have made on their own.

In other words, Google has found that expropriating others' intellectual property is a relatively inexpensive way of doing business on a colossal scale—provided you can get away with it.

*   *   *

Google has demonstrated over and over that it has little respect for others' intellectual property; little respect for anyone outside Google who creates intellectual property; and little respect for trademark, copyright, and patent law.

Google's strategy is to use others' intellectual property without permission. When the owners complain, Google delays, obfuscates, and seeks to have the laws reinterpreted in its favor.

It's a brilliant strategy because it allows Google to monetize others' intellectual property, puts the burden of enforcement on those whose rights have been violated, and arguably costs Google less than obeying the law.

And it's a strategy that almost guarantees Google will win. Google understands that the digital economy creates new opportunities for evading intellectual property laws. Google understands that if it can get away with not obeying the rules, then it will achieve a huge competitive advantage, because its costs will be lower than everyone else's.

These are not isolated incidents. Google stands accused of systematically infringing all types of intellectual property rights (including trademarks, copyrights, patents, and trade secrets) for all major types of content (including books, movies, music, and news). And Google stands accused in multiple countries.

In Part II, I'll discuss the political philosophy behind Google's attempts to justify this behavior.

Chapter Four

Security Is Google's Achilles' Heel

The online world that we have come to depend on is a dangerous place. It presents serious safety hazards to you and your family: Your private information, such as account numbers and passwords, can be stolen; your identity can be hijacked; and your reputation can be besmirched.

Google makes the online world much more dangerous.

We've seen that Google does not respect your privacy. We've seen that Google does not respect others' property rights. So it should come as no surprise that Google does not respect your online security needs.

Google's mission is to make information accessible; why place it behind security barriers? Google wants to speed information access; why install speed bumps? Google wants to drive the cost of information down to zero; why invest in securing something that's free?

Most people's priorities include safety and security. Psychologist Abraham Maslow showed that humans have a hierarchy of needs.[237] The most basic human needs are physical, such as the needs for food and water. The next most basic need is to be secure. Not just secure in body, but secure in property, finances, and other resources.

Security is not one of Google's priorities. Google's corporate website contains a page titled "Our Philosophy: Ten things we know to be true." Here, in plain English, are the "core principles that guide [Google's] actions." Securing your data is not one of them. In fact, security isn't even mentioned; the principles focus on speed, access, and availability.[238]

Google only pays lip service to security. There is a separate page that describes Google's Security Philosophy. Unfortunately, the page doesn't inspire confidence:

We've learned that when security is done right, it's done as a community. This includes everybody: the people who use Google services (thank you all!), the software developers who make our applications, and the external security enthusiasts who keep us on our toes. These combined efforts go a long way in making the Internet safer and more secure.[239]

Notice that Google delegates the responsibility for security to users, developers, and people bizarrely described as "security enthusiasts." To the extent that Google does take responsibility, it is reactive rather than proactive: most of Google's Security Philosophy page is devoted to "reporting security issues."

* * *

In February of 2007, a student at Los Rios Community College googled his own name and was shocked by what he saw. One of the links was to a database containing his name, date of birth, and social security number. The database provided similar information for about 2,000 students.[240]

How did this happen? Google's search bots crawl and copy the entire Web. (Google is able to provide lightning-quick results by searching its indexed copy of the Web rather than the actual Web.) Though information contained in private folders on Web hosts is normally not found by Web surfers, it can be harvested by Web crawlers and indexed by search engines if the folders are not password protected.

Google didn't break the law, but it did act like an automated hacker. Google never stopped to consider that a folder with no links pointing to it must be private, because securing others' private data is not something Google thinks about.

* * *

Google exposes users to numerous security risks, but it resists taking steps to eliminate them.

Google collects information about individual users that is unprecedented in both quantity and quality. In fact, Google is rapidly acquiring Total Information Awareness.[241] Google logs most users' online searches. Google tracks, records, and cross references most clicks. Google knows where users go, what users seek, what users read or view, and how often and how long they do these things.

Google stores a current copy of the more than one trillion Web pages. Google aggregates more content than anyone, and only Google can track access to Google aggregated content. Android mobile phones track users' locations. Google is gathering voice prints and face prints. There are Google products that collect your bank and credit card account numbers, your phone numbers and email addresses, and your calendar and business documents.

It is hard to exaggerate the damage that could be done if the private information that Google gathers and stores fell into the wrong hands.

The risk of Google, its employees, or its business partners willfully making users' private information public is small. It's not in Google's business interests to let this happen. But as a student at Los Rios Community College discovered, it can happen.

Google operates what is probably the world's largest private computer network. Its distributed architecture makes it more vulnerable to attacks from hackers, because information is stored in multiple locations and there are many entry points.

Google's products also pose security risks. Google often releases "beta test" versions to the public. The traditional approach is to supply the beta version to a limited group of customers for field testing prior to general release. Google's method subjects products to large-scale field testing, but it also exposes a wider audience to possible security flaws.

These problems are compounded by Google's corporate culture. Google is run by data mining engineers who see privacy and security as obstacles to data gathering, access, and use. Google fails to adequately warn users of specific security risks, and it evades responsibility when they arise.

Google's radical free business model encourages lax security. Products such as Gmail devalue your data on a number of levels. From Google's perspective, when your information is stolen or leaks out, it's no big deal. What did you expect for free?

Google's hiring practices—emphasizing top grades from top schools, the ability to solve Mensa brain teasers, and the stamina to survive a gauntlet of interviews—may sound impressive. However, these hiring practices produce a monolithic culture with tunnel vision.

This tunnel vision prevents Google from seeing many of the security risks. For example, storing documents indefinitely increases the chances they will be hacked. Disclosing users' contacts can lead to harassment. Tracking users' locations may facilitate stalking.

Google's data mining engineers have not only failed to anticipate these risks, they have been caught off guard by the public's negative reactions. Google does not even perform a cursory review of a new product's privacy and security implications. Google believes it is up to users to detect and report security problems and that the problems should only be fixed when not fixing them would jeopardize the product's widespread acceptance.

Data protection authorities from several countries express frustration that Google has repeatedly disregarded users' privacy.[242] Safeguarding users' privacy is not part of Google's culture. Neither, apparently, is obeying privacy laws. Google was highly intransigent when asked to comply with a California privacy law.[243]

Likewise, when some of Google's search result links were corrupted, Google did not warn users about the danger. Google is more concerned about protecting Web publishers and advertisers from revenue loss than about protecting users from viruses and identity theft.

Even Google TV presents unnecessary security risks. Google TV brings the Web to the biggest screen in your home using the Chrome Web browser. But the browser has no user controls, and you can't install security software on Google TV. That means you can't block undesirable websites or pop ups. Google TV gives you the entire Web—including the stuff you don't want.[244]

A new Google security threat has emerged. Google is collaborating with the National Security Agency (NSA) to combat foreign hackers. That may help Google secure its network from external attack, but it raises the specter of information about individual users falling into the hands of a government spy agency.

*   *   *

Some pundits believe that releasing beta (test) products to the general market is a great idea. Instead of telling the market what it wants, they say, engage the market in an ongoing conversation. Solicit feedback from end users, and use the feedback to debug and fine tune products. Embrace the wisdom of crowds.

There's just one problem: beta products almost always have bugs, and some of the bugs may adversely affect privacy and security.

Robert Hansen, CEO of security consultancy SecTheory, has documented numerous security problems found in Google products. For example, in early 2007 he discovered a flaw that enables hackers to access data indexed by Google's PC search product, Google Desktop.[245]

Hansen later discovered that private corporate information was inadvertently revealed by Google Calendar. Though Google Calendar gives users the option to keep calendar entries private, many corporate users don't realize they need to select this option to keep their calendar entries from being disclosed on the Web.[246] Understandably, there is a tendency to believe that a product's default settings are best for most users.

Hansen found that Google Gadgets, tiny programs that users can embed in personalized home pages, can be hijacked by data thieves.[247] For example, a harmless-looking program that displays local weather information can be used to monitor the user's Web searches. The risk is compounded by the fact that anyone can upload one of these little applications.

Hansen also unearthed security holes in Google Buzz,[248] Google's Chrome browser,[249] and an open source software tool called Goolag. The latter was developed by a company called the Cult of the Dead Cow and uses

Google's search engine to look for vulnerabilities in websites.[250] While Goolag was designed to help security professionals find and resolve website security risks, it can also be used by hackers to identify sites that are most vulnerable to cyberattacks.

In fact, tricking Google to serve up malicious links to Web searchers has become something of an art. It's called "Black Hat SEO." (SEO = search engine optimization.) Instead of serving as a conduit between searchers and content publishers, Google unwittingly acts as a conduit between hackers and their victims. Though Google responds to reports about new security threats, security specialists complain that the company is reluctant to share information with them.[251]

*   *   *

Google's network infrastructure was built for speed, scalability, and efficiency—not security.

Think of Google's network as the world's most powerful supercomputer with a copy of the entire Internet stored in its memory. The network was constructed using inexpensive servers, a distributed architecture, and virtualization technology. It exploits Moore's Law—the law predicting that computing power and memory will continue to increase as prices decrease—on a global scale.

To wit, only Google has built an infrastructure that scales with the Internet's exponential growth. Google's innovative network design gives the company a huge competitive advantage.

Unfortunately, one attribute that does not scale well is security.

Google's Internet evangelist, Vint Cerf, has admitted as much. When asked about the possibility of a two-tier Internet that would provide businesses with better security, he replied, "My bias right now tends to be it's every man for himself. You need to be suspicious whether you're inside the trusted cloud or not, and when it fails, the house of cards tends to collapse."[252]

Translation: Security-wise, you are on your own when you use the Internet, and don't expect much help from Google.

Here is why. Google's founders' original goal was to index the entire Web. They quickly realized that would require files much too big for a single server to handle. So they developed a virtual file system called BigFiles. BigFiles treats the individual hard drives on networked PCs as sectors within a very large virtual drive. To ensure rapid access, they decided to store at least three copies of every file, with the different copies in different locations. Over time, BigFiles was enhanced and renamed BigTable.[253]

Google's BigTable[254] is in many ways like the ill-fated passenger steamship, the *RMS Titanic*. We now know that the *Titanic* was vulnerable because it was not divided into watertight compartments and did not have a double hull. A single breach anywhere on the *Titanic* could sink the entire ship. Likewise, Google's BigTable lacks the data equivalent of watertight compartments and a double hull.

Why did Page and Brin choose a relatively insecure design? Their main objective was to stockpile the world's information in a quasi-public space—an information commons. Above all, they wanted to make it easy for anyone to add data, share data, and combine data (to create "mashups").

BigTable takes virtualization to new heights. It's one thing to treat many individual hard drives as sectors on a large virtual hard drive. It's another to treat hundreds of thousands of computers in data centers scattered around the globe as part of a colossal supercomputer. In Google's network, the data and applications are so highly distributed that even Google doesn't know exactly where they are at any given moment. Think of BigTable as virtualization on steroids.

BigTable puts all of Google's security eggs in one basket. It creates an irresistible target for hackers. And it flies in the face of common sense risk mitigation strategy. Like the ancient Library of Alexandria, BigTable puts all of the books (information) in one place. A single fire (cyberattack) could result in a catastrophic loss.

Put another way, with BigTable Google is too big not to fail.

Google is obsessed with speed. When you use Google's search engine, it reports not only the number of results but also the time it took (down to the nearest one-hundredth of a second) to deliver them. Google has even launched an initiative "to make the Web faster"[255] based on Google's free alternative to the domain name system (DNS) that serves as the Internet's automated phonebook.[256]

Unfortunately, security barriers slow things down. The more layers of security there are, the better the overall security. But it's like deploying a series of speed bumps. You can't have both robust security and maximum speed.

Another reason that Google's network is vulnerable to hackers is that its servers use the free, open source Linux operating system. Linux is completely transparent—it has no secrets. Because no one owns Linux, no single entity is empowered to issue periodic security updates. Linux machines are an inviting target for hackers.[257]

Google's distributed architecture is inviting because once a hacker penetrates the network, he can get at everything. In this case, "everything" means petabytes of data (one petabyte equals one billion megabytes). Another ramification of a distributed architecture is that it may be difficult to determine exactly what was stolen. Knowing what was stolen is essential to taking the appropriate precautions. For example, if you know that a specific batch of credit card numbers was taken, then the cardholders may be advised to deactivate the affected accounts.

Hackers target Google because—to again paraphrase bank robber Willie Sutton—that's where the information is. In fact, Google is the world's central banker of information. Unfortunately, it has no vaults or armed guards.

* * *

Google does not warn users when they are exposed to serious security threats.

In early 2008, *USA Today* reported that hackers were inserting mischievous links in Google's search results. When a user clicked on one of the corrupted links, it took the user to the correct site but his PC also downloaded rogue software from an invisible server. The rogue software could be used, among other things, to install a keystroke logger capable of observing and reporting user names and passwords. Google contacted websites affected by the attack but did not warn users.[258]

Google didn't warn users because Google has a conflict of interest. Google works for advertisers and publishers—not users. Google makes money off search advertising and is reluctant to do anything that would discourage searches.[259] However, that's no excuse: the consensus today is that Enron and WorldCom should have warned investors when things started going wrong. Not doing so allowed their situations to spin out of control.

Google's official blog offered some security guidance about one month after *USA Today* broke the story. However, it was advice about recognizing email phishing attacks.[260] Instead of apologizing for the hazardous search results and promising to do its best to prevent a reoccurrence, Google told users that they need to be more security conscious.

Here's yet another example of how Google responds to security problems. In 2007 Google bought GrandCentral, a company that offers users a single phone number for all of their phones. One morning the service went down, but there was no mention of the problem or estimate of when service would be resumed on Google's website. People who came to depend on the service were left completely in the dark. GrandCentral co-founder Craig Walker apologized after service was restored, acknowledging that a phone company can't just quietly disappear. "We'll do a better job keeping you informed in the future," he said.[261]

* * *

Google's free email service, Gmail, is fraught with security problems. Spammers have used Gmail to sneak past spam filters. Users who don't have Gmail accounts may not realize that messages they send to Gmail users are scanned by Google's robots and stored on Google's servers. Gmail also stores copies of draft messages as users compose them. Archived messages sitting on Google's servers may be hacked.

Spammers' exploitation of Gmail is particularly ironic. One reason that Google's founders developed a search engine was that they felt existing search engine results were overrun with spam. Google's founders were also reluctant to accept advertising because they considered unsolicited and indiscriminant advertisements to be spam. As other email providers came to trust Gmail, however, spammers realized they could use Gmail as an open relay to sneak past spam filters.[262]

Offering unlimited storage of users' email and other documents is part of Google's radical free business model. However, Google's practice of keeping copies of everything also creates unnecessary security risks. To hackers, private documents are buried treasure.

Storing copies of everything on Internet servers is irresponsible. Deleting private information that is no longer needed by the users is common sense.

*   *   *

While Google's distributed network presents myriad doors and windows for hackers to break into, Google's centralization of information puts all of the user's security eggs in one basket. From a user safety vantage point, Google is like an automobile without seatbelts, airbags, or structural reinforcement.

Greg Conti makes the point with sparkling clarity in his book *Googling Security*. The current trend is to consolidate communications, giving users the convenience of a universal address book and centralized access to email, calendars, and other forms of communication. However, this convenience is bought at a price: "Consolidating these applications creates a single point of failure: one exploited vulnerability or successful subpoena will reveal all of the user's communications."[263]

Google continues to compound the risk. In mid-2010, Google introduced a feature that lets users sign in to multiple accounts simultaneously. Billed as a convenience, the feature lets users access multiple Gmail accounts and Google Apps and switch between them.[264]

However, it's also a convenience for hackers. If hackers succeed in accessing your Google account management page, then they can access your Gmail, Calendar, Reader, and so forth. The information that can be gleaned and the damage that can be done is mindboggling.[265]

* * *

Does Google take data security seriously?

Google hired a magician and mentalist for one of its top security jobs. Eran Feigenbaum, Director of Security for Google Apps, became famous for performing death-defying stunts on the NBC television show *Phenomenon*.[266] For example, he played Russian roulette with six pneumatic nail guns, only one of them loaded, by pointing and firing five of them at his forehead.

Magicians and mentalists are entertainers. Magicians create illusions. Mentalists pretend to read minds and/or predict the future.

Feigenbaum claims that working as a magician is good training for a security job because "Hackers are trying to find vulnerabilities in our systems, things we haven't thought about; trying to get us to look at something over here when they're doing something over there and make use of that vulnerability."[267]

Do hackers "get us to look at something over here when they're doing something over there"? Or is Google trying to distract attention from its security vulnerabilities?

Feigenbaum is responsible for securing enterprise applications associated with Google's cloud computing service. That could require a magician. Whatever risks an Information Technology department faces within its own facilities, the risks posed by storing crucial business data on remote servers and accessing vital applications via the Internet are far greater. Yet Feigenbaum told IT executives, "It is incumbent upon you as security officials to know what the security controls of your cloud provider are."[268]

Public disclosure of confidential business information is just one danger. Documents could be lost or corrupted. Hackers could secretly modify documents. If a company relies on remote access to applications, then network outages could disrupt vital operations.

Perhaps Google's cloud computing enterprise customers need to hire their own magicians to disguise data stored on Google's servers and mentalists to access it when Google's network goes down.

*   *   *

Google products have been used by mischief makers to create innovative and dangerous security threats.

Researcher Samy Kamkar demonstrated how to stalk someone using geographic location data from Google's Street View database. In a security conference talk entitled "How I Met Your Girlfriend," Kamkar described how to lure the victim to a website that uses JavaScript to determine the person's media access control (MAC) address. Assuming the victim accesses the Internet via a wireless LAN, the address can be compared with the database of MAC addresses collected by Google's Street View cars.[269]

Kamkar's technique, which he calls "XXXSS," may not be a significant threat today, but it shows that the information collected and organized by Google can also be accessed and used by people with bad intentions.

Likewise, some of Google's products and tools can be used by pirates to redistribute content. For example, the Android operating system's open architecture creates opportunities for distributing illegal copies of mobile games.

According to Android game developer Hexage, there are far more illegal copies of its game Radiant in use than legal copies. In fact, 97% of Radiant players in Asia have illegal copies. Another mobile game developer, the South Korean company Com2US, also complains about Android game piracy.[270]

Google is developing a system that enables application developers to check the authenticity of copies through Google's servers. If a copy is found to be illegal, then the developer can disable it. However, this does nothing to stem the flow of illegal copies and puts the burden of policing them on developers. Once again, Google shifts the responsibility for security to others.

Google favors attributes that scale well. Apparently, responsibility is not one of them.

* * *

Sure enough, Google reported a major security breach in late 2009.

Here's how Google described the attack: "In mid-December, we detected a highly sophisticated and targeted attack on our corporate infrastructure originating from China that resulted in the theft of intellectual property from Google."[271] Other reports suggested that the hackers broke into Google employees' computers and stole valuable source code.[272]

Google's account was perplexing: "As part of our investigation we have discovered that at least twenty other large companies from a wide range of businesses—including the Internet, finance, technology, media and chemical sectors—have been similarly targeted. We are currently in the process of notifying those companies, and we are also working with the relevant U.S. authorities." Were the companies targeted directly, or was their data on Google's network targeted? If the former, why would Google need to inform them? If the latter, the statement is misleading.

In the very same blog post announcing the attack, Google's Chief Legal Officer suddenly switched gears, lecturing users to avoid sharing personal information online and clicking on suspicious links. It was a clever attempt to draw attention away from the fact that Google's network was hacked, to suggest that users (rather than Google's engineers) need to be more vigilant, and to shift responsibility for security to others.

There is no longer any need to speculate. Security is Google's Achilles' heel. The Chinese hacker attack proved it. By all accounts, it was an extensive attack; Google even raised the possibility of pulling out of China.

Then reports began surfacing that Google overreacted to the incident. Though Google reported that other companies were also targeted, Google was the only company to publicly accuse China.[273] A research report described in *Forbes* magazine claimed that the hackers were amateurs.[274] According to a WikiLeaks document, U.S. diplomats have good reason to believe that the attack was ordered by the same Chinese official who conceived the Great Firewall of China.[275]

Others are more concerned about the damage. John Markoff of the *New York Times* wrote that the hackers broke into a password system that controls access for millions of Google users. That raised the specter of the hackers coming back later for more information.[276]

The manner in which the attack transpired is evidence of Google's vulnerability. Reportedly, a Google employee in China clicked on a link in an instant message. The link took the employee to a malicious website used by the hackers to access the employee's PC. From there, they gained access to the PCs of Google software developers. By the time the attack was over, the hackers had penetrated one of Google's key software repositories.[277]

Google responded to the attack by loudly complaining about China's policy of censoring the Internet.[278] Google began redirecting users from google.cn to its uncensored site in Hong Kong (google.com.hk), but within six months Google agreed to stop redirecting users, and its license to operate google.cn was renewed. Google created an international incident over China's censorship policy just long enough to ride out the storm over Google's compromised password system.

Google tried shifting attention to users, making China's censorship policy the issue, and enlisting help from the National Security Agency. But nothing could hide the fact that Google's network was hacked in a big way. Contrast that to the way Microsoft responded to a security breach affecting its software update service; instead of blaming others or changing the subject, Microsoft overhauled the service.[279]

* * *

Google's strategic alliance with the National Security Agency (NSA) creates more security dangers than it eliminates.

The news that Google asked the NSA to help defend its network against cyberattacks was first reported in a front-page article in the *Washington Post* in February of 2010.[280]

The alliance between Google and the NSA opens a Pandora's box of privacy and security issues. Is this the start of a dangerously cozy relationship between the Internet's dominant information gatekeeper and the U.S. Government?[281] Is there an understanding that Google will share information about users (foreign and domestic) with the NSA?

Google operates the world's biggest computer network. Google employs some of the world's top engineers. Google could have convened a special task force to identify the weaknesses exploited by the hackers and devised a strategy to prevent reoccurrence. Instead of taking responsibility for the vulnerability and correcting it, Google chose to inflate the power and sophistication of the hackers by calling in the NSA.

The alliance creates a host of new security concerns. Both Google and the NSA are extremely secretive. We don't know precisely what they are doing together. Will Google share information about its one billion users with the NSA? Will the NSA be permitted to monitor Google's users?

A more important question presents itself: who will be monitoring the joint Google/NSA activity? If a strategic relationship between the largest government intelligence organization in the U.S. and the biggest data mining operation in the world is justified, then surely the empowerment of an independent organization to monitor the alliance is also warranted.

Google by itself has more power than most countries. Recognizing Google's extraordinary clout, author Jeff Jarvis coined the phrase "The United States of Google."[282] Google owns and operates the world's largest computer network and is using it to tackle complex problems such as automatically translating text from one major language to another.[283] Google is increasingly seen by other countries as an agency of the United States government. U.S. Secretary of State Hillary Clinton gave a foreign policy address that praised Google for making "the issue of Internet and information freedom a greater consideration in their business decisions."[284] Google publicly pressured U.S. trade officials to bring a World Trade Organization (WTO) complaint against China for its Internet censorship practices.[285]

There is already enough reason to worry about Google's power being placed at the disposal of the U.S. Government. As Google Chairman Eric Schmidt told CNBC, "...the reality is that search engines, including Google, do retain this information for some time and it's important, for example, that we are all subject in the United States to the Patriot Act and it is possible that all that information could be made available to the authorities."[286]

Google's embrace of the NSA increases the risk of the U.S. Government accessing the mother lode of sensitive, intimate, and private information about individual U.S. citizens as well as citizens of many other countries.

*   *   *

Google does not provide adequate data security and does not have a satisfactory security strategy.

Imagine that another Fortune 500 corporation—let's use Bank of America as an example—had its password system hacked. Customers would demand a full investigation: what data was stolen, what steps were taken to minimize the damage, and how does the company plan to prevent another attack? Customers, consumer advocates, and banking authorities would all demand that Bank of America take full responsibility.

Google's response, in contrast, is all spin and no substance.

Google does not want people to notice that security is its Achilles' heel. Google hired a magician to handle security for enterprise customers. When Google suffered a major security breach, it claimed at least twenty other companies were also attacked, lectured users on the ABCs of security, suddenly turned China's longstanding policy of Internet censorship into an international incident, and ran to the National Security Agency for help.

To wit, Google does everything but accept responsibility for making its infrastructure secure.

Chapter Five

Googleopoly

Google is a monopolist.

Google's mission "to organize the world's information and make it universally accessible" is a recipe for destroying competition. And it's working: over the past decade, Google has come to dominate online information access.

Google handles about four out of five Web searches in the free world. Google controls roughly 90% of the global search advertising business. Only one company, Google, serves most Internet users, advertisers, and Web publishers. Google dominates PC and mobile search advertising (handling more than 98% of mobile searches[287]), and Google is on a trajectory to extend its monopoly to other forms of advertising: advertising in online video, maps, books, local, and other types of content.

For a growing percentage of users, Google *is* the Internet.

If we were talking about the market for a specific commodity, then the situation would not be as troubling. But we are talking about something fundamental to almost everything we do: information access. With its vast network infrastructure, Google has built an unsurpassable lead in Web indexing and search services.

Officially, Google denies it is a monopoly, but occasionally the firm's executives admit to Google's extraordinary market power. Google Chairman Eric Schmidt stated, "Our model is just better. Based on that, we should have 100% share."[288] Peter Greenberger, Google's head of industrial relations, opined "Anything that benefits the Internet ecosystem will benefit Google."[289] Amit Singhal, ranking team head, confessed that Google's search service has the power to choose the Internet's winners.[290]

Google looks and acts like a monopoly. Most advertisers have no choice but to do with business with Google; if they don't, they can only reach about

20% of the online market. Advertising via AdWords means submitting to an arbitrary process: in Google's purported "auction" the highest bidder doesn't necessarily win, and Google may change the formula for its secret but critical quality score at any time without warning.

Google has concocted a devious strategy for rapidly penetrating dozens of new markets and milking them for traffic, content, and behavioral data. Google uses its search advertising monopoly to subsidize free products and services—products and services that competitors would have to charge for to operate viable businesses. That practically guarantees Google an instant, large chunk of any market, enabling it to extend its monopoly reach to every form of content, every major hardware platform, and every corner of the Web. And Google's strategy preempts most competitive threats; who would invest in a business proposing to compete against free products?

In fact, Google is on track to monopolize the consumer digital media ecosystem.[291] Google is increasingly the Internet's information gatekeeper and e-commerce toll collector. And Google is muscling into other products that create and use information such as mobile phones (with its Android operating system) and television (with Google TV).

When you use Google's search service, you see the Internet that Google wants you to see. Even Sergey Brin admits that Google exercises control over people by "determining what information they get to look at."[292] When you use an Android mobile phone, you are connected to Google's mobile Web. When you search within books, compose Gmail messages, and organize your Picasa digital photographs, you do it all within Google's mysterious black box. Google is rapidly becoming the Internet version of a Company Town—a place where one company controls almost everything you could want or need.

Google has learned from Microsoft's public relations mistakes. Namely, it understands the importance of flying under the radar. Google claims everything it does is either to drive innovation or to benefit users without locking them in. Google's public relations strategy has not only shielded Google from antitrust enforcement, it's enabled Google to achieve the most powerful monopoly in modern times.

The danger posed by Google's unique form of monopoly—
Googleopoly[293]—is far greater than (and qualitatively different from) any
threat ever posed by corporate giants Standard Oil, AT&T, or Microsoft.
Even Harvard Law School Professor Lawrence Lessig, a Google admirer,
admitted that Google was on course to exceed Microsoft's peak power.[294]

* * *

Others also see Google as a monopolist.

The U.S. Department of Justice (DOJ) announced in late 2008 that it
would file an anti-monopolization lawsuit to block the proposed advertising
deal between Google and Yahoo![295] As a team, Google and Yahoo! would
have controlled more than 90% of the search advertising market. As DOJ
special prosecutor Sanford Litvack said, "…Google had a monopoly and that
[the advertising pact] would have furthered their monopoly."[296]

Thomas O. Barnett, Assistant Attorney General in charge of the
Department's Antitrust Division, observed: "The arrangement likely would
have denied consumers the benefits of competition—lower prices, better
service and greater innovation."[297]

The DOJ's Christine Varney had serious concerns about Google even
before she was appointed Assistant Attorney General for Antitrust. She told
attendees at a conference: "For me, Microsoft is so last century. They are not
the problem… Google has acquired a monopoly in Internet online
advertising." Though she believes that Google acquired its dominance
legally, she added that Google is "quickly gathering market power." She sees
Google becoming a "…repeat of Microsoft… there will be companies that
will begin to allege that Google is discriminating… not allowing their
products to interoperate with Google's products."[298] Varney was troubled by
Google's acquisition of DoubleClick as well as by the proposed advertising
deal with Yahoo!

The DOJ is far from alone. European Union member states believe
Google is a monopoly. For example, Germany's Justice Minister, Sabine
Leutheusser-Schnarrenberger, said "All in all, what's taking shape there to a

large extent is a giant monopoly…" and called on Google to be more transparent.[299] Google Watch dedicates its website to monitoring "Google's monopoly, algorithms, and privacy policies."[300] A wide range of parties— from individual authors to publishers to Amazon.com—believe that the Google Books Settlement alone grants the company monopoly power.[301] And *Wall Street Journal* publisher Les Hinton calls Google "a digital vampire."[302]

Antitrust authorities are not out to punish Google just for being big. The DOJ estimated that a Google-Yahoo! partnership would control 90% of the search advertising market and 95% of the wholesale search market. Given the Internet's winner-take-all dynamic, those numbers are too close to 100% for comfort.

* * *

Google's search advertising monopoly is often underestimated.

Most estimates of Google's search market share refer only to Google's retail operation. For example, comScore reported Google's U.S. retail market share as 65.1%,[303] and Hitwise estimated it at just below 70%.[304] However, Google also provides wholesale search services to sites such as Ask.com and AOL. Consequently, Google's total search market share is higher: 71.4% (comScore) and 74% (Hitwise).[305]

Google's share of markets outside the U.S. tends to be even higher. For example, Google's search market share is 91% in both the UK and France; 93% in Germany, Spain, and Switzerland; 90% in Italy; 87% in Australia; 78% in Canada; and 89% in Brazil.[306] ComScore notes that "8 in 10 European searches occur on Google sites."[307]

Google's search advertising revenue share is even higher. I calculated Google's U.S. revenue share for the second quarter of 2010 to be a whopping 93.8%.[308] Meanwhile, Google's lead over Yahoo! and Microsoft continues to grow. Given that Google's search market dominance is much greater in Europe, it's likely that Google's search advertising revenue share in Europe is even greater.[309]

Though Google does not dominate the search advertising market in China and Korea, Google was allowed to team up with its only major competitor in Japan, Yahoo Japan Corp.,[310] to create a monopoly.[311]

Google's overall impact on the online economy is greater still. Web publishers can spend years increasing their rank in Google's search results, because Google ranks pages based largely on the number and quality of links to each page. As the website searchneutrality.org noted, Google's $23 billion in revenue (2008) was tiny compared to "the hundreds of billions of dollars of other companies' revenues that Google controls indirectly through its search results and AdWord listings."[312]

Google argued in an op-ed in the *Financial Times* that the company's search business should not be regulated.[313] The next day, the *Financial Times*'s editors offered their response: "Google should be watched carefully."[314] The very same day, the *New York Times* also expressed concerns about Google's search service.[315] While no one wants to discourage innovation, it's widely agreed that Google has little search advertising competition and many tempting opportunities to abuse its monopoly power.

Few Internet users realize the extent and power of Google's search advertising monopoly.

* * *

Google employs misleading arguments to deflect accusations that it is a monopoly.

Google's favorite defense is, "Competition is just one click away."[316] But it's a deceptive argument because it assumes that Google's customers are users. In reality, Google's customers are advertisers, and advertisers can't transfer their search campaigns to other providers with just one click. Even if they could transfer their search campaigns with one click, no other provider comes close to reaching 80% of the search market.

Google cites polls by Forrester and JP Morgan showing that most consumers use multiple search engines and would be willing to switch search providers. Again, that wrongly assumes Google's customers are users.

Google says that it can't be a monopolist because it offers consumers free products. Google's antitrust lawyer Dana Wagner said, "We want to be Santa Claus. We want to make lots of toys that people like playing with. But if you don't want to play with our toys, you've got us."[317] Google apparently believes that users are guileless children who can be bought off with a bag full of toys.[318]

It's yet another disingenuous argument: Google does not produce revenue and profits from free products—it produces revenue and profits from advertising.

Besides, Google's "free" products aren't really free. Each time you use one of Google's free products, you pay Google in tracking data and the incremental loss of privacy that goes with it.

Companies selling competing products pay an even higher price because they don't have a monopoly search business to subsidize their products. Put another way, if all Web-based products were free, then only Google could afford to provide them. As a website called "What If Google Does It?" makes disturbingly clear, Google's free products have the ability to stop new business ideas dead in their tracks.[319]

Google's free products are actually quite costly over the long run. By reducing the number of competitors, they deprive consumers of alternative choices. Free information and content diminish the incentive to produce quality content. That, in turn, limits the diversity of available information and content. When Google's free products take over a market, an environment is created in which future products don't need to serve users' interests, because now there is only one supplier. And free products can't fund important extras that consumers expect, such as customer service, enhanced features, and data security. Plus, by inundating the Internet with monopoly-subsidized free products, Google is torpedoing a trillion-dollar sector of the economy, severely damaging what should be the biggest source of jobs and growth during the current global downturn.[320]

Google wants you to believe it can't be a monopolist because its "Don't be evil" motto forbids it. However, that has not stopped Google from violating users' privacy and infringing others' copyrights. Scofflaws always manage to convince themselves that they are justified in breaking the law.

Google also wants you to believe that it is too wrapped up in the development of innovative technologies to be a monopolist. However, many of Google's most popular products and services rely on technology that was acquired rather than developed in-house.[321] For example, Google Earth is based on technology developed by Keyhole, and Google Voice is based on technology developed by GrandCentral. Google's video sharing service was created by and is still known as YouTube. Google's mobile advertising technology comes from its recent acquisition of AdMob. Even Google's crown jewels—AdWords and AdSense—employ technology developed by other companies (Overture and Applied Semantics).[322]

The flipside of this argument is that there is so much innovation going on that an Internet monopoly couldn't last long enough to matter. That may be true over the long run. However, Google wants us to simply trust that whenever competition is needed it will "sneak out of nowhere."[323] That's an obviously self-serving argument: there's no guarantee that competition will appear automatically just in time to prevent a monopoly—particularly with Google snapping up more than 70 emerging competitors and offering so many free products that it has surrounded itself with an ever-expanding "no competition" zone.

Google downplays its acquisitions as being in different or nascent markets. That's another deceptive argument. Google has discovered that the online economy offers an alternative path to monopoly. Instead of acquiring other search providers, Google's strategy is to dominate the entire value chain by purchasing companies such as DoubleClick, YouTube, and AdMob.

Google understood that to create a search advertising monopoly you need traffic, reach, and content; an array of (subsidized) free products to undermine potential competition; and inoculation against antitrust enforcement.

* * *

Google recognizes the extraordinary market power that it has acquired—even if others don't.

The full extent of Google's market power is not immediately evident. Even Google's hired Chairman (Eric Schmidt) needed time to grasp it. "I didn't really understand the power of Google until I was here for several years. Looking back, even looking at the memos I wrote in the first year I was here, you could see (Google co-founders Larry Page and Sergey Brin) viewed Google at the level it is today. They saw it, I didn't."[324]

The Internet lowers entry barriers, but it also permits rapid concentration of power. Comparing the Internet to traditional newspapers, Schmidt observed: "[the] fundamental point for newspapers to understand is that Internet distribution does not work if it is built on the economics of scarcity, but only works with ubiquity and abundance economics."[325] Speaking to the *New York Times*, Schmidt said: "The brutal economic answer is that the Internet does in fact change other people's businesses because of this massive distribution. ...We should just acknowledge that and not hide from it."[326]

Google's chief economist, Hal Varian, has developed a theory to explain it all: Googlenomics.[327] The theory consists of two major components, one macroeconomic and the other microeconomic. The macroeconomic side deals with Google's "seeming altruistic behavior" in giving products and services to users at no charge. Google does this, Varian explains, to create more Internet traffic and tracking data which, in turn, enables Google to sell more advertising.

However, the microeconomic component is most important. This is where the traffic and user behavior is analyzed, enabling Google to predict consumer behavior, attract more users, and sell more ads. It's a giant data feedback loop that's constantly tweaked to maximize performance. Summarizing Googlenomics, Varian says that on the Web, data is ubiquitous and cheap, while the ability to analyze and exploit that data is scarce.[328]

Writer Steven Levy concludes: "Varian, of course, knows that his employer's success is not the result of inspired craziness but of an early recognition that the Internet rewards fanatical focus on scale, speed, data analysis, and customer satisfaction."[329]

Chairman Eric Schmidt describes how Google exploits network effects: "…we get more users and that gets us more advertisers. More advertisers gives us more cash, more cash gives us more data centers, more data centers means we can get more engineers who want to build even bigger data centers… that cycle is very real at Google."[330]

As an article in the *Economist* notes, "Its costs are mostly fixed, so any incremental revenue is profit. It makes good sense for Google to push into television and other markets, says Mr. Varian. Even if Google gets only one cent for each viewer (compared with an average of 50 cents for each click on the web), that cent carries no variable cost and is thus pure profit… This infrastructure means that Google can launch any new service at negligible cost or risk."[331]

Google Chairman Eric Schmidt takes the idea a step further, stating that Google realizes the benefits of ownership without incurring the costs and risks of ownership: "I think the solution is tighter integration. In other words, we can do this without making an acquisition. The term I've been using is 'merge without merging.' The Web allows you to do that, where you can get the Web systems of both organizations fairly well integrated, and you don't have to do it on an exclusive basis."[332]

In other words, Google doesn't need to shoulder the costs and risks of producing the information people want in order to make money from it. All Google needs to do is control access to the information—generating traffic and tracking data in the process. It's an ideal cost-benefit arrangement: Google uses its monopoly to force others to bear the costs while Google reaps the benefits.

And make no mistake about it—Google knows exactly what it is doing.

Google is so confident, in fact, that it is using its market power to replace standards with its own solutions, knowing it is the one company that can create a de facto standard almost overnight. For example, Google has entered the URL shortening market. As blogger Jesse Noller commented, "It's not that Google suddenly came out with a (better) thing then [sic] bit.ly—Google simply came out with something which 'does the job' to the technical specifications they think are superior, sitting on Google's nearly unbeatable infrastructure and then threw the weight of their brand behind it."[333]

Think of the implications: If Google chooses to offer an online product for free and integrate it with its monopoly search system, then it is all but impossible for other companies to compete against that product. Who would want to invest in a product facing such overwhelming odds? Google claims to be a leading force for innovation, but the long-term effect of extending its search and search advertising monopoly is to squash new entrants and, consequently, discourage innovation.

What Google is ignoring to its own peril is that clearly dominant companies do not merit the same degree of freedom as non-dominant competitors. Dominant firms are held to a higher antitrust standard precisely because they have more opportunities to abuse their power.

However, monopolies are not created by people who are shy or hesitant. As author Janet Lowe described in her book *Google Speaks*, "In one strategy meeting, Brin and Page were annoyed at the presentation. Page complained that the engineers weren't ambitious enough.... We want something big, said Page. Instead you proposed something small. Why are you so resistant?"[334]

* * *

Google's goal is to control access to the world's information.

Google is unabashed about its mission "to organize the world's information and make it universally accessible and useful." However, in order to make the world's information universally accessible to others, Google must first have universal access to the world's information.

Google knows quite well that its real goal is exclusive access to the world's information. As Chairman Eric Schmidt told *Wired*, "One day Larry and Sergey and I were sitting in a room and Sergey looked at us and said, 'It's obvious what our strategy should be. It's to work on problems on a scale no one else can.'"[335] Organizing the world's information was the right kind of problem.

Schmidt admitted at a conference that Google wants it all: "Ultimately our goal at Google is to have the strongest advertising network and all [of] the world's information."[336]

Google understands that it's not necessary to create or own the information—it just needs to be the dominant conduit. As Google spokesperson Gabriel Stricker said: "Our vision remains to be the best conduit that we can be, connecting people between whatever their search is and the answer they are looking for. For that reason we are not interested in owning or creating content."[337]

The scale on which Google is organizing others' information is unprecedented. Google co-founder Larry Page said "The perfect search engine... would understand exactly what you mean and give back exactly what you want... Google became successful precisely because we were better and faster at finding the right answer than other search engines at the time."[338] Google continues to acquire exclusive access to information. As Google Chairman Eric Schmidt said, "We are very early in the total information we have within Google."[339]

Hal Varian, Google's chief economist, doesn't try to hide Google's strategy. He told writer Steven Levy that anything that increases Internet use ultimately enriches Google, since more eyeballs on the Web lead inexorably to more ad sales for Google.[340] Varian also told author Ken Auletta, "The Internet makes information available. Google makes it accessible."[341] Clearly, Varian believes Google is the only game in town.

Of all of the possible corporate mascots, Google chose to install a life-sized replica of a Tyrannosaurus Rex—one of the most fearsome predators that ever lived—at its corporate headquarters. The T-Rex is a fitting symbol of Google's determination to devour the world's information.

* * *

How did Google become a monopolist?

They say that history is written by the victors. Google attributes its phenomenal success to its superior search engine and search algorithm (a true statement), user focus (a bit of a stretch), and innovation (largely a myth). The untold story is that Google bought most of its traffic from companies including Yahoo!, AOL, and Ask.com.[342]

Users didn't choose Google's search service just because it was better. Ironically, it was Yahoo! (now Google's biggest competitor) who put Google in front of a large audience. Yahoo! outsourced its search to Inktomi and then switched to Google in 2000. That drove Google's search market share from roughly 5% to 50%. Three years later, Yahoo! realized it had made a strategic blunder, and it acquired Inktomi and Overture (which had earlier acquired AltaVista). Meanwhile, Google exploited its search lead to buy additional traffic. Google signed wholesale search deals with AOL (still the leader in dial-up access), Ask.com, and MySpace (the leading social networking site at the time). Google also provided search for hundreds of high-traffic websites. And Google cut deals with Adobe and other software firms to make Google Toolbar available for their products as a downloadable add-on.

Most users don't choose Google's search service on their own—they are directed to Google by existing service and software providers.

Google created a perpetual feedback loop[343] (that in the hands of non-monopolists would be a "virtuous circle") to achieve Googleopoly. This unbeatable feedback loop exploits the fact that Google has the only platform that enables users to reach all content, publishers to reach all advertisers, and advertisers to reach all users.[344] Google Senior Vice President Jonathan Rosenberg publicly boasted about Googleopoly's invincibility: "So more users more information, more information more users, more advertisers more users, more users more advertisers, it's a beautiful thing, lather, rinse, repeat, that's what I do for a living. So that's, someone alluded to the engine that can't be stopped."[345]

Google's perpetual feedback loop didn't just appear on its own. Google systematically acquired more than 75 strategically positioned consumer Internet companies including DoubleClick, AdMob, Android, Keyhole, Picasa, GrandCentral, Postini, and Urchin.[346] However, it was Google's acquisition of YouTube in November of 2006 that really tipped the balance and gave Google an overwhelming lead. YouTube generates the second largest number of searches in the world and now accounts for 25% of Google searches.[347] Approximately three-quarters of Google's gains in search market share over the past four years can be attributed to YouTube.[348]

DoubleClick gave Google most of the users, advertisers, and publishers that it didn't already have. By acquiring DoubleClick, Google gained 800 million ad viewers, the top 1,500 or so Internet advertisers, and relationships with 17 of the top 20 websites.[349]

Google's acquisition of AdMob has all but ensured the extension of Google's monopoly to the mobile market. Google's largest search competitors, Yahoo! and Microsoft, are not significant players in mobile advertising. It has been estimated that Google (including DoubleClick and YouTube) has an astounding 1,500,000 advertisers—far more than any mobile competitor. An article by Simon Buckingham at Appitalism.com— since removed from the Web—found that Google changed its advertising clients' default settings so that their ads were served not only to PCs but to IP-enabled mobile devices.[350] The combination of Google and AdMob gives Google 75% of the in-app (displayed within applications) mobile advertising market.[351]

Marc Rotenberg, executive director of the Electronic Privacy Information Center, was alarmed by Google's acquisition of AdMob: "We've reached a point in Google's evolution in which Washington agencies and Congressional committees need to look more closely at the company's dominance of Internet services."[352]

YouTube gave Google 80% of online video viewers. According to comScore, Google dwarfs competitors in number of viewing sessions and number of minutes viewed. Thanks to lax antitrust enforcement, Google has become the dominant global Internet TV service.[353]

In fact, through vertical media concentration Google has created what could be called the Google Internet TV Network. Leveraging its base of users, advertisers, and Web publishers—as well as products such as its Android device and Chrome Web browser operating systems—Google is positioned to extend its dominance of PC video to mobile devices and even high definition television (HDTV).[354]

Google has assembled most of the components needed to dominate not just the Internet but all Web-based consumer media for a very long time—and it did it right under the antitrust authorities' noses.

* * *

Google falsely portrays antitrust investigations as something faced by all big companies.

Julia Holtz, Google's senior competition counsel, wrote: "This kind of scrutiny goes with the territory when you are a large company."[355] Well, except for the fact that it's not true. Global Fortune 1000 companies are by definition large, yet 99% of them are not being investigated for antitrust violations.

Ms. Holtz also said, "We've always worked hard to ensure that our success is earned the right way—through technological innovation and great products, rather than by locking in our users or advertisers, or creating artificial barriers to entry."[356] But as Foundem and other customers have discovered, Google sometimes manipulates search results to take competitors out of the game.

Google insists that complaints by competitors are just sour grapes and should be ignored. Naturally, most antitrust investigations are prompted by competitors' complaints. Microsoft was investigated in response to allegations from (among others) Netscape. What matters in the end is not who complained but whether the complaints have merit.

Ms. Holtz told the *New York Times*, "We haven't done anything wrong."[357] That's sweeping absolution given that there have been multiple complaints by private parties about Google's actions; the DOJ twice opposed the Google Books settlement as a violation of antitrust, copyright, and class action law; and the DOJ opposed Google's planned advertising deal with Yahoo!.

Google Fellow Amit Singhal suggests that Google's search service appears anticompetitive because, "This stuff is tough."[358] He's referring to the difficulty of searching billions of documents and displaying the results in less than one second. However, it's also tough to compete against a dominant search service that uses constantly changing human-engineered algorithms and filters to determine who rises to the top and who sinks to the bottom.

Singhal argues that computers and algorithms are inherently unbiased and therefore can't be anticompetitive:

> Google ranking is a collection of algorithms used to seek out relevant and useful results.... Our algorithms use hundreds of different signals to pick the top results for any given query... Those signals and our algorithms are in constant flux, and are constantly being improved. On average, we make one or two changes to them every day.[359]

It's preposterous to claim that algorithms can't be biased. If it were possible to design an objective algorithm, then there would be no justification for ever changing it. Google makes daily changes because it wants to promote and demote certain Web pages. These are purely subjective decisions. The fact that they are embodied in algorithms has absolutely no bearing on whether or not they are anticompetitive.

Singhal finds the prospect of an independent examination of Google's search engine alarming: "Lately, I've been reading about whether regulators should look into dictating how search engines like Google conduct their ranking."[360] However, it's not necessarily a choice between letting Google or government officials decide who should rank highest in search results. A reasonable dose of transparency and accountability is all that would be needed to reassure everyone that Google is not acting anti-competitively.

Google insists that if a website ranks low in search results, then it must be because that site is somehow lacking. According to Singhal, "We do have clear written policies for websites that are included in our results, and we do take action on sites that are in violation of our policies or for a small number of other reasons (such as legal requirements, child porn, spam, viruses/malware, etc.)."[361] However, a number of Web publishers complain they were demoted without warning or explanation. It's up to antitrust authorities and the courts to determine whether Google's policies and practices are anticompetitive and, consequently, illegal.

Once every decade or so, a company acts in ways that threaten the survival of competition in its industry. It's not because it is big—it's because it is abusing its monopoly power.

* * *

Why is Googleopoly a bad thing and who is harmed?

A card game analogy can be used to better understand Googleopoly. By raising the search rank of its own content, Google deals itself aces.[362] Using human raters and quality scores, Google deals bad cards to competitors. With its online dominance, Google alone can see and count everyone else's cards. Google decides the ante, who can play which hands, and who can bid. When the dealer has unchecked power, there's no way to keep the dealer honest.[363]

Google's secret weapon is its Total Information Awareness. As Eric Schmidt said, "We can suggest what you should do next, what you care about. Imagine: We know where you are, we know what you like."[364] Commenting on the power of Internet-connected devices, Schmidt said, "You can literally know everything."[365] To wit, the Internet is the ultimate tracking and surveillance technology.[366] When Google executives talk about "innovation without permission," they mean unfettered use of others' data and content.

A search monopoly decides what information is found. A search advertising monopoly decides who wins and who loses. The first company to lock up all major information silos and device platforms controls information at both its sources and destinations.

Information is power. Googleopoly is absolute power.

* * *

If Google is a monopoly, then what is its strategy?

Based on its actions, Google's monopoly strategy appears to have five main components[367]:

Google hides conflicts of interest to gain user trust—Google claims to work for users, but it is paid by advertisers. This is like a physician who sends patients to a diagnostic lab without disclosing that he is the owner. Google says it is focused on serving users, but in reality Google exploits users to make money from advertisers. Google has acquired a critical mass of user trust and parlayed it, under false pretenses, into a veritable cash machine.

Google systematically buys, co-opts, and eliminates competitors—Google uses its exclusive broad view of the market to identify and buy the most important emerging companies such as Keyhole, GrandCentral, and YouTube—often paying more than their current value. Google lures companies such as Yahoo! and Ask.com into search advertising deals to prevent these companies from becoming competitors. (In fact, when a dominant company strikes deals with potential competitors they can justifiably be accused of market collusion.) And by offering free products and services, Google forces existing competitors to surrender their market share and discourages the establishment of new competitors.

Google uses highly dubious "auctions" to manipulate prices—Google purports to operate advertising keyword auctions. However, in these "auctions" the highest bidder doesn't necessarily win. In addition, Google sets individual reserve prices. The process is kept hidden from participants; they have no way of knowing what it takes to win and no way of even knowing whether the auctions are conducted fairly. Rather than encouraging competition between advertisers, Google's auctions appear to be designed to ensure maximum revenue for Google.

Google excludes competitors from accessing needed information— Google owns or controls access to critical data that others would need in order to compete. For example, Google has digitized millions of books to create an exclusive repository. Only Google is able to organize this information and make it searchable. In some cases, Google uses its monopoly power to acquire exclusive control. In other cases, Google uses its huge scale advantage to gather metadata (such as profiles of demographic groups, companies, and the entire market) that no one else can hope to acquire.

Google discriminates against emerging competitors and self-deals— Google uses human raters to adjust its search rank algorithms. The purpose of this exercise appears to be to lower competitors' (such as TradeComet, MyTriggers, and Foundem) search rank and increase their advertising price per click. Meanwhile, Google uses inside information about competitors, partners, and users to Google's advantage. For example, Google's search engine favors faster-loading websites such as those with Google's text ads over those with Yahoo's and Microsoft's display ads.

There are also allegations that Google is paying big advertising agencies to funnel display ads to Google. Google calls the payments "incentives."[368] Critics call them "kickbacks."

Each of these strategies is employed systematically. Google's monopoly strategies are purposeful, well planned, and well executed.

* * *

A seminal court ruling in March of 2007 determined that Google is a publisher and therefore has editorial power over search results.

The case began in early 2006 when KinderStart, a search engine for parents of young children, sued Google for removing its pages from Google's search results. Google responded by accusing KinderStart of trying to game its search algorithm and of operating a low-quality site (specifically pointing to a part of its site with visitor-posted content). KinderStart replied that Google's quality guidelines are too vague. A federal judge dismissed KinderStart's complaint, ruling that Google is free to manage its search results in any way it chooses.

With no prior judgment that Google was a search monopoly, Google obtained a lower court decision against KinderStart that could be cited in the future as corroborating its right to treat Web publishers any way that it wishes.[369]

* * *

Many other companies claim they have been harmed by Google's capricious actions and lack of accountability.

Ethan Siegel, CEO of Orb Audio, says that he let Google change his ad campaign and that it nearly destroyed his company.

It all began when Google offered to optimize his ad campaign. Since Google took 90% of Orb Audio's advertising budget and produced 90% of its sales, it sounded like a great idea. But when the changes were implemented, Orb Audio's sales dropped 30% while its costs increased 30%.

Orb Audio makes and sells round speakers for home theaters and PCs. It sells directly to consumers, advertising exclusively online via AdSense.

One thing Siegel didn't realize: by altering its campaign, Orb Audio lost four years of history that had entitled it to better rates and ad placements. And there was no reset button—he couldn't just go back to the way things were before the changes.

Sales dropped $100,000 per month for six straight months. Meanwhile, Orb Audio's daily advertising budget increased $500 to $1,000 per day.

In this case, Google made amends by giving Orb Audio substantial advertising credits. While its business suffered in 2007 and 2008, by 2009 Orb Audio was back on track.[370]

* * *

MyTriggers, a vertical search company started by ex-NexTag employees, sued Google for driving the company out of business by raising its minimum bids for advertising keywords anywhere from ten to one hundred times what they had been.

MyTriggers runs three shopping comparison websites: mytriggers.com, comparisonsearches.com, and shopbig.com. MyTriggers acquired traffic by advertising through AdWords, and Google extended the firm a $250,000 line of credit. Just as MyTriggers was finalizing the lease on a large datacenter, the firm's business crashed.

Google changed MyTriggers' AdWords quality score, driving up the cost of its minimum bids. The company was forced to lay off most of its employees and shut down its marketing.

MyTriggers had an unpaid bill of $335,000 with Google, and Google decided to take the company to court. MyTriggers responded by suing Google for violation of Ohio's state antitrust law, the Valentine Act.

MyTriggers made two potentially important claims. First, MyTriggers alleged that Google cut deals with select shopping bots to ensure more favorable quality scores. Second, MyTriggers claimed that Google maintains a whitelist and that if a shopping bot isn't included, it is essentially blacklisted by Google and its search partners.[371] The Ohio Attorney General filed an amicus curiae in support of MyTriggers.

Google's defenders point out that a 2008 insurance claim by MyTriggers undermines the company's case. The claim says that overheating in MyTriggers' datacenter caused servers to crash, which in turn caused a drop in the firm's AdWords quality score.[372] However, MyTriggers' complaint is that its low quality score persisted long after it eliminated the overheating problem by moving to a new datacenter.

Google always tries to shift the blame to someone else. However, MyTrigger's problem is that it ran into the Google quality score brick wall: no transparency, zero flexibility, and an unhelpful appeals process.

* * *

Totlol was founded to aggregate the best YouTube videos suitable for children. It was praised by TechCrunch writer Erick Schonfeld as a great alternative to Saturday morning cartoons. Totlol's developer, Ron Ilan of Vancouver, Canada, developed filters and other controls for parents.[373]

Ilan built Totlol around the YouTube application programming interface (API). An API allows a software program to interface with another program or device. Unfortunately, Ilan found that Google's YouTube API was something of a trap. After he developed Totlol, Google changed the API's terms of service. Namely, Google said use of the API for commercial purposes required YouTube's written permission. Ilan requested permission but never even received a response.[374] Apparently, Google doesn't like sites that make money by adding value to YouTube's service. Ron Ilan was forced to shut down the service despite having attracted thousands of parents.[375]

YouTube did issue this statement, though: "Updates to our API Terms of Service generally take months of preparation and review and are pushed out primarily to better serve our users, partners and developers. When new Terms of Service are ready, we notify our developers through as many channels as possible, including on our developer blog."[376] In other words, the changes are for everyone's benefit, and if the timing of their release seems suspicious, then it's just a coincidence.

* * *

Navx is a French company that operates a police radar speed trap location database. Though radar detectors are illegal in France, providing speed trap location information is not.

Navx relied heavily on Google AdWords to sell its services. The company spent hundreds of thousands of dollars per year on AdWords, which brought it most of its new subscribers. Without warning, Google terminated Navx's AdWords account—just as the company was about to close a second round of funding. Navx suspects that Google saw its service as competing with Google's geolocation services.[377]

France's antitrust authority concluded that Google discriminated against Navx. The French antitrust authority didn't say that Google couldn't enforce content restrictions, but it did say that the policy should be clear and the enforcement transparent. Google was given five days to restore Navx's AdWords account and four months to clarify its content policy and enforcement process.[378]

* * *

Skyhook Wireless has registered serious complaints against Google.

If Skyhook's accusations are proved in court, Skyhook Wireless could become for Google what Netscape became for Microsoft: the cornerstone of a far-reaching DOJ anti-monopolization lawsuit.

According to Skyhook's legal complaint, Google not only decided to develop and market its own version of Skyhook's technology after lengthy discussions with the firm, it used thuggish tactics in an attempt to replace Skyhook's solution with its own. The company claims that Google pressured Motorola and others to stop shipping Android mobile phones with Skyhook's location-based software.

Specifically, Skyhook Wireless alleges that Google's Vice President for Engineering Andy Rubin called Motorola's CEO Sanjay Jha and told him that Skyhook's software was not compatible with Android and that shipments of units with the software should be stopped.[379]

There is a pattern of behavior here. Google uses others' intellectual property without permission, betting that it can generate enough profit from the property to pay for any future settlement. In a nutshell, Google knows that having by far the largest stable of users, advertisers, and publishers, it can make more money from the owner's intellectual property than the owner would likely make on his own.

Skyhook's business, location-based services, is extremely valuable and strategic to Google. With this asset, Google can dominate both the local and mobile advertising businesses. These are potentially huge businesses. For starters, there are more than twice as many mobile phone users worldwide as

Internet users. Plus, mobile advertising could become the most lucrative form of advertising as local businesses seek to pull in impulse and convenience buyers.

Perhaps that's why Eric Schmidt suggested that Android, despite being offered for free, could become a $10 billion per year business.[380]

* * *

Many pundits argue that Facebook is giving Google serious competition and that consequently Google can't be a monopoly. The tech industry press is enamored with this narrative because conflict always makes good copy—particularly when it's between billionaire titans in Silicon Valley. The industry press focuses on how many users Facebook has, how much more time they spend on Facebook, and how many Google employees have defected to Facebook.

It's a dubious comparison, however. Though both Google and Facebook make money from advertising, the similarities end there. For example, Facebook depends on users spending time on its site, while Google speeds users on to other sites.[381] Facebook serves more display ads than anyone, while Google relies mainly on text ads.[382] Facebook has a low clickthrough rate, while Google has a high clickthrough rate.[383]

The point is that, unlike Google, Facebook relies on volume. It's important to remember that the dot-com bubble was fueled by an obsession with volume (as measured by the number of visitors and page views). However, Google's 2009 revenue was about 25 times greater than Facebook's. And Google is strategically positioned to dominate the Web for many years.

Don't get me wrong: Facebook is a force to be reckoned with and should enjoy plenty of growth in the years ahead. But that does not make Facebook a Google-slayer.

Facebook is not a serious threat to Google's monopoly for a number of reasons. Google is serving everyone on the Internet; Facebook is serving the subset of users seeking the best social network. Most of Google's users interact with Google many times each day; about one-half of Facebook's users do not even visit the site daily.[384] Facebook's reach will always be dwarfed by Google's because while Google is going for the whole Internet pie, Facebook is focused on a slice (albeit a very large slice).

Google is perfecting and expanding a proven model: monetizing access to information. Facebook faces more of an uphill climb. Facebook is the trailblazer in monetizing social networks (given MySpace's earlier but unsuccessful attempt). Yahoo!'s experience suggests that display advertising (favored by Facebook) can only take an online business so far.

There's a subtle but important fact that most people miss. Google has beaten Facebook in the race to sneak through the rapidly closing privacy window. Specifically, Google perfected its winning business model (involving the creation and monetization of user profiles) in time to avoid the current privacy backlash. Facebook has already been forced to limit tracking which, in turn, limits its ability to produce and grow revenue. New privacy legislation would stunt Facebook's growth much more than Google's.

Facebook's potential golden goose—detailed knowledge of users' intimate personal relationships—is also its Achilles' heel. Knowledge of relationships is powerful because purchases are often influenced by family and friends. But in the current environment, this is precisely the sort of private information that people don't want to see companies exploiting.

Ironically, it was Google who taught Facebook how to better organize online friends.[385] For years, Facebook imagined that people want all of their friends placed in one big group. Actually, most people have different types of friends with whom they share different information and experiences. Facebook responded to Google's public explanation by franticly overhauling its service in 2010.

Google demonstrated that it has a much deeper understanding of how to run an Internet business than Facebook.

* * *

A global information monopoly is a dangerous thing.

By locking up all of the major information silos and dominating search and search advertising, Google controls:

- The information that is available—influencing education, news, public opinion, and elections.

- The information and content that is published—the sources of our beliefs, freedoms, and diversity.

- The ability to innovate and compete—the engines of job creation and economic growth.

- Our privacy and safety—the most fundamental human needs after food and shelter.

- All forms of sovereignty—individual, national, religious, and cultural.

Google is turning the Internet into Googletown: a place run by and for Google. You can click on whatever links you want, but nine times out of ten it is Google who determines what you get.

Perhaps that's the reason legendary antitrust lawyer Gary Reback is leading the charge for a full-scale DOJ investigation of Google.

Chapter Six

A Morass of Hidden Conflicts

Google is not an honest broker.

Google serves as a broker in two key areas. As a search broker, Google mediates between users and Web publishers, helping users find the right content. As a search advertising broker, Google mediates between advertisers and users, helping advertisers present relevant ads to interested users.

In both cases, the parties depend on Google to mediate in a fair and balanced manner.

Conflicts of interest are inevitable for brokers. An honest broker discloses its potential conflicts of interest up front. Google tries to hide its conflicts of interest. As Google's vice president of engineering admitted, "We are, to be honest, quite secretive about what we do."[386] By failing to divulge potential conflicts of interest, Google exposes users, customers, and partners to unnecessary risks.

When confronted about its many conflicts of interest, Google changes the subject, launching into an elaborate presentation designed to convince us that the company is the most trustworthy in history. It features "Don't Be Evil," a line in the sand that Google promises never to cross, and Google the corporate Santa Claus, with his bag of free products and services for users.[387] Instead of addressing its conflicts of interest, Google lectures us about openness, transparency, and good security practices. By the time Google is done giving its answer, we've almost forgotten that the question was whether we can trust a company that hides its conflicts of interest.

Experience teaches us that we shouldn't trust people just because *they* say we should. It's wise to be cautious and even skeptical about new relationships. Partners must earn our trust over time by demonstrating that they do not cause or threaten harm. It all boils down to authenticity. Are they who they say they are? Do they do what they promise? Do they live by the values that they espouse? Are they up-front about risks?

Having potential conflicts of interest is not an automatic disqualifier. All businesses have them—they are unavoidable. If a business discloses its potential and actual conflicts of interest, and operates in an open and transparent manner, then you still may want to work with that business. A forthright business is a good partner because it gives you the information you need to protect yourself and make well informed decisions.

Google increases the risk to you by hiding its conflicts of interest. If you do not know Google's conflicts of interest, then you do not know what assets need to be protected. You have a greater chance of being blindsided. By hiding its conflicts of interest, Google prevents you from mitigating the risks, increasing both your chances of being harmed and the likely severity.

President Ronald Reagan often said, "Trust, but verify." Few people have attempted to confirm Google's honest broker status. Those who try invariably run into a brick wall.

* * *

Google claims that everything it does is for the good of others.

Google asserts that it always puts users' interests first. "Focus on the user and all else will follow."[388] However, advertisers provide most of Google's revenue. Google also insists that all of its applications and tools are designed to serve users. But that's only half of the truth: Google's applications and tools are designed to *track* as well as serve users.

In reality, Google cares about many of the same things that concern other online businesses, but it is better at feigning altruism. For example, Google is a leading proponent of "open systems," arguing that open systems are better for everyone:

> *At Google we believe that open systems win. They lead to more innovation, value, and freedom of choice for consumers, and a vibrant, profitable, and competitive ecosystem for businesses. Many*

companies will claim roughly the same thing since they know that declaring themselves to be open is both good for their brand and completely without risk.[389]

It simply isn't true that open systems produce "more innovation, value, and freedom of choice." Many successful products and services employ proprietary technology. In fact, Google mentions three in the very same blog post: IBM mainframes, the Apple iPod, and the Apple iPhone.

Note also how Google takes a gratuitous swipe at other companies, suggesting that many support open systems for selfish reasons. The implication is that only Google's support for open systems is pure.

There are different degrees of openness. The Linux operating system is an example of maximum openness. The free software license includes the source code, and anyone who changes or adds to the source code must share the changes with other licensees.

Contrary to Google's claim, this radical type of open system has major disadvantages. Products based on freely available source code are easy targets for hackers. Having to share changes and additions with other licensees discourages innovation; most inventors don't want to give away their inventions.

Might Google have an ulterior motive for supporting radical openness? It's easier for Google to collect information from products that are completely open. Harvesting information from proprietary systems is much harder. However, many proprietary systems support interoperability between different vendors' products (offering consumers freedom of choice) without giving away the source code.

Google wants others' systems to be radically open but has a clever excuse for keeping many of its own systems closed:

> *There are two components to our definition of open: open technology and open information. Open technology includes open source, meaning we release and actively support code that helps grow the Internet, and open standards, meaning we adhere to accepted*

standards and, if none exist, work to create standards that improve the entire Internet (and not just benefit Google). Open information means that when we have information about users we use it to provide something that is valuable to them, we are transparent about what information we have about them, and we give them ultimate control over their information. These are the things we should be doing. In many cases we aren't there, but I hope that with this note we can start working to close the gap between reality and aspiration.[390]

When Google refers to "open information," it is being disingenuous. The attribute that all open technologies have in common is that they permit other vendors to participate. However, Google considers the information that it collects about users proprietary.

The rest is even more misleading. Google uses most of the information it has about users to provide something that is valuable to advertisers. Nor is Google transparent about the information it collects; only when government authorities asked to see the raw data collected for Street View did Google admit it had recorded wireless LAN transmissions. And Google gives users very little control over the information Google compiles via online tracking.

Google is a champion of transparency—others' transparency. Google complies with most government requests to remove content from its services or to hand over private user data because it is required by law.[391] Google's promise to inform users is yet another masterpiece of prevarication: "Whenever we can, we notify users about requests that may affect them personally." In fact, Google's refusal to share information about its internal processes is a common complaint among Google's customers and partners.

When asked about the misuse of information, Google Chairman Eric Schmidt emphasized that users need to be more transparent:

The only way to manage this [use of information for harmful purposes] is true transparency and no anonymity. In a world of asynchronous threats, it is too dangerous for there not to be some way to identify you. We need a [verified] name service for people. Governments will demand it.[392]

However, when asked whether Google should be more transparent, Schmidt expressed a very different view:

In the eyes of sophisticated people, we gain trust by being transparent.[393]

In other words, only a tiny elite demand transparency of Google. The average user doesn't require Google to be transparent because he knows he can always go elsewhere if his trust is violated:

All of our testing indicates that the vast majority of people are perfectly happy with our policy. And this message is the message that nobody wants to hear so let me say it again: the reality is we make decisions based on what the average user tells us and we do check. And the reason that you should trust us is that if we were to violate that trust people would move immediately to someone else. We're very non-sticky so we have a very high interest in maintaining the trust of those users.[394]

However, *Wall Street Journal* columnist Holman Jenkins challenges the assertion that Google's users can just walk away:

Some might be skeptical that a user with, say, a thousand photos on Picasa would find it so easy to walk away. Or a guy with 10 years of emails on Gmail. Or a small business owner who has come to rely on Google Docs as an alternative to Microsoft Office. Isn't stickiness— even slightly extortionate stickiness—what these Google services aim for?[395]

Google claims that it is an unbiased information and advertising broker: that it always puts users first, is performing noble and important work, supports open systems for the common good, provides all of the transparency that you really need, and earns your trust each and every day.

Unfortunately, these claims don't square with reality.

* * *

Google is closed, opaque, and secretive.

A report by One World Trust, a UK-based independent think tank, ranked thirty international organizations in terms of accountability. The subjects included ten intergovernmental organizations (IGOs), ten international non-governmental organizations (INGOs), and ten transnational corporations (TNCs). Google received the lowest overall score due to its nearly complete lack of openness and transparency.[396]

Google supports closed systems in markets that Google dominates. For example, Google wants mobile phone networks to be open, but insists that AdWords, AdSense, and search advertising syndication should remain closed:

> In many cases, most notably our search and ads products, opening up the code would not contribute to these goals and would actually hurt users. The search and advertising markets are already highly competitive with very low switching costs, so users and advertisers already have plenty of choice and are not locked in. Not to mention the fact that opening up these systems would allow people to "game" our algorithms to manipulate search and ads quality rankings, reducing our quality for everyone.[397]

Google promotes open systems for markets that Google doesn't already control because open systems erase competitive advantages derived from proprietary technologies. If you can convince an industry to phase out proprietary systems in favor of open systems, then everyone is sent back to the starting line and the race is done over. It's a clever way to dethrone the market leaders.

In markets Google controls, however, it argues that open systems aren't necessary and would only invite abuses such as spam.[398]

Similarly, Google demands transparency of everyone but Google. However, as a publicly-traded company Google is expected to be transparent. For example, Google does not give earnings guidance to investors and analysts. Yet it acts like it is doing investors a favor: "...we believe that artificially creating short term target numbers serves our shareholders poorly."[399]

* * *

Google has a long list of liabilities that it avoids discussing.

The DOJ was within hours of filing an antitrust suit against Google for its proposed advertising agreement with Yahoo![400] when the deal was abandoned.[401] The FTC pressured Google Chairman Eric Schmidt to resign from Apple's Board of Directors.[402] And the DOJ twice opposed Google's proposed book settlement for violations of antitrust, copyright, and class action law.

Google also has liabilities in Europe. The European Union has launched a formal antitrust investigation of Google.[403] Three companies in the EU— the UK's Foundem, France's Ejustice.fr, and Germany's Ciao GmbH—allege that Google discriminates against niche search competitors and favors its own content in search rankings.[404]

Google has security liabilities. The hacking of its main password system could cause incalculable harm to Google's users, Google's business customers, and Google's government customers. Google doesn't talk about threats to its international business, even though it accounts for 53% of its revenue. How comfortable are foreign businesses and governments using Google's products and services now that the company is collaborating with the National Security Agency (NSA)?

Because Google repeatedly violates privacy norms, authorities in several nations are watching Google closely and may block or restrict some of its products and services. This is not a hypothetical concern: Google already reports that "Google products—from search and Blogger to YouTube and Google Docs—have been blocked in 25 of the 100 countries where we offer our services."[405] A group consisting of data protection authorities in several countries has published a letter asking Google to do more to safeguard private information.[406]

Google's former head of government relations continued to communicate with Google personnel after he went to work at the White House. A privacy flaw in Google Buzz revealed that Andrew McLaughlin, Deputy Chief Technology Officer for the Office of Science and Technology Policy, was in contact with more than two dozen Google lobbyists and lawyers. McLaughlin was reprimanded; many think he should have been forced to resign.[407]

Proposed privacy rules for behavioral advertising are another threat to Google's investors. Support has been growing for comprehensive privacy legislation that would give consumers more control over how private information is collected and used by firms such as Google.[408] There is growing support for Do Not Track rules that would allow users to opt out of being tracked online for advertising purposes.[409] The FTC issued a report endorsing privacy protections (including a Do Not Track mechanism) for consumers.[410]

Viacom's lawsuit accusing Google of copyright infringement is another liability. Google claimed during the discovery phase that Chairman Eric Schmidt's emails were accidentally deleted. (That's hard to believe given Google's obsession with archiving even draft messages.) Though Google won a lower court decision, Viacom is appealing the ruling.[411] If Viacom prevails, Google could be open to numerous actions by intellectual property owners.

Google faces multiple patent infringement complaints concerning its Android operating system. Android is gaining traction in the fast-growing smart phone market and can be used in other devices. Given that there are more mobile phone users than Internet users, unfavorable court decisions could materially affect Google's financial performance.

Google has so far benefitted from its lack of transparency. If Google's luck runs out, however, the company could take a big tumble.

* * *

Google's primary source of revenue, ad auctions, is a mysterious black box.

Google's AdWords permits advertisers to bid on text ads that appear on search result pages. The original idea was that ads had to be clearly identified (labeled as "sponsored links") and displayed separately from the organic search results. When Google added competitive bidding and per-click pricing to AdWords, Google's business took off like a rocket.

Google has backpedaled on the original concept, however. Now there are often two sets of ads on search results pages. One set is displayed separately in the rightmost column. The other set is placed directly above the organic search results. Both sets of ads are displayed against a low-contrast, shaded background. The "sponsored links" label has been replaced with the more accurate (though perhaps less noticeable) "ads" label.[412]

According to Merriam-Webster's Dictionary of Law, an auction is defined as "a public sale of property to the highest bidder."[413] However, Google's AdWords auctions are not conducted in public, and the winner isn't necessarily the highest bidder.

Google took Overture's keyword auctions, which ranked ads based on bid price, and added another ranking factor: the click-through rate. If an advertiser bids $1.50 per click for an ad predicted to generate few clicks, and another advertiser bids $1.00 per click for an ad expected to produce many clicks, then the advertiser bidding $1.00 wins.[414]

New York Times reporter Miguel Helft observed: "Not all advertisers like Google's approach. Many say that despite efforts by Google to be more transparent, they remain in the dark about what goes on inside the company's ad machine."[415]

The problem isn't merely that advertisers can't see how Google's ad auctions work. It's that advertisers have no way of knowing whether the auctions are conducted fairly. Google doesn't need to disclose the exact process to reassure advertisers. Google simply needs to hire an independent auditor to monitor the process and confirm that it is fair. Unfortunately, Google chooses not to do this.

Given Google's dominance of search and search advertising, there isn't enough competitive pressure to keep Google honest. Meanwhile, government agencies chartered to protect the public from fraud—the Federal Trade Commission (FTC), the Department of Justice (DOJ), the Securities and Exchange Commission (SEC), and the Commodity Future Trading Commission (CFTC)—have failed to examine Google's ad auctions.

The one thing we can be sure of is that Google's ad auctions are designed to benefit Google. Given Google's lack of transparency and accountability, even if Google's ad auctions are conducted fairly today, there is nothing to stop Google from conducting the auctions unfairly tomorrow.

In fact, there are reasons to suspect that Google's ad auctions are not conducted fairly. The process is opaque. The highest bidder doesn't necessarily win. Google has created mechanisms that could be used to manipulate prices. If Google did self-deal by manipulating AdWords prices, how would anyone know?

Google bids on keywords to promote its own products and services. That could be unfair for two reasons. Google could know exactly how much it must bid to beat the competitors. Since Google is paying itself (transferring money from one account to another), it receives an exclusive discount. Competitors, in contrast, must bid more or less blindly.

Rather than being open, transparent, and neutral, AdWords is closed, opaque, and tilted in Google's favor. It is a mysterious black box. There is no independent audit, and the appeals process is totally opaque.

Others suspect that Google benefits from advertisers' inability to see how AdWords functions.[416] According to search marketing consultant Adam Audette of AudetteMedia, "Hiding the complexities of AdWords makes Google the most money. There's at least the potential for a conflict of interest."[417] Google even avoids answering questions about new AdWords features by simply declaring that they are in beta test. Google often lists products and features as beta versions years after they are released.

In testimony before the U.S. House of Representatives, Harvard Business School assistant professor Benjamin Edelman explained that Google AdWords is not an auction because prices are not determined solely by supply and demand.

Edelman testified that Google manipulates a variety of factors to influence prices. For example, if a company is the sole bidder on a specific keyword, then the company pays a reserve price set by Google. There are different reserve prices for different purposes. There is a minimum price for an ad to appear, a minimum price for appearing in the space directly above the search results, and even minimum prices associated with particular ads and particular keywords.[418]

Edelman goes on to explain that reserve prices are not the same for all advertisers. Google could increase an advertiser's fees based on knowledge of the advertiser's ability to pay. The minimum bids affect other advertisers as well: if one advertiser's minimum bid is raised, then competing bidders may need to raise their bids as well. By setting secret minimum bids, Google acts like what on eBay is considered a shill: a separate account created by a seller for the purpose of bidding up prices in his or her own auctions. Google can also manipulate prices by changing the number or prominence of advertisement slots on a page.

Cade Metz, a reporter with the *UK Register*, also challenges Google's representation that AdWords is an auction.[419] Metz points out that AdWords advertisers can't bid their way to the top. According to Metz, "AdWords is an auction where you don't know the rules, [and] the rules are always shifting." In addition, Google reserves the right to eliminate an advertiser's ads—a phenomenon known as the "Google Slap." Metz observes that Google's third-quarter revenue soared 31% at a time when other companies were experiencing reduced demand. Google attributed the growth to "quality improvements." Given Google's lack of transparency, it's difficult to determine whether these quality improvements benefitted advertisers as much as they benefitted Google.

Even after Google's manipulation of AdWords prices was exposed, the company's chief economist Hal Varian continued to insist that AdWords prices were determined by auctions. Speaking in response to a report by SearchIgnite criticizing the planned deal between Google and Yahoo!, Varian said, "First and most importantly, the report fails to acknowledge that ad prices are not set by Yahoo! or Google, but by advertisers themselves, through the auction process. Since advertisers set prices themselves via an auction, the prices must ultimately reflect advertiser values. That process will remain completely unchanged by our agreement."[420] Varian also disputed SearchIgnite's claim that Yahoo! would be able to compare the prices fetched for Yahoo!'s and Google's ads and display the more expensive advertisement. According to Varian, the agreement prohibited the parties from examining each other's ad prices. But that is an admission that such price manipulation is possible. Without an independent audit, there would be no way of knowing whether Yahoo! and Google were conspiring to drive up prices.

There is evidence that Google has manipulated AdWords for its own benefit. In 2008, Google audaciously added a feature called "automatic matching" and configured the default setting as "on." Automatic matching extends AdWords campaigns to keywords not selected by the advertiser using money left in the advertiser's daily budget. Though advertisers can opt out at any time, this maneuver exploits the fact that many customers fail to opt out in a timely fashion or simply never get around to it.[421]

Google claims that it treats its AdWords ads the same as ads from any other advertiser. However, Google has been accused of favoring its ads by highlighting them, equipping them with a special dropdown box, and using longer titles than other advertisers are permitted.[422]

There have also been complaints that Google's "quality score," which the firm says is based on the relevancy of the advertiser's keywords to its text ad and user search queries, makes it harder for small advertisers to win keyword auctions at reasonable prices.[423] Changes in the quality score formula can knock down previously successful campaigns, leaving small advertisers baffled. Aaron Wall of SEOBook suggests that Google favors big brands (because they have larger advertising budgets and are likely to attract more clicks) and may even use small advertisers as probes to identify effective keywords for their larger competitors. Wall mockingly describes Google's attitude: "Thanks for sharing the keyword data needed to tell the brands what to bid on, and best of luck getting traffic from somewhere else."[424]

One thing we know for sure: there is a huge click fraud problem. Click fraud occurs when a person or computer clicks on an ad just to generate a charge to the advertiser. Though Google pays website owners each time someone clicks on an AdSense ad, the amount that Google receives from the advertisers is far greater. Google benefits from click fraud, and some feel the company really isn't interested in stopping it. There are other companies that specialize in helping advertisers detect click fraud. One of them, Click Forensics, reported in 2010 that the overall click fraud rate was 18.6%.[425]

Google is an online advertising player, referee, and scorekeeper rolled into one. If the process were transparent and accountable, then that wouldn't necessarily be a problem. Google's determination to hide what goes on in its mysterious black box breeds healthy suspicion.

* * *

Advertisers call it "click fraud." Google calls it "click spam." Is it a crime or just an annoyance?

Consider the case of home mortgage company Lendingexpert.com. Owner Samuel Baruki Cohen's strategy was to use online advertising to keep down costs. Suddenly, Cohen noticed that the number of ad clicks increased sharply. The additional clicks generated higher advertising fees but no additional mortgages. Tellingly, the number of mortgage applications submitted also did not increase. Lendingexpert.com's search engine marketing specialist, Nicole Berg, determined that the company was a victim of click fraud. For example, she found that a single IP address accounted for 200 clicks, costing the company $200.[426]

No one accuses Google of encouraging click fraud. Author David Vise points out, however, that Google could do more to prevent, detect, and stop it: "Google has the data, but not the incentive."[427] Plus, Google puts the burden of enforcement on the advertisers. Unlike credit card companies, Google expects to be paid for charges that are under investigation. Click fraud sleuth Jessie C. Stricchiola helped expose the problem in 2001: She told Vise that Google is less responsive than Yahoo! and that it often brushes off click fraud complaints.[428]

Click fraud creates additional revenue for Google. If the general perception were that Google does nothing to combat click fraud, advertisers might start abandoning Google. However, as long as Google investigates the complaints and issues some refunds, it is able to keep a lid on advertiser anger. Google's handling of click fraud is analogous to Google's handling of copyright infringement. Google creates opportunities for abuse, shields its internal operations, and puts the burden of reporting and proving violations on the victims.

Some observers believe that click fraud is a bigger problem than Google admits. Competing pay-per-click search engines estimated that prior to implementing safeguards, 40% of clicks were fraudulent. Much of the fraud was committed by software robots.[429]

*   *   *

Search rank is crucial to being found on the Web. Studies by Chitika Research show that the top position may attract more than twice the traffic of the second position. Likewise, there is a large advantage to landing on the first page of search results as opposed to the second page.[430]

Users trust Google largely because of the oft repeated claim that its search engine is unbiased—that search results are determined by an algorithm.

At Google we do not manually change results.[431]

Our third philosophy: no manual intervention... The final ordering of the results is decided by our algorithms... not manually by us. We believe that the subjective judgment of any individual is... subjective, and information distilled by our algorithms... is better than individual subjectivity.[432]

Google's search results are solely determined by computer algorithms that essentially reflect the popular opinion of the Web. Our search results are not manipulated by hand. We're not able to make any manual changes to the results.[433]

Yet on occasions Google has admitted that is not true:

[When] we roll[ed] out Google Finance, we did put the Google link first. It seems only fair right, we do all the work for the search page and all these other things, so we do put it first... That has actually been our policy, since then, because of Finance. So for Google Maps again, it's the first link.[434]

There is plenty of evidence, too. A number of companies have reported suddenly losing their high rankings in Google's search results, often with devastating effects. Some of the companies believe that they were purposely demoted by Google for competitive reasons. All of the companies complain that demotions occur without warning or explanation, and that the only recourse is to submit a formal complaint and wait for Google's response.

SearchNeutrality.org charges that Google routinely uses penalty filters to remove specific search results or demote them beyond the first three pages—effectively rendering them invisible to most users. Google originally created penalty filters to deal with spam and companies that it felt were trying to trick its search algorithms. Meanwhile, some websites are granted immunity from penalty filters or "whitelisted." According to SearchNeutrality.org,

Google increasingly uses penalty filters against potentially competing vertical search and directory services.[435]

Google justifies secrecy surrounding its search algorithm as necessary to avoid spam and gaming of the system. Or as Eric Schmidt clumsily put it, "We don't actually want you to be successful. The fundamental way to increase your rank is to increase your relevance."[436]

Contrary to what Schmidt says, Google's secrecy prevents Web publishers from learning how to legitimately achieve the highest possible ranking. Google claims to believe in competition, open source collaboration, and the wisdom of crowds, but Google's secrecy prevents these forces from coming into play. Worse, Google's secrecy makes it impossible for outsiders to confirm that Google treats all legitimate Web publishers fairly.

The fundamental problem is that Google misrepresents its search service. Google does not clearly state that the purpose of its search service is to gather information about users and sell it to online advertisers (whose text ads appear above or to the right of the search results). Consequently, most users don't even realize that their privacy is being compromised.

Why is it wrong for Google to pretend that it works for users when it actually works for advertisers? Imagine a real estate agent representing a buyer and failing to disclose that he is also the listing agent for some of the properties he is showing that buyer. The buyer needs to know that the real estate agent stands to benefit more from the sale of specific properties.

Google's founders recognized there were potential conflicts of interest from the start. In Appendix A of their 1998 academic paper, "The Anatomy of a Large-Scale Hypertextual Web Search Engine," Larry Page and Sergey Brin wrote:

> ...we expect that advertising funded search engines will be inherently biased towards the advertisers and away from the needs of the consumers... Since it is very difficult even for experts to evaluate search engines, search engine bias is particularly insidious.[437]

Google's search dominance creates an additional problem. Users depend on search engines to find information on the Web. A dominant search service is like a single source of information. In a free society, it's important to have multiple sources of information.

The danger only grows as users come to trust Google. A study sponsored by Northwestern University showed that college students often click on the top search result. The study found that many of the 102 students believe as a matter of faith that the top result is the most relevant and reliable.[438]

Combine blind acceptance of Google's search rankings with Google's market dominance and you get something approaching information tyranny. For devoted Google users, the company's search engine becomes an information bottleneck; these users erroneously assume that Google is an omniscient source.

Search dominance threatens a free society down to its foundation. Freedom requires separation of powers, checks and balances, and choice and competition. Like the Tower of Babel, a single global information portal is a product of hubris. A dominant search engine is the ultimate Company Town—a town in which one company provides everything.

Google's search service is not completely automated and algorithmic, as Google has long pretended. Google uses "human raters" to judge the quality of some websites and move them up or down in the search rankings.[439] Amit Singhal admits that the human raters tweak Google's search algorithm 600 times per year. However, Google does not divulge the grading protocol used by its human raters, the qualities it looks for in human raters, or the safeguards employed to prevent personal biases from interfering with their work. And Google has admitted that it demotes websites that "in our opinion, provide an extremely poor user experience."[440]

The potential for abuse is tremendous. Using human raters makes Google prosecutor, judge, jury, and executioner. Websites that Google demotes or blocks have little or no recourse.

Google search is not neutral and unbiased.[441] As Ben Edelman's research shows, Google hardcodes its search engine to favor Google-owned content (and products and services) over non-Google-owned content in the search rankings. This keeps users on Google's properties and promotes the use of Google products and services, giving Google more advertising opportunities.

Google has purposely injected bias in its search results. Google announced in April of 2010 that site loading speed would be taken into account when determining search rankings.[442] Some webmasters point out that this discriminates against Web pages with multiple photos and sophisticated display ads.[443] It favors sites with Google's simple text ads.

Even Google's famous PageRank algorithm is biased. Web pages are ranked by the number of sites that link to them and the number of links to the linking sites. This means, in practice, that Google's search engine favors online content over offline content, advertising-funded content over subscription-based content, brands over non-brands, and technology content over non-technology content.

There is also a not-so-virtuous circle at work here: commercial websites tend to rank higher in Google Suggest (suggestions that pop up as you type in a query) than non-commercial websites.[444]

Google's search rankings put Google's interests first.

* * *

TradeComet.com LLC accuses Google of anti-competitive behavior.

TradeComet.com operates a business-to-business search engine called SourceTool.com that connects industrial product buyers with suppliers. Within a period of months, the site grew to 650,000 visits per day. ComScore judged SourceTool.com the "Second Fastest Growing Internet Site in the World."[445]

SourceTool.com is run by Dan Savage. He made money by running AdSense ads and advertising on AdWords—receiving about $0.10 for each AdSense click and paying about $0.05 for each AdWords click. At its peak, SourceTool.com was spending $500,000 per month advertising on AdWords. Then Google suddenly raised his reserve price to anywhere from $1 to $10 per click. Savage discovered this only after his traffic dwindled dramatically.

Savage suspected that Google didn't like his narrowly focused search engine competing with Business.com, one of Google's content partners. *New York Times* writer Joe Nocera wondered if the problem was that Google doesn't like sites engaging in ad arbitrage. Google wouldn't say precisely what the problem was, but it offered Savage some advice about how to improve performance. Savage made the adjustments to little avail—he received just 1% of his former traffic.[446] Google ultimately attributed SourceTool.com's problem to changes in its "impartial" algorithm.[447] Nocera concluded:

> *The problem with monopolists, of course, is that they just can't help acting like monopolists, even supposedly benign monopolists like Google and even when they are not consciously trying to rub out the competition. They are always right and everybody else is wrong. They have disdain for their own customers, knowing those customers have nowhere else to turn. They tell small fry like Mr. Savage to stop bugging them.*

TradeComet.com's suit filed in the Southern District of New York was dismissed for improper venue; Google's standard contract says that any legal action must be brought in California. TradeComet.com pointed out that Google enforces that clause selectively; in any event, it would be unfair to try the suit in Google's backyard.[448] Tradecomet.com continues to pursue the suit.

A Web-based entertainment industry news site also claims that Google destroyed its business. Studio Briefing launched a blog and then signed up for Google's AdSense program, which pays websites for hosting ads provided by Google. The company complained that after a few months it received a form letter stating that StudioBriefing.net had been dropped from the AdSense program for failing to comply with Google policy. However, no specific violations were identified, and repeated requests for clarification proved fruitless. Studio Briefing also alleges that the website disappeared from Google's search results, and that Google cancelled its participation in the AdWords program "due to one or more serious violations of our advertising policies related to Landing Page and Site Quality."[449]

What's odd about this case is that Google reinstated StudioBriefing.net several weeks later. The company was happy to be back in business, but owner Lew Irwin wanted to understand what caused the disruption. With no clear explanation from Google, he could only guess that Google tends not to like entertainment industry content.[450]

The European Commission (EC) has also received complaints that Google demotes the search results of companies it perceives as competitors. Foundem is a UK-based vertical search engine that drills deep into websites for travel, real estate, and employment opportunities. For example, Foundem can respond to a specific travel query with a list of flights and prices—not just links to travel sites.

Foundem claims that for three-and-a-half years it all but disappeared from Google's search results while continuing to rank high in Yahoo!'s and Bing's search results. For example, in a search for prices on a specific motorcycle helmet, Foundem ranked #1 on Yahoo!, #7 on Bing, and #144 on Google. That demotion dramatically increased Foundem's per-click cost for AdWords advertisements.

To its credit, Google eventually responded to Foundem's complaints, lifting a penalty filter, but only after years of irreparable damage to Foundem's business. Foundem jumped to #5 on Google and was whitelisted on AdWords to ensure reasonable costs.

Unfortunately, just submitting complaints and waiting for Google to review them can be a hefty penalty for companies that rely on search and search advertising. First, the company must document precisely what happened. Then the company must present its case to Google. Meanwhile, its business suffers and may never fully recover.

Two other companies filed similar complaints with the EC: the French company Ejustice.fr and Ciao GmbH, a German company acquired by Microsoft. Like Foundem, ejustice.fr is a vertical search site whose search ranking was demoted without warning. Ciao was a long-time AdSense participant that, according to Google, only began complaining about

Google's terms and conditions after it was purchased by Microsoft. The EC found sufficient merit in the complaints to launch an official antitrust investigation of Google.[451]

*   *   *

Google has many other potential and real conflicts of interest.

Google's search-within-search feature lets users stay on Google's site while searching certain large websites. The users aren't actually searching the websites; they are searching copies of the websites on Google's servers. A conflict of interest arises when Google displays ads for competing sites in a secondary search box.[452]

Google's cloud computing solutions are fraught with potential conflicts of interest. Believe it or not, one of Google's selling points for cloud computing is security. Google likens storing data on your local PC to keeping cash hidden under your mattress.[453] Google already scans (cloud-based) Gmail messages for the purpose of displaying targeted advertising; there is every reason to expect Google to scan cloud computing data and documents.

Some of Google's conflicts of interest are more subtle. Google promotes free content over subscription-based content because Google wants easy access to all of the world's information. By offering information aggregation services such as Google News and Google Finance, Google depresses the value of subscription-based services.

Google invests in companies that serve search advertising customers by helping them craft search advertising campaigns. Such investments could put pressure on the companies to favor Google over Yahoo! and Bing when designing campaigns.[454]

Google entered the lead generation business with a product called Comparison Ads. Google compares products such as home mortgages and then sends leads to participating advertisers. However, because Google displays the more lucrative Comparison Ads as the top search result, Google can capture customers before they see an advertiser's own ad. As *Search*

Engine Journal puts it, "Google Comparison Ads are effectively competing against Google's own advertisers."[455]

Google's Chrome Web browser has potential conflicts of interest. The other major browsers have a search bar (for typing keywords) and an address bar (for typing URLs). While the search bar uses a search engine (most often Google), the traditional address bar simply looks up the Web address entered.

Chrome combines these two bars into what Google calls its "Omnibox." Google offers search suggestions as the user types in the Omnibox.[456] A user trying to reach a specific brand may be presented with suggestions that divert the user from the intended brand and that consequently serve as a form of advertising. Google's latest innovation (for which Yahoo! claims several patents), Google Instant, favors big brand names that are most readily constructed from partially spelled words, pushing what Google wants rather than what the user is seeking.[457]

Google also has political conflicts of interest. Google Chairman Eric Schmidt campaigned for Barack Obama, was a member of Obama's transition advisory board, and was expected to be offered a White House post. Despite his obvious personal bias, Schmidt warns politicians to expect the development of an online "truth predictor" that would "hold politicians to account." Schmidt added "We [at Google] are not in charge of truth but we might be able to give a probability."[458]

Schmidt illustrates how Google makes something inappropriate seem innocuous. Google has a decided preference for one political party. It is hardly in a position to ascertain which politicians are most honest. Presenting judgments as probabilities isn't a strategy for eliminating bias—it's a strategy for disguising it. Some people may be impressed when told that there is an 83% chance that what Senator Smith said about health care policy is not true, but at the end of the day it is just an opinion with a number stamped on it.

The problem is further compounded by the fact that Google has an expansive public policy agenda. Google has been a target of antitrust investigations; Google has an interest in discouraging new privacy laws and regulations; and Google is affected by policy decisions concerning the wireless spectrum, the nation's power grid, and electronic medical records—just to name a few.

Given the propensity of users to click on the top search results, Google could influence elections merely by promoting and demoting relevant Web pages by one position. Because Google's search engine lacks transparency, it would difficult for anyone outside Google to detect small, politically-motivated promotions and demotions. It's also likely that Google has exclusive tracking data on politicians' online campaigns and could use this data to assist its favorite candidates.

There is growing concern that Google uses its search engine to help boost its own products and hurt competitors' products.[459] Technorati, a specialized search engine, complains that its search rankings have fallen precipitously on several occasions. Barry Diller, chairman of travel site Expedia, accuses Google of favoring Google travel sites.[460]

Commenting on Google's acquisition of ITA Software, an online travel service, Diller said, "I think it is disturbing that Google is moving into serving individual spaces, rather than being search neutral. It is a dangerous step because it is inevitably going to cause problems with customers and regulatory authorities."[461]

Google publicly opposes rules that would require major search engines to operate transparently or comply with "search neutrality" standards. In a guest editorial in the *Financial Times*, Google's vice-president of search product and user experience Marissa Mayer said:

> *These algorithms embody rules that decide which information is "best", and how to measure it. Clearly defining which of any product or service is best is subjective. Yet in our view, the notion of "search neutrality" threatens innovation, competition and, fundamentally, your ability as a user to improve how you find information.*[462]

Mayer went on to argue that any type of search neutrality rules would inhibit innovation. She not only ignored mounting evidence of abuse by

Google, but she warned against making Google's search engine transparent on the grounds that that would invite abuse by "spammers."

Pot, meet kettle.

* * *

Google is in business to make money. By pretending that it is in business to make the world a better place, Google creates an elaborate smokescreen to hide its conflicts of interest—conflicts inherent to being a search and search advertising broker.

Despite the Google myth-making machine's success, knowledgeable and influential people are increasingly skeptical. Google tries to avoid the conflicts-of-interest issue by offering a choice: trust it or go elsewhere.

Unfortunately, it's not that simple. Google dominates search and search advertising. Google has inside information on practically everyone. Google's information asymmetry gives Google power over users, publishers, and advertisers. We can't just go elsewhere.

The problem isn't that Google is big—the problem is that Google hides and denies conflicts of interest. Fair representation, full disclosure, and truth in advertising are the answers.

Chapter Seven

Unchecked Power

Google is the most powerful company in history.

When Google's founders began their research project in 1996, they understood that the digital economy was just taking shape, and they made a series of momentous discoveries. They recognized, for example, that the expanding online universe would revolve around search. They concluded that quickly finding information needles in the Web's burgeoning haystack required an automated, algorithmic process. And they knew that if they built a scalable network replicating the entire Web, then they could handle problems no one else could even dream of tackling.

Later, when they recognized how valuable tracking and profiling users is to advertisers, they found that—thanks to their scalable network and database—they were ideally positioned to profit from the idea.

Google's founders also had keen business insights. They knew, for example, that despite the Internet gold rush there were huge, untapped opportunities. They believed that anyone sufficiently ambitious and aggressive could reap untold rewards. And they saw that there was a remarkable first mover advantage still waiting to be exploited.

Acting on these profound insights, Google raced to acquire scale, scope, and reach. It quickly amassed power that others didn't even realize was available. Slowly, other companies and later governments began to realize what was happening. By then it was too late: Google had pulled so far ahead that competing with Google head-on was all but impossible.

Power is not automatically a bad thing. Power can be used to advance charitable causes. Power is essential to a free society; citizens grant their government a monopoly of force in exchange for the rule of law, recognition of citizens' fundamental rights, and due process. A legitimate government is accountable for how it exercises power and is subject to checks and balances.

Power can also be abused, and that's why it should always be constrained. As Milton Friedman observed, "The power to do good is also the power to do harm."[463] And as Lord Acton famously quipped, "Power tends to corrupt, and absolute power corrupts absolutely." History teaches us to be wary of unchecked power.

By seizing the first mover advantage, Google acquired extraordinary power over the digital economy. Google acted so quickly, in fact, that there was no time to institute needed checks and balances. Knowing it was almost home free, Google mastered one more skill: evading accountability.

Fifteen years after what started as a university research project, Google's unchecked power has mushroomed, threatening everything from online competition to individual freedom.

* * *

Google is by far the largest Internet business.

Google has more than *one billion* users. Google dominates both search and search advertising. Google handles more than *two billion* Internet searches per day.[464] Google's tentacles extend to every major type of content, every major hardware platform, every nook and cranny of the Web, and every corner of the globe.

Google has indexed over *one trillion* Web pages.[465] If you spent one minute scanning each page indexed by Google, then you would need more than 38,000 years to scan them all. Gmail's data repository is equivalent to about 1.74 billion music CDs. If you printed the information Google processes each day, then you would need to cut down 1.2 million trees. The most popular YouTube video has been viewed over 200 million times.[466]

Google has the most online advertisers (well over *one million*[467]), and virtually all Web publishers are its clients. Google Translate handles 57 languages, covering most of the world's population. Google YouTube is the world's largest video-sharing site with 43% of the market—more than ten times the nearest competitor. Google has over 500 products and services[468] covering almost every imaginable type of information.

Digital technology has ignited an information explosion. According to Google Chairman Eric Schmidt, "Between the birth of the world and 2003, there were five exabytes of information created. We [now] create five exabytes every two days."[469] An exabtye is one quintillion (10^{18}) bytes.

It's hard to visualize such a large number. One exabyte is roughly 20,000 times the amount of information contained in all of the books ever written. It would take 50,000 years to watch a one-exabyte DVD-quality video.[470]

It's no coincidence that Page and Brin named their company after the largest number with a moniker, the googol. The pair recognized from the start that the Web would spark the digitization of all existing information and content and the rapid creation of new digital information.

Google is the only company capable of handling such huge volumes of data. Schmidt added: "Plot that curve. The information explosion is so profoundly larger than anyone ever thought. But that's what this opportunity creates. We want to enable it to be more organised."[471]

When Google's executives say they want to "organize the world's information and make it universally accessible," they mean they want to record, store, copy, and distribute the world's information. Recording the world's information requires, figuratively, global eyes and ears. Storing and distributing it requires, quite literally, the world's biggest computer, the world's biggest storage network, and a global-scale file system.

Google is master of the googol-scale world. While many scientists and companies are developing nanotechnology—solutions on the scale of molecules—Google is pioneering the other end of the spectrum—solutions on the scale of the world. Working at this level requires vast infrastructure and entirely new tools.

To its credit, Google has developed a search engine capable of finding a needle in the global information haystack in less than one second. Few people fully appreciate how difficult it is to do that. Think of Google as a library the size of a large city, the United States, the planet Earth, or the entire solar system. Then think of the file system and navigation tools needed to instantly find a specific item in that library.

The most powerful search engine is the search engine that indexes the most information and has the most users. That's why Google is obsessed with extending its reach to all major forms of content, all major devices, and every corner of the Web. It also explains why Google admonishes others to be "open" and "transparent."

How might we gauge Google's power? We can calculate Google's search market power by dividing the total volume of searchable information by the number of viable search competitors. It is a very large number because Google has indexed an enormous volume of data and has only one truly viable search competitor.

The Internet is a double-edged sword. One edge empowers users by connecting them to information, content, and each other. It provides a universal language for exchanging text, graphics, audio, and video at the speed of light. And it spans the entire globe.

The other edge empowers Internet companies. It enables companies with the vision and ambition to gather and organize the world's information, reach most consumers, and analyze data on a scale never before contemplated.

By thinking big, Google's founders created the most powerful company in history.

* * *

Google poses a much greater threat than Microsoft ever did.

Ken Auletta, writing in the *New Yorker*, said:

> *Andy Grove, the former chairman and C.E.O. of Intel, who was an enthusiastic supporter of Google's founders when they started the company, in 1998, believes that there may be more worry about Google than there was about Microsoft. "Microsoft's power was intra-industry," he told me. "Google's power is shaping what's happening to other industries." Because of this, he says, Google is increasingly seen as a company "on steroids, with a finger in every industry."*[472]

There are several key differences between the Google of today and the Microsoft of the 1990s. Microsoft dominated how information was produced and visualized; Google determines what information is found, read, viewed, heard, distributed, and monetized.

Microsoft acquired monopoly power before most consumers had personal computers. Google acquired monopoly power after most consumers had Internet access.

When Microsoft began selling its mobile operating system, there were only hundreds of millions of mobile phone users, and wireless was still predominantly narrowband. When Google introduced its free mobile operating system, there were billions of users, high-speed digital networks, and a soaring smart phone market.

Microsoft's software was primarily machine-based, and much of it was installed at the factory. Google's software is mainly cloud-based and is easily accessed and used over the Web.

Microsoft was a pre-Internet company with the scale, scope, and network effects of a company rooted in the physical world. Google is an Internet company with far greater scale, scope, and network effects.

Neither Microsoft nor Yahoo! can compete with Google. While search is Google's core competency, it's just a sideline for Yahoo! and Microsoft. Google operates the world's largest computer grid with over one million servers in multiple data centers. Google processes hundreds of millions of searches each day with sub-second response time. Google indexes tens of billions of Web pages daily, maintaining its own copy of the entire Internet.[473]

Google has mastered at least 26 sources of market power[474] including economies of scale (e.g., one billion users), economies of scope (e.g., search engine interfaces for more than 110 languages), time (e.g., fastest search), standards (e.g., Google is the wholesale search standard), bundling (e.g., Google Toolbar), and network effects (= audience x advertisers x publishers x traffic).

Google's search algorithm is based on over 200 relevancy variables ("signals") and formulas ("classifiers") that have been honed and refined with feedback from trillions of actual searches. For example, Google has learned the myriad ways people misspell or mischaracterize their searches.[475]

Google's huge audience is a big advantage. Google can afford to pay more to acquire additional traffic because Google has big leads in both number of users and number of advertisers.

Microsoft monopolized PC operating system software but was stopped by the DOJ when it tried to buy Intuit, the leading maker of PC financial software, and again when it tried to strangle Netscape's Web browser. The antitrust authorities permitted Microsoft to dominate the horizontal operating system market but stopped Microsoft from extending its dominance to vertical markets.

Google, in contrast, is using its search advertising monopoly to extend its dominance to digital information such as maps and location data; mobile operating systems; video streaming; news; and several other areas.

Instead of responding to Google the way they responded to Microsoft in the 1990s, the antitrust authorities (in this case the FTC) approved Google's acquisitions of DoubleClick and AdMob, enabling Google to achieve monopoly power in both the horizontal search market and key information and content vertical markets.

In short, Microsoft's monopoly power was kept in check by antitrust authorities; Google's monopoly power has been allowed to mushroom out of control.

* * *

Most users see only one half of the Internet information bonanza.

The Web not only makes it easier to publish information; the Web makes it easier to harvest, store, and apply information.

In the past, there were separate bottlenecks associated with collecting, saving, and analyzing information. The Internet, with its underlying digital technology, changed everything. Now information and content are just streams of 1s and 0s.

Users know from experience that the Web makes an incredible amount of information available to them. They are somewhat aware, due to concerns over privacy and security, that the Internet also makes information about them available to businesses, governments, and hackers.

What most users don't yet fully appreciate is that everything they do online can be recorded, creating unique "digitalprints."

Digitalprints consist of both obvious and non-obvious information. Most users know that they may remain logged on for months to websites such as Yahoo! and Amazon and that they are automatically recognized when they return to those sites. However, literally everything we do online can be recorded, and it's the details that make a user's digitalprints unique. For example, your digitalprints may include information about the time you spend on individual Web pages, how often you click on links, and even the way that you move the on-screen cursor with your mouse. If it can be observed or measured, it can be included in your digitalprints.

One of the factors driving the recording and permanent archiving of online information is described by Nicholas Carr in his book *The Big Switch: Rewiring the World, from Edison to Google*. Carr explains that just as electricity evolved from a few homes with private generators to power plants serving many homes, computing is evolving from personal computing to cloud computing. It's more cost-efficient for electricity customers to be served by a central power plant than it is for customers to install and operate their own generators. Likewise, it's more cost-efficient to run applications and store documents in the Internet "cloud" than on users' individual PCs.

Cloud computing is leading inexorably to the permanent archiving of all information and content. It's not just books, research papers, and business memos that are being stored, though; it's what you searched the Web for last Tuesday and that draft email message that you thought you deleted.

You may prefer that most of this information be destroyed. Google has learned, however, that even the information that you discard reveals something about you and can be used to select and target you with greater precision. And Google doesn't mind going through your online wastebasket.

Governments and big corporations are beginning to realize that because the Internet is an open network with extensive archives, it can never be fully secure. This has given rise to a countertrend. Namely, sensitive information that never belonged on a public network—such as military and confidential business information—is increasingly being stored elsewhere to prevent theft, unwanted disclosure, and improper use. Unfortunately, most consumers don't have that option.

It's the half of the information bonanza that you can't see that can really hurt you.

* * *

Google is moving toward Total Information Awareness.

Following the September 11, 2001 terrorist attacks, a former U.S. national security advisor to President Reagan, Admiral John Poindexter, proposed that the U.S. intelligence community make aggressive use of surveillance and information technologies to identify and track terrorists. An office was established in early 2002 for what became known as the Total Information Awareness program. However, responding to fears that the technology could be used to spy on ordinary citizens, Congress defunded the program in 2003.

Ironically, a similar program was conceived by Google and continues to move forward.

Google deserves credit for inventing a way to handle the exponential growth of information. However, not all information should be "universally accessible." Most Internet users do not want information about their online behavior sold to advertisers. Content creators and publishers do not want their copyrighted works to be freely accessible. And governments do not want national security secrets placed online.

Despite the many concerns and common sense objections, Google is intent on finding, logging, copying, storing, distributing, and analyzing every bit of information it can get its hands on. As Google Chairman Eric Schmidt said, "We are very early in the total information we have within Google. The algorithms [software] will get better and we will get better at personalisation."[476]

In fact, Google is pursuing its own version of Poindexter's Total Information Awareness program.[477] Google logs, stores, and analyzes three major categories of information: personal information, market information, and the world's information.

Personal information includes identity, intentions, location, and associations. Personal identity includes everything from IP (Internet protocol) addresses, email addresses, and phone numbers to voiceprints, bank account details, and personal genomes. Personal intentions include keywords searched, ads clicked, and calendar appointments. Personal location includes, for example, mobile phone waypoints, maps to destinations, and Google Goggles (an application that can purportedly search for information about landmarks using digital photographs taken with Android mobile phones). Personal associations include contact lists, discussion groups, social networks, and more.

Google acquires market information by monitoring online advertising supply and demand and by detecting search trends, fads, and growth spurts. Google harvests the world's information by periodically crawling more than one trillion Web pages, digitizing books, and by acquiring satellite images of the Earth's surface. Yet these are just a few examples.[478]

Google doesn't really believe that all of the world's information should be accessible to the public. In fact, there is an entire category of information that Google believes should be hidden away and carefully guarded. The information that Google considers exempt includes Google's search algorithms and filters, the AdWords auction process, details concerning Google's infrastructure, and almost everything that goes on inside Google.

Google knows that it is its right to keep certain information secret. Google just needs to understand that others have the same right.

* * *

Unchecked power breeds arrogance.

Google demonstrates this simple truth almost every day. For example, in an interview with *BusinessWeek*, Google Chairman Eric Schmidt was asked whether Google has acquired too much power over where people go on the Web. Schmidt responded, "…to say Google is too powerful implies that users are somehow making a wrong choice."[479]

Schmidt's response typifies Google's tactic of shifting responsibility. If Google is too powerful, then shame on users. Schmidt not only refuses to acknowledge that Google could be too powerful, he refuses to acknowledge that Google's lack of transparency prevents most users from seeing how much power Google has amassed.

When asked why users should trust Google, Schmidt flippantly responds, "Because we say so."[480] Instead of demonstrating that the company is accountable, Schmidt expounds on how easy it would be for disgruntled users to go elsewhere.

At times, Schmidt's arrogance borders on threatening. "There are many, many things that Google could do, that we chose not to do. One day we had a conversation where we figured we could just try to predict the stock market. And then we decided it was illegal. So we stopped doing that."[481]

Schmidt acknowledged that Google executives have the power to detect financial market trends before others. The only thing that stopped them was the realization that it was illegal. However, notice the ambiguity: If they were just batting around an idea, then what did they stop doing?

Google claims that its search engine is unbiased: "All rankings are decided algorithmically, and the focus is on user benefit, not advertiser or commercial benefit."[482] But the head of Google's search ranking team, Amit Singhal, acknowledges that Google is "the biggest kingmaker on this earth."[483] And Google Senior Vice President Jonathan Rosenberg admits that Google dethrones others: "We won't (and shouldn't) try to stop the faceless scribes of drivel, but we can move them to the back row of the arena."[484]

However, if Google's search engine is unbiased, Google would only be identifying kings—not making and breaking them. Google arrogantly believes that it can have it both ways: bragging that its search service is a kingmaker while continuing to peddle the myth that it is unbiased.

Chairman Eric Schmidt confesses that it took time for him to fully grasp Google's dominance. "I didn't really understand the power of Google until I was here for several years," he said.[485] Obviously, it wasn't a humbling experience.

Google also demonstrates its arrogance by pretending it is universally adored by users, Web publishers, and advertisers. In reality, Google is a target of frequent complaints. For example, users complained that they were promised but never received $10 for signing up with Google Checkout, the company's answer to PayPal. Several users even filed complaints with the Federal Trade Commission (FTC).[486]

Google demonstrates the height of arrogance when it acts (as it often does) without warning or explanation. For example, Google's Blogger service shut down several music blogs after receiving copyright infringement complaints.[487] Google certainly has the right to cancel copyright infringing blogs, but what if some of the bloggers were innocent? Google has little patience for warnings and appeals.

Google acts as if its dominant market share is a mandate to do as it pleases.

* * *

Meet J. Edgar Google.

J. Edgar Hoover was the first director of the Federal Bureau of Investigation (FBI). While Hoover is credited with advancing forensic science and building the FBI organization, he is also accused of illegally assembling dossiers on leading politicians and dissidents.[488]

Google is creating dossiers on Internet users—dossiers that could be dangerous if shared with governments. As author Andrew Keen said:

> *They have amassed more information about people in 10 years than all the governments of the world put together. They make the Stasi and the KGB look like the innocent old granny next door. This is of*

immense significance. If someone evil took them over, they could easily become Big Brother.[489]

No one can match Google's ability to track and analyze users' online behavior. Google employs techniques such as click tracking, forms, cookies, logged server requests, JavaScript, and Web beacons (tiny images) to gather the data.[490]

Google's free products collect more data. According to search engine optimization expert Danny Dover, Google Health captures information that includes the user's physical characteristics, medical conditions, procedures, test results, doctors, prescriptions, allergies, and immunizations.[491]

The full extent of the information that J. Edgar Hoover gathered about individuals only came to light after his death.[492] Likewise, users don't know the full extent of the information that Google is collecting about them. The Freedom of Information Act (FOIA) does not apply to Google.

There are, however, some differences between Google and J. Edgar Hoover. Google not only gathers information about users, Google influences the news people get, the videos they watch, and the books they read.

Google understands the threat its power poses to other people and organizations. Eric Schmidt has said as much: "Every government sort of has some group that's busy trying to figure out what we're up to. Because information is power."[493]

* * *

Many people fear that Google has become too powerful.

In a letter to EU authorities concerning Google's planned acquisition of DoubleClick, the European consumer group BEUC (European Bureau of Consumers' Unions) said: "Never before has one single company had the market and technological power to collect and exploit so much information about what a user does on the Internet. The unprecedented and unmatched databases of user profiles appear also to be in clear violation of users' privacy rights."[494]

Commenting on Google's emergence as the Web's information gatekeeper, Seton Hall associate professor of law Frank Pasquale said:

> *Google knows more and more about us, but right now there's almost nothing we can do to find out exactly what it does with that information. We want to make powerful entities on the Internet accountable.*[495]

Ken Auletta, author of *Googled, The End of the World as We Know It*, also sees unprecedented power: "...there has never been a company whose influence extended so far over the media landscape, and which had the ability to disrupt so many existing business models."[496]

Others feel it's time to put the brakes on this runaway locomotive. Germany's *Der Spiegel* wonders if Google knows too much and quotes author Gerald Reischl suggesting that Google's "machinations, hunger for power and dominance need to be scrutinized."[497]

Questioning the proposed Google-Yahoo! deal, Google customer Michael Menis, Vice President of Global Marketing Services at InterContinental Hotels Group, said, "Anytime you have this level of consolidation or control by one company in any industry should raise concerns."[498]

A *BusinessWeek* article asked, "Is Google Too Powerful?" Perhaps the correct answer in 2007 was, "No." The article drew attention to the rapid growth of Google's global audience, the concentration of power over information and content in one company's hands, and Google's destructive, anti-competitive strategy.[499] The question at the time should have been whether Google was on a course to become too powerful.[500]

Some commentators believe concerns about Google's unprecedented power are exaggerated.[501] However, what one person sees as paranoia another person may consider heightened awareness. We should be concerned when any person or entity acquires too much power. We should be doubly concerned when that person or entity is secretive and unaccountable.

Google understands that having the biggest audience enables it not only to protect its market lead but to extend it.[502] For example, Google cut a deal with Mozilla, maker of the Firefox open source browser, to make Google's search page the browser's default home page and make Google the default search provider in Firefox's search bar. To seal the deal, in which Google paid Mozilla royalties, Mozilla agreed to incorporate and keep the details of the arrangement secret. To some, it looked like the champions of the open source browser became "an extension of Google" overnight.[503]

It's easy to underestimate Google's power—and hard to overestimate it.

* * *

Just how unaccountable is Google?

When Google went public, the company structured its stock so that the top three executives are minimally accountable to other shareholders. The three received special shares with privileged voting rights. As the founders admitted in their IPO letter: "...New investors will fully share in Google's long-term economic future but will have little ability to influence its strategic decisions through their voting rights."[504]

What this means is that Google is a publicly-owned, privately-controlled corporation. While that's a perfectly legal arrangement, it shows that Google does not practice the sharing, openness, and universal access that it preaches. A publicly-owned, privately-controlled corporation is less accountable to outside shareholders.

Google is not even accountable to the U.S. Supreme Court. When the Chairman of the Homeland Security Committee, Senator Joe Lieberman, asked Google to take down content intended to incite violence and promote terrorism, Google refused, claiming the content was protected speech.[505] Actually, the U.S. Supreme Court is the final arbiter of what types of speech are protected under the U.S. Constitution; the Court ruled that speech inciting violence is not protected.[506]

Unaccountability is part and parcel of Google's "innovation without permission" culture. Google is an enthusiastic participant in the free software/open source community that believes that proprietary software inhibits innovation and that developers should be free to copy, modify, and share code. This "techtopian" philosophy is an essential ingredient for mashups—new applications created by combining data and/or functionality from two or more sources.

Google literally believes that it does not need permission to do anything that it considers good. For example, Google's Chrome Web browser automatically updates itself without asking the user's permission.[507] Google changed the default settings for its advertisers' accounts without asking permission, generating hundreds of millions of dollars in additional revenue.[508]

Instead of first asking for permission, Google waits until the complaints roll in and then asks for forgiveness. Google Chairman Eric Schmidt told the *Financial Times,* "Whack-a-mole is our life."[509] He was referring to the purely reactive arcade game in which players must knock down a plastic mole whenever one pops out of one of numerous holes. Schmidt goes on to explain that he sees his job, in part, as protecting Google's freewheeling culture: "I want to have checks and balances. But it would be terrible to put a chilling effect on creativity. We have to find a way to continue to be creative with some more oversight."[510]

That attitude might be justified if Google was a tiny startup. But Google is the world's largest Internet company—a position that comes with responsibilities. Instead of proactively avoiding expected problems, Google prefers to react to problems after they've been pointed out by others. Instead of preventing copyright infringement, Google puts the burden on copyright holders to assert their rights—often after damage has been done.

Surely the public would not tolerate this attitude in other industries. For example, imagine pharmaceutical companies launching new products without testing them, and then insisting that determining the efficacy and safety of the drugs is the sole responsibility of patients and their doctors.

Though Google does not produce pharmaceuticals, the company's actions can endanger users. For example, one woman complained that when

Google populated her Google Buzz account with her email contacts, it gave contact information for her friends and family to her abusive ex-husband.[511]

Instead of acting more responsibly, Google prefers to lecture others about how they can better protect themselves. For example, Google responded to complaints about Google Buzz by producing a video about teen safety.[512]

Google refuses to believe that its problem is a lack of internal controls. Asked about the challenge of managing such a large company, Chairman Eric Schmidt said, "The word 'control' is not such a strong word at Google."[513] But he has also complained about how difficult it is to get Google employees to email a one sentence summary of what they did over the previous week.[514]

Larry Page and Sergey Brin worry about anything that could hinder innovation. According to author Ken Auletta, "Larry and Sergey believe that if you try to get everybody on board it will prevent things from happening… If you just do it, others will come around to realize they were attached to old ways that were not as good… No one has proven them wrong—yet."[515]

Eric Schmidt defends Google's practice of making products available before they've been thoroughly tested. According to the *Financial Times*, "…Schmidt counters that the 'launch first, correct later' approach is vital to the ultra-creative and flexible company DNA that has produced the world's most popular search engine, Gmail, and Google Earth…"

Schmidt also takes satisfaction in knowing that legislation has not yet caught up to changes wrought by the information economy: "We are in the information business and everyone has an opinion about information. But the laws [covering these areas] are inconsistent."[516]

It's just a small step from there to the belief that Google should be exempt from accountability and even many laws. In an on-stage interview, Eric Schmidt explained that Google's cause transcends the concerns of conventional businesses: "The goal of the company is not to monetize everything, the goal is to change the world… We don't start from monetization. We start from the perspective of what problems do we have."[517]

Google not only resists accountability, it undermines efforts by others to hold Google accountable. For example, Google's website traffic measurement service, Google Trends, competes with companies that track Google such as comScore and Nielsen Online.[518] Advertising executives point out that it is a conflict of interest for the leader in online advertising to also be in the business of measuring and reporting online performance.[519] To wit, it enables Google to act as witness, prosecutor, judge, and jury.[520]

Being unaccountable means not having to abide by your own rules. Google's official position is that it never manipulates search results. But Google has admitted that its search service isn't neutral. Google spokesman Gabriel Stricker said, "Sometimes that means that our own properties could come up first, such as in case that you cited, maps, and that happens when it gives them a quick answer that benefits users. But apart from those situations, these are organic search results that are determined algorithmically and change all the time."[521] There have also been complaints about Google selectively blocking advertisements.[522]

Google desperately needs a large dose of accountability.

* * *

The Google Books settlement further illustrates why Google should be made more accountable.

The Google Books settlement is a proposed agreement between Google, the Authors Guild, and the Association of American Publishers.[523] One problem with the settlement is that it tacitly accepts Google's exclusive authority to scan, digitize, store, and search books. Writing in the *New York Review of Books*, Harvard Professor Robert Darnton said, "The settlement creates a fundamental change in the digital world by consolidating power in the hands of one company..." He also called the settlement, "a tipping point in the development of what we call the information society."[524]

The settlement empowers Google to seize and monetize others' intellectual property. For example, it creates opportunities for Google to sell targeted advertising, temporary online access to content, and print-on-demand excerpts.

Google exploited a broader industry effort to digitize printed books. Writing in the *Globe and Mail*, Toronto attorney Grace Westcott said, "The position of power Google will occupy, as owner of a database comprising the combined holdings of the greatest U.S. research libraries, is simply breathtaking. And worrisome."[525]

Though most libraries support scanning as a way to ensure the long-term survival of books, many have misgivings about the deal. Carole Moore, Chief Librarian at the University of Toronto, told the *Economist*, "Some librarians worry that this gives the Internet firm enormous power. This is a more powerful monopoly than we've ever seen for access to 20th-century material."[526]

Appointing just one company to scan rare and fragile old books may be the wisest course. But the privilege should be balanced by the obligation to provide access to other search companies and to share advertising revenue with the appropriate authors, publishers, and libraries.

However, that will only work if Google operates in a transparent and accountable fashion.

* * *

Google's extraordinarily rapid acquisition of power has created a dangerous environment—one in which Google's power could veer out of control.

Google is already destroying privacy, intellectual property, and online security. Through aggressive use of acquisitions, partnership deals, and the radical free business model, Google is destroying competition. And Google's hidden conflicts are destroying fairness and trust.

Now it is time to connect the dots. What is Google's attitude toward Internet users? What are Google's values and ethics? Does Google have a hidden agenda? We will answer those questions in Part II.

Part II

Why Google Inc. Is Destructive

Chapter Eight

The Google Mind

Google treats Internet users like laboratory animals. Google studies users' behavior by manipulating their perceptions and observing their reactions.

Google tracks users online more closely and accurately than totalitarian governments monitor citizens in the physical world. And Google constantly adds to its tracking capabilities—sometimes in ways that are shockingly intrusive. As mentioned earlier, Google has patented a system for monitoring the way you move the on-screen pointer with your PC's mouse.[527] It's also been reported that Google is developing a method for listening to background sounds picked up by your PC's microphone.[528]

Google is equally adept at shaping users' perceptions. For a company that doesn't like corporate public relations, Google has one of the most effective public relations strategies. It's so slick that most people don't realize that they are being fed a 21st century industrial fairy tale. Google's image is an air-brushed celebrity self-portrait: Google is making the world a better place; Google is focused 100% on end users; Google is driving Web 2.0 openness, transparency, and authenticity; and Google is the most ethical company in history.

Google is intensely interested in the workings of the human mind. Naturally, it comes at the problem from an engineer's perspective ("based on facts and data and analysis"[529]) and applies what it learns to employees as well as users.

For example, Google gets the most out of employees by pampering them. Perhaps that's why Dr. David Rock, a psychologist, calls Google "the Club Med of corporations."[530] And Google gets the most out of users by observing and recording their actions—usually without informing them and almost always without their consent.

Google's tracking and profiling of online users represents the latest developments in the field pioneered by Ivan Pavlov and B. F. Skinner: behaviorism. The Russian scientist Pavlov is remembered for his research concerning what he called "conditional reflexes." For example, he studied how dogs salivate when presented with food. The American psychologist B. F. Skinner went even further, tracing all human behavior (including verbal responses) back to environmental stimuli.

It's not surprising that behaviorism appeals to data mining engineers. Unfortunately, it doesn't leave any room for the things (such as free will) that make us human.

* * *

Google plays with your mind.

Google has a repertoire of psychological tools that it uses in dealing with the press, users, advertisers, Web publishers, and the courts.

Eric Schmidt could justifiably add "Chief Psychologist" to his title of Chairman of the Board. Ask Schmidt a probing question, and he responds with a question of his own: "Do you believe we have good values?" Suddenly, the focus has shifted from Google to you. Schmidt turns a question about the propriety of Google's actions into a question about your assumptions.

Sometimes Google resorts to reverse psychology. Google dares us to catch the firm doing wrong, betting that most people will interpret Google's self-assuredness as proof of innocence.

That tactic was tried by presidential candidate Gary Hart in 1988 with disastrous results. Reporters didn't believe Hart when he denied he was having an extramarital affair, so he dared them to follow him around. He thought he was no longer being watched. But he was wrong.

Google acted similarly in what is now known as the Wi-Spy scandal. Google programmed its Street View cars to scan, identify, and record the locations of Wi-Fi networks. When German authorities asked to see the raw data, it turned out that Google was also recording unencrypted user data.[531]

Google demands—and receives—a tremendous amount of trust. In fact, Google's primary source of power is the trust placed in it by one billion users.

How does Google command so much trust? Google has transformed trust into a psychological weapon. An experienced person knows that trust must be earned and the recipient's trustworthiness must be periodically verified. Taking reverse psychology to new heights, Google tries to convince us that trust is something that most people give freely. If you don't trust Google, it means you are uncharitable.

For example, when *New York Times* reporter David Carr asked Schmidt if he should "...be worried that I am putting all of my digital eggs in one multicolored, goofy-lettered basket," Schmidt replied, "That depends on what you think of our company and our values. Do you believe we have good values?"[532]

Later in the interview, Carr realized that his assessment of Google's values was a red herring: "Google continues to insist that my IP address is not me, but a motivated government with a subpoena in hand could find me, lots of me, on Google's servers." The only thing that really matters is whether the private information stored on Google's servers is vulnerable.

Eric Schmidt uses other techniques to deflect attention from troublesome issues. After a speech in Abu Dhabi, Schmidt was asked by someone in the audience: "All this information that you have about us: where does it go? Who has access to that?" Schmidt replied that the information goes to Google's servers and that Google employees, operating under careful rules, have access. The questioner followed up by asking "Does that scare everyone in this room?" Schmidt shot back: "Would you prefer someone else? Is there a government that you would prefer to be in charge of this?"[533]

Schmidt cleverly presented a false dilemma. Should we put Google in charge of our information or should we put the government in charge? We are so busy pondering the two choices that we forget there is a third choice: give users control over what Google does with their private information.

By now you get the picture. Google influences our perceptions by turning tough questions around on us, daring us to prove them wrong, and presenting us with false dilemmas. As we have seen, Google is adept at shifting responsibility. And as we will see, Google believes that it can further influence people by choosing the right words and metaphors.

You don't grow as big and as fast as Google without doing many things right. However, Google's virtues have been inflated to mythical proportions. Google isn't evil—but neither is it trustworthy. By playing mind games, Google disarms its critics and bamboozles the public.

* * *

Google's executives pretend to be egalitarian, but they are hardcore elitists.

Elitists believe that they know what's best for others. They consider themselves most qualified to determine what information deserves the highest rank, who should win and who should lose, the borders and place names on maps, and even what users really want (Google Instant) as opposed to what they think they want. They are so convinced of their superiority that they would appoint themselves the world's supreme information authority.

Elitists permit themselves to stretch the truth when they feel it does more good than harm. Google pretends that everything it does is for users, that it cares about users' privacy, and that its search engine is unbiased. In reality, Google knows that it works for advertisers, that privacy is an obstacle to data collection, and that it uses human raters to override its algorithms and filters.

Most companies revere their users. To the *Goog-elite*, users are mainly a rich source of behavioral data. Google doesn't serve users—users serve Google. As Mike Elgan observed, in Google's business model you (the user) are the product.[534]

Google decides which rules should apply to Google. If something is good for Google, then it is good for America, the Internet, and the world. But there are rules that were never meant for Google, because those rules would impede Google's ability to pursue innovation-without-permission.

The Google elitists are primarily data mining engineers with their peculiar prejudices and blind spots. Engineers tend to believe that technology is the answer to all problems. As author Ken Auletta told an audience, "They don't understand things you can't measure, and you can't measure fear... People are afraid of how much info Google has collected."[535]

Elitists are unapologetic about their double standards. Google wants others to always share their information; Google shares its information only when it suits Google. Google apparently cooperated with *Fortune* when the magazine was preparing a feature article titled "100 Best Companies to Work For."[536] But when someone asked for Google's Equal Employment Opportunity (EEO) data under the Freedom of Information Act (FOIA), the company fought the request, claiming that the composition of its workforce by race and gender is a trade secret.[537]

The Google elitists have developed a monolithic culture. The company is obsessed with hiring people who received top grades from top schools. (Interestingly, Steve Blank, who teaches classes on entrepreneurship at Stanford, points out that the most successful startups "are founded by dropouts."[538]) Prospective Google employees are often asked to solve Mensa-style brain teasers. The Google Labs Aptitude Test includes questions such as, "What is the optimal size of a project team?" and, "What's the coolest hack you've ever written?"[539] Google even created an "airport test" consisting of one question: "If your flight got canceled, and you were stuck in the airport for three hours with this guy or this girl, how happy would you be about that?" The purpose of that question was to identify people who share the founders' tastes.[540]

Companies with monolithic cultures are plagued by blind spots. When everyone in the company thinks the same way, it's easy to get blind-sided (as in, for example, the Gmail and Google Buzz privacy blowups). A diverse organization can draw on multiple perspectives. A company of clones has only one perspective.

Google brags that its culture encourages innovation. The firm claims that employees are expected to share their opinions and ask the top executives tough questions.[541] In reality, Google's monolithic culture breeds yes men. Google is a highly biased sample of the world's population; Google hires people who share the founders' elitist attitudes.

Term?

The Google elitists are intoxicated with the scale and scope of their network infrastructure. Speaking to the *New York Times* about language translation tools, Vic Gundotra, Vice President of Engineering at Google, said, "We can take approaches that others can't even dream of."[542] No wonder they believe they are justified in acting without permission.

The flipside of elitism is insularity, and that is one trait that undermines Google's psychological tactics. You can't pretend to be egalitarian and make derogatory remarks about users in the way Google's Jonathan Rosenberg did when he complained about the Internet's "faceless scribes of drivel."

The Google elitists want you to think they are egalitarian. But this is one mind game they are sure to lose.

* * *

It takes hubris to treat Internet users like laboratory animals.

Google's hubris is so unique that it deserves its own name: *goobris*.[543] Google demonstrates its goobris in many different ways. Google's founders appointed themselves to organize the world's information. Google implies that its purpose is nobler, that its values are more worthy, and that its ethical standards are higher than those of other companies. Google promulgates the myth that Googlers are smarter than everyone else. Google uses others' intellectual property without asking permission. Google determines what constitutes protected speech and decides how to label disputed territory.

When something goes wrong, Google determines who is responsible. When Google's network is hacked, Google lectures users about good security practices. When Google is sued for patent infringement, Google accuses other companies of trying to harm the tech industry and community.

It takes hubris to name your company after the largest named number, googol. It takes even more hubris to name your corporate headquarters after one to the power of googol (Googleplex).

Being a product of the utopian dot-com era is one reason Google has so much hubris. Like other *techtopians*, Google's engineers believe there are technological solutions to all problems.

vs. T.S.'s *The Vision of the Anointed*

Goobris is reminiscent of the dot-com hubris exemplified by Michael Saylor, founder, Chairman, and CEO of MicroStrategy, a maker of business decision support software.[544] During the dot-com era, Saylor predicted his company would last as long as the Roman Empire.[545] But as Excite co-founder Joe Kraus wisely observed, "Nothing deceives like success."[546]

MicroStrategy became embroiled in an accounting scandal. In early 2000, Saylor and other MicroStrategy executives agreed to a settlement with the Securities and Exchange Commission (SEC). Within weeks, MicroStrategy's stock lost more than 95% of its value, and Saylor is said to have lost more money ($6 billion) in one day than anyone with the exception of Microsoft's Bill Gates.[547]

Google's founders dodged the dot-com crash and became giants in a field of Lilliputians. It's understandable that Larry Page and Sergey Brin began to see themselves as Masters of the Universe. But even Google's founders can be deceived by success.

For example, Page and Brin believe that if you are brilliant and talented in one area, then you are probably brilliant and talented in other areas. Put another way, Google's founders are like the multitude of actors, singers, and scientists who think they know best how to save the world.

Goobris leads to visions ranging from grandiose to bizarre. Eric Schmidt gave a speech describing a future in which Internet-connected devices anticipate what the user wants to know—"the age of augmented humanity."[548] For now, however, he is content to run your daily life.[549] Sergey Brin wants Google to be part (the "third half") of your brain.[550] Following a speech by Eric Schmidt in Abu Dhabi, Gawker.com suggested that Google's leaders had become delusional.[551]

More recently, Google revealed that it has developed self-driving cars and that the cars have already logged over 140,000 miles on public roadways. But not to worry: "Safety has been our first priority in this project."[552] And Google plans to give the U.S. Government competition by publishing an alternative inflation index.[553]

Eric Schmidt said it took him several years to fully grasp the power of Google. He slowly came to understand that Google has the ability to tackle problems too large for anyone else. Now Schmidt believes that with enough data and using artificial intelligence, "we can predict where you are going to go."[554]

Google's aspirations are frightening. In Isaac Asimov's Foundation science fiction series, he tells a story about scientists who specialize in "psychohistory," a discipline that enables them to predict the future. However, the scientists are not able to predict individual events; they are only able to predict broad trends and general outcomes.

Google, however, believes it can predict everything: individual events ("where you are going to go"), broad trends (such as flu epidemics), and general outcomes (such as election results). Perhaps that's because Google is not afraid to use tools that Asimov never contemplated—tools such as search engines that determine what information gets found and what information gets lost.

Google's hubris has even been noted by one of Larry Page's mentors. Speaking to author Ken Auletta, Stanford computer science professor Terry Winograd said: "Larry and Sergey believe that if you try to get everybody on board it will prevent things from happening... If you just do it, others will come around to realize they were attached to old ways that were not as good... No one has proven them wrong—yet." But Winograd also sees a potential weakness in Google's strength: "Not from an institutional, political point of view but from this personal and engineering point of view. 'We would never do that sort of thing'—they believe that in their hearts... [They believe they] are smart enough to make sure that it won't happen by accident." That, Winograd concludes, signals "a certain amount of technical arrogance."[555]

Eric Schmidt dismisses people who worry about Google's growing power as simply fearful of change. He told Auletta that because Google is "run by three computer scientists we're going to make all the mistakes computer scientists running a company would make. But one of the mistakes we're not going to make is the mistake that non-scientists make. We're going to make mistakes based on facts and data and analysis."[556]

Though he probably doesn't realize it, Schmidt admitted that Google is only good at solving technical problems. Google wants to treat all problems as math problems. But you can't solve a complex ethical or political problem just by feeding numbers into a computer. No wonder Google has trouble dealing with matters of principle such as property rights.

Another example of goobris is the way that Google Maps handles place name disputes. On the Japanese version of a map, Google labeled a disputed archipelago in the East China Sea with both the Chinese name Diaoyu and the Japanese name Senkaku. The government of Japan demanded that Google remove the Chinese name. A Google spokesperson responded with an email stating, "We work to make information in Google Maps and Earth as discoverable as possible... This is especially important for disputed features that have conflicting claims." In other words, Google places itself above rival nations.[557]

In ancient Greek tragedy, hubris was exemplified by individuals who attempted to defy the gods. Google seems to think that its computer scientists are the gods and Internet users are the mortals.

* * *

Google's leaders take big risks—for others.

We admire companies that take risks—companies that gamble with their own money and assets. Google is different: when Google takes risks it is gambling with others' private information, intellectual property, data security, and businesses.

With its massive infrastructure and one billion users, Google can harvest information at nearly zero incremental cost. From a cost perspective, users' private information is worth more to the users than to Google. Sergey Brin told the *Economist,* "Ambition is a very important part of our culture."[558] With others shouldering most of the risk, Google can afford to be reckless.

Google has often gambled and lost. Google bet it could circumvent Overture's patent. Google bet that its BigTable design would be sufficiently secure. Google bet that it could digitize books without the copyright holders' permission. Google bought YouTube knowing that YouTube was infringing video copyrights. Google launched products such as Android knowing that it lacked necessary licensing agreements and would probably be sued— possibly by multiple parties. Google played a game of chicken with China over censorship.

Google wants you to think that reckless ambition is synonymous with innovation. It is not.

* * *

Google pretends to be neutral. In reality, Google is politically biased.

Everything Google's leaders do and say has a political angle. Perhaps that's why Google executives have been called "ideological technologists."[559] They don't just want to develop new technologies and succeed at business. Google's leaders have social goals; they want to change our culture, society, and politics. They envision a future in which Google and government work together to make the world a better place.

Google claims to be neutral and unbiased, but that simply isn't true. Google understands that information is power—and Google is not shy about using that power. In fact, Google is one of the most political companies in the Fortune 500. Google makes backroom deals with politicians and government officials;[560] Google supports specific policies and candidates; and Google's CEO Eric Schmidt is the chairman of a Washington, DC think tank.[561]

Given Google's numerous conflicts of interest, Google's political activities should raise a red flag. A search service could be used to promote and demote candidates, causes, and policies. For example, an AdWords ad triggered by the keyword "Obamacare" (purchased by the U.S. Department of Health and Human Services) can easily be mistaken for the top organic search result.[562] Google claims to be neutral, but it often takes sides.

Google's political bias can even be seen in its unconventional mission. Most corporate missions focus on delivering value to customers for the benefit of the company's shareholders and employees. Google's mission is to change the world in ways that challenge tried and true ideas about private property, individual rights, and the role of government.

For example, one of Google's top priorities is universal access to information. The implication is that all users should enjoy equal access. However, the guiding principle in our free-market system is that there should be equal opportunity but not necessarily equal outcomes.

Google's founders told us in their IPO letter that Google is a different kind of company—a company with social and political goals:

> *We aspire to make Google an institution that makes the world a better place... With our products, Google connects people and information all around the world for free.*[563]

That can only mean one thing: Google wants to impose its values on everyone else. For example, when Google says that it wants to make the world a better place it assumes that we all agree on what that better place would look like. But that runs counter to the ideal of a society in which each individual is free to pursue his or her personal goals.

> *We have also emphasized an atmosphere of creativity and challenge, which has helped us provide unbiased, accurate and free access to information for those who rely on us around the world.*[564]

Google frequently makes self-congratulatory statements. However, what would you think of a person who tells you that he is unbiased, accurate, and generous? You would probably consider that person naïve at best; every human has biases, makes errors, and acts out of self-interest. But what if he made that claim month after month, year after year? In time you would wonder who he is trying to fool.

Is Google trying to fool us? When Google's founders were students at Stanford University, they produced a paper in which they said, "We expect that advertising funded search engines will be inherently biased."[565] If they have changed their minds, then they should say so and explain why.

Sergey and I founded Google because we believed we could provide an important service to the world—instantly delivering relevant information on virtually any topic. Serving our end users is at the heart of what we do and remains our number one priority.[566]

Google's executives want us to believe they aren't in business for the money. Instead, they want us to think that they are providing free products for the purpose of making the world a better place. It's merely a happy coincidence that they are making money hand over fist.

Deep political ties can be a problem for any big company, but they are particularly problematic for Google. Google collects and stores a tremendous amount of information—information that could give Google leverage over individuals and even organizations. Does Google use this information to help its political allies? Would we know if it did?

Former Vice President of the United States Albert Gore, Jr. visited Google in February of 2001. Page, Brin, and Omid Kordestani, Senior Vice President for Worldwide Sales and Field Operations, asked Gore to serve as a senior advisor and invited him to join Google's board of directors. Gore, sponsor of the Supercomputer Network Study Act of 1986, received a large chunk of pre-IPO Google stock (reportedly worth more than $30 million)[567] and subsequently launched a cable TV channel (Current TV).[568] Gore's net worth grew from roughly $2 million (while in office) to approximately $100 million—largely thanks to Google.

What advice could Gore, who had no relevant private sector experience when he first visited the company, have given to Google? According to one account, Gore advised Google on "international issues."[569] Another source says Gore advised Google on "search quality" issues.[570] It seems most likely that Google saw Gore as an influential politician with numerous government connections.

Google is anything but neutral and unbiased about politics. *USA Today* reported that 98% of the federal campaign contributions made by Google employees in 2004 went to Democrats.[571] Google CEO Eric Schmidt endorsed Barack Obama, actively campaigned for him, and was a member of the President's Science and Technology Advisory Council[572] and Transition Economic Advisory Board.[573] Larry Page and Eric Schmidt contributed $25,000 each to Obama's inaugural celebration.[574]

While most companies seek business advice, Google frequently solicits political advice. Google is enthralled by linguist George Lakoff's theory that the way that we use language—particularly the way we frame issues—is crucial to influencing people.

Lakoff, a professor at the University of California at Berkeley, assigns linguistic family metaphors to what he sees as America's two major opposing political camps: "progressives" and "conservatives." He likens progressives to the "nurturant parent model" and conservatives to the "strict father model."[575]

Lakoff suggests ways that progressives can counter successful conservative word frames. For example, he recommends that progressives use "stronger America" instead of "strong defense"; "broad prosperity" instead of "free markets"; "better future" instead of "lower taxes"; "effective government" instead of "smaller government"; and "mutual responsibility" instead of "family values."[576]

Lakoff has been invited to speak at Google on several occasions. He was introduced at Google's headquarters in 2007 as someone who studies how "language may well mold cognition." He began his talk by describing Google as "the major force in the world for the democratization of information." He went on to discuss the "democratization of knowledge about politics." He believes that emotion is a prerequisite to reasoning. That is, he disputes the enlightenment view that reason is dispassionate. He criticized the United States' founding fathers for believing that human rights are based solely on reason—a belief that he feels led them to the false conclusion that people can be largely self-governing. And he explains away the success of ideas that he doesn't like with this condescending argument: ideas that are repeated over and over "become part of your brain."[577]

Google's interest in Lakoff's theory is, to say the least, worrisome. As the Web's dominant information gatekeeper, one of Google's major goals should be to minimize ambiguity. However, Lakoff promotes just the opposite: the use of metaphors and word choices to make people think what you want them to think.

The problem isn't that Google has political views. The problem is that while Google claims to be unbiased and neutral, Google is also intensely interested in the way that information can be used to advance or defeat various political causes.

There's not much difference between George Orwell's theory that language (newspeak) can be used to deceive people and George Lakoff's theory that language (framing) can be used to convince people.

*   *   *

Google is really of two minds.

One Google is elitist, arrogant, reckless, political, and morally lax. The other Google manipulates people using mythology, air-brushed images, reverse psychology, and language.

In other words, Google looks at itself and others from radically different perspectives. While Google's data mining engineers see themselves as natural leaders, they see others as subjects to be tested and controlled. It's a condescending view that only reinforces their megalomania.

Chapter Nine

Don't Be Evil?

Google says, "You can make money without doing evil."[578]

The implication is that most businesses make money by doing wrong, but Google is showing us that there is an ethical way to make money.

However, when we consider whether a person or company is ethical, we should not rely exclusively on their testimony. Only others are qualified to judge whether they have good values and act in ways that are consistent with those values.

* * *

Is Google an ethical company? To answer that question, we must first examine Google's values.

Values are the things that matter most to people—the things that consistently guide their actions. Values are judged not by what people say, but by what they do.

Most people consider qualities such as honesty, respect for others, fairness, responsibility, empathy, and cooperation to be good values. There are additional characteristics, such as moderation, that others would include on the list. A good way to verify that a trait qualifies as a good value is to check whether it is compatible with the Golden Rule.

Does Google have good values? Most people would say "no" once they become familiar with Google's beliefs and record of behavior. However, Google skillfully frames issues using words carefully selected to make the company appear principled and virtuous—words such as "open," "universal," and "transparent."

Google claims credit for values it doesn't consistently embrace. Google stages a grand morality play, but it is pure theater.

Google's "Don't be evil" motto has attracted a tremendous amount of attention; it has won the acclaim of like-minded people for its directness and succinctness; and it has spurred seemingly endless commentary and debate. No other major corporation trumpets its moral superiority so blatantly and shamelessly.

However, Google engages in ethical sleight of hand. When Google says "Don't be evil" it implies that Google is the opposite of evil. It's a clever public relations stunt that so far has been very successful. But Google never defines the words "good" and "evil." It's all highly subjective.

When Eric Schmidt was asked how Google defines evil, he replied flippantly, "Evil is whatever Sergey says is evil."[579]

Most people think of "evil" as the worst extreme on the ethical scale. Evil is sinful, depraved, abhorrent, despicable, corrupt, disastrous, or hurtful. Evil is what we fear most. When asked to name a truly evil character, most people will say the devil, Adolph Hitler, Pol Pot, Charles Manson, or Joseph Stalin.

"Don't be evil" sets the ethical bar way too low. It should go without saying that a large, successful company isn't evil. However, there is a vast expanse between "good" and "evil" on the ethical scale; most of what is unethical falls short of evil.

What makes Google a different kind of company is not its high ethical standards but its moral conceit. "Don't be evil" is as much an indictment of the business world as it is a guiding principle. Does Google really believe the typical company makes money by doing evil? If so, Google should identify the evil deeds most often committed by other businesses and promise to never perform the same acts.

There is further proof of Google's moral conceit. Google excuses misdeeds such as redistributing others' intellectual property without permission by claiming it is in business to make "the world a better place." And when Google established a philanthropic arm, Google.org, it was set up as a for-profit organization.[580] Using the for-profit structure, Google.org remains free to fund startups, partner with venture capitalists, and lobby the

U.S. government. But at least Google is consistent: Google sees its business as a gift to humanity and its gift giving as a business.

Google is the master of the ethical double standard. Google admonishes others to be open and transparent while keeping its search engine closed and opaque. Google sees nothing wrong with scanning your email messages but resists calls to be more accountable.

Google portrays itself as morally superior, but it breaks the same rules that it expects others to follow.

* * *

You can't trust Google Inc.

Google systematically misrepresents its business; mistreats Web publishers and advertising customers, sometimes causing serious harm; and uses others' intellectual property without payment or permission.

No individual or company is perfect. As the saying goes, "To err is human…" If we were talking about a few isolated incidents, then Google could be forgiven. But we are talking about misbehavior that is intentional, that has been going on for years, that involves numerous products and services, and that spans multiple dimensions of Google's business.

The problem isn't Google's popular search engine. Google has the best search engine technology and the most complete and up-to-date index of the Web. What is untrustworthy is the company and corporate culture behind the search engine. Or as the *Financial Times* put it, "The world has every reason to applaud Google, but few reasons to trust it."[581]

Google feeds off the confusion created by new technology to deceive users, the public, and even the courts. Google exploits the fact that most Internet users don't realize how much online tracking and profiling takes place. Google exploits the widespread but mistaken belief that computerized processes are inherently fair. And Google exploits opportunities created by digital and online technologies to reinterpret the Fair Use Doctrine and other aspects of intellectual property law.

In fact, Google's main business is a grand deception. Google pretends that it works mainly for users, but Google makes almost all of its money off advertisers. Google claims that serving users is its top priority, but Google doesn't provide users with customer service. And Google claims it offers free products because it wants to be a corporate Santa Claus, but Google doesn't mention that users pay for these products with their loss of privacy.

Google's free products are a Trojan horse. Google lures users with free products and then uses the products to collect the data that enable Google to sell targeted advertising. Think of Google's free products as software equivalents of George Orwell's telescreens in *Nineteen Eighty-Four*.

For example, Google's Gmail free email service saves copies of every email message that the user composes, sends, or receives. That includes messages received from non-Gmail users and draft messages that the user decides not to send. Then Google's software robots scan the emails for advertising keywords.

Google perpetrates this grand deception in a variety of ways. Google's website claims that even the company's advertising products are designed to serve users.[582] Google executives publicly deny that the company is in business to make money: "The goal of the company is not to monetize anything."[583] Google continuously expands its portfolio of free products.

However, that's not the only reason you can't trust Google Inc.

Google treats advertisers and Web publishers unfairly. Google portrays AdWords and AdSense as auctions despite the fact that the highest bidder does not necessarily win; bidders are not told exactly what they must do to win; key parameters such as the bidder's secret "quality score" may be changed without notice or explanation; and bidders are not provided a full accounting of how much they paid and what they received for their payment.

By operating AdWords and AdSense in an opaque fashion, Google is free at all times to implement new rules or make other changes designed to maximize Google's revenue.

Google would not be able to get away with treating customers this way were it not for the fact that it has a search advertising monopoly. A huge number of online businesses rely heavily—and sometimes exclusively—on

Google to bring in new customers. Many companies complain that they experienced a sudden decline in business when Google demoted them (in terms of "quality score" or search rank) or blocked their accounts. This almost always occurs without warning and often without adequate explanation.

Google treats others unfairly by pretending that its technology is neutral and unbiased, by operating its search and search advertising services in a closed and opaque manner, and by refusing even the most basic forms of accountability such as third party audits.

Advertisers and Web publishers are at Google's complete mercy. Google can change algorithms and filters at any time. Google has even changed AdWords' default account settings, causing customers to incur charges for additional services that they did not request. (This is another example of Google's deceptive practices; Google puts the burden on users and advertisers to opt out of things that they never agreed to in the first place.)

And there is one more major reason that you can't trust Google.

Google uses others' property without payment or permission. Google infringes copyrights, trademarks, and patents—and facilitates infringement by others—while aggressively protecting its own intellectual property. And Google is being sued, has been sued, or is accused of copyright infringement by almost every major content industry (books, videos, music, and news).

To wit, Google monetizes the works of other individuals and companies, reaping illicit profits and depriving the creators of fair compensation.

It's important to understand how Google achieves this. Google games the legal system by exploiting gray areas in the law and operating as close to the boundaries as possible. Google does not engage in outright piracy, directly selling others' content. Google's strategy, instead, is to sell advertising by organizing content and making it accessible (or at least searchable). Sometimes this is done by stretching the definition of "fair use." Other times it's accomplished by putting the burden on the copyright holders to identify their content and request that it be removed, creating a brief but damaging window of exposure. In either case, Google exploits the fact that most intellectual property law was written prior to the Internet era.

For example, Google purchased YouTube knowing that the company's video sharing service makes it easy for users to upload copyrighted videos without permission. As we saw earlier, the statement of undisputed facts in the *Viacom v. Google* (YouTube) legal battle revealed that Google discussed using the window between upload and removal to pressure copyright owners into signing advertising deals.

Google Books is another example. Google copied and digitized a large number of copyrighted books without the copyright owners' permission, provoking groups representing authors and publishers to sue Google. A settlement was proposed between Google and two groups. The Department of Justice opposed the proposed Google Books settlement for violating laws in three different areas (copyright, antitrust and class action).

Other companies have been caught stretching the truth and even lying. But only Google has built a business producing $30 billion in annual revenue around the false claim that it is a corporate Santa Claus delivering free toys every day of the year.

Other companies have been caught mistreating some of their customers. But numerous advertising customers have complained that Google suddenly terminated their accounts or hit them with huge price increases. And Google generated additional advertising revenue by spending money left over in customers' daily budgets ("automatic matching") without first asking for their permission.

Other companies infringe copyrights, trademarks, and patents. But only Google abuses others' intellectual property knowingly, systematically, and daily. In fact, Google admonishes others to share their intellectual property while Google hides and guards its own.

You may be able to trust Google's search engine, but you can't trust Google Inc.

* * *

Google's Code of Conduct for employees lacks specificity, clarity, and accountability. The Code consists of eight chapters filled with meaningless platitudes, vague guidelines, and few if any penalties.[584]

For example, the first chapter is titled "Serve Our Users" and contains the following sections: Integrity, Usefulness, Privacy and Freedom of Expression, Responsiveness, and Take Action.

The Integrity section consists of just two sentences:

> *Our reputation as a company that our users can trust is our most valuable asset, and it is up to all of us to make sure that we continually earn that trust. All of our communications and other interactions with our users should increase their trust in us.*

Notice that this section makes no reference to objective standards. Employees are urged to earn and increase user trust, but there are no guidelines about how best to do that, no strictly prohibited actions, and no penalties for failing to comply.

Google's policy regarding drugs and alcohol is contained in the second chapter, "Respect Each Other." Google's policy regarding illegal drugs says:

> *Illegal drugs in our offices or at sponsored events are strictly prohibited. If a manager has reasonable suspicion to believe that an employee's use of drugs and/or alcohol may adversely affect the employee's job performance or the safety of the employee or others in the workplace, the manager may request an alcohol and/or drug screening. A reasonable suspicion may be based on objective symptoms such as the employee's appearance, behavior or speech.*

While the use of illegal drugs in Google's offices and at Google-sponsored events is strictly prohibited, the use of illegal drugs elsewhere is not. If a manager believes an employee's use of drugs is adversely affecting that employee's job performance or workplace safety, the manager may request a drug screening. However, managers are not required to request drug tests. There is no assurance that such a request would be approved. And there is no mention of penalties for failing drug tests.

Chapter Three is titled "Avoid Conflicts of Interest." Here is how Google defines "conflict of interest":

> *When you are in a situation where competing loyalties could cause you to pursue a personal benefit for you or your friends or family at the expense of Google or our users, you may be subject to a conflict of interest.*

Amazingly, this definition completely ignores conflicts of interest for Google. More telling are the questions employees are advised to ask themselves to identify potential conflicts of interest; the questions deal exclusively with appearances. For example, employees should ask themselves, "Would this relationship or situation embarrass me or Google if it showed up on the front page of a newspaper or the top of a blog?"

The remaining chapters are Preserve Confidentiality, Protect Google's Assets, Ensure Financial Integrity and Responsibility, Obey the Law, and Conclusion. The guiding principles appear to be: avoid doing anything that could harm Google; avoid the appearance of impropriety; and do not violate laws dealing with trade controls, competition, insider trading, or bribery. While there is nothing wrong with these principles, they show that Google looks out for its own interests as much as the next big corporation.

What is troubling, however, is that Google leaves most ethical decisions to the employee's judgment. Nikesh Aurora, head of Google's European operations, said: "We try not to have too many controls. People will do things that they think are in the interests of the company. We want them to understand the values of the firm, and interpret them for themselves."[585]

Google's Code of Conduct isn't wrong. But its main message to employees—that they should not do anything that might harm Google—is hardly suggestive of superior ethics.

* * *

The more people learn about Google's values and practices, the more likely they are to see Google as an unethical company.

An organization called Intelligence Squared was established to promote Oxford-style debates on timely and controversial topics. In November of 2008, six panelists were invited to debate for and against the motion: "Google Violates Its Don't Be Evil Motto."

Arguing for the motion were Harvard professor Harry Lewis, University of Chicago Law School professor Randal C. Picker, and University of Virginia professor Siva Vaidhyanathan. Arguing against were writer and investor Esther Dyson, Jim Harper of the Cato Institute, and author of *What Would Google Do?* Jeff Jarvis.

Given that "Don't Be Evil" sets a low ethical standard, you might think that it would be easy to defeat the motion. Two audience polls were taken: one before the debate and the other after the debate. The pre-debate poll tallied 21% "For," 31% "Against," and 48% "Undecided." The post-debate poll results were 47% "For," 47% "Against," and 6% "Undecided." In other words, coming into the debate, most of the audience was either against the motion or undecided. After the debate, equal percentages were for and against the motion. The majority of the initially undecided were convinced by the debate that Google *does* violate its "Don't Be Evil" motto.[586]

The more people learn about Google, the more concerned they become. Google rejects traditional Judeo-Christian values—the values that most companies look to for guidance—while claiming to be morally superior.

* * *

Google claims there is more to "Don't Be Evil" than meets the eye.

Speaking to ABC News in 2004, Larry Page said, "We have a mantra: 'Don't Be Evil,' which is to do the best things we know how for our users, for our customers, for everyone. So I think if we were known for that, it would be a wonderful thing."[587]

Fair enough. But who determines what is best for users? Should Google decide? Should users decide? Or should some other party decide?

The problem is that Google's founders define morality based on their own sense of what is right and wrong. That gets the Golden Rule exactly backwards. It is the height of goobris to define morality around your own beliefs and then ask that others judge you by your own definition.

Most people understand that morality—if it is to be anything other than self-serving—must come from a higher authority. For Christians, morality is defined by the Bible. For Jews, morality is defined by the Torah. For Muslims, morality is described by the Koran. Even agnostics and atheists with a strong sense of morality point to objective and external sources such as common law, natural law, or the U.S. Constitution.

Morality isn't something that individuals can define for themselves. The purpose of morality is to guide individuals' behavior and provide a basis for judging those individuals. Anyone can invent a moral system that suits their tastes and interests and then simply proclaim that they are moral. A worthy moral system is one that individuals subscribe to in advance and that sometimes requires them to forego actions that suit their own interests or tastes. Moral people don't do what they want—they do what is right.

To understand Google's moral system, we need to identify Google's moral values. Unfortunately, the only values that Google talks about are technological values such as "openness," "transparency," and "neutrality." Google has never publicly discussed its moral values. And Google may not want to: Google knows that the day it tells us its moral values is the day it begins to be accountable.

It's revealing that Google chose to state its guiding principle as a double negative—"Don't Be Evil" rather than "Be Good"—because a double negative is weaker and more nuanced than a positive statement. With the many ethical and legal complaints registered against Google, it seems fair to say that Google does not believe the alleged abuses qualify as "evil."

Is "Don't Be Evil" really Google's guiding principle? Though a company as large and powerful as Google is confronted with ethical dilemmas every day, it's doubtful that doing evil is ever a viable choice for a business. "Don't

Be Evil" is mainly a linguistic frame designed to make Google appear morally superior.

* * *

When Google says, "Don't Be Evil" it means something specific, but it's not what most people would think.

"Evil" is a techtopian code word. To techtopians, people who claim specific software or online information as their private property are evil.

Techtopians believe that everything digital and/or online should be shared and that no one should have to pay or ask permission to use it. Though techtopians insist the slogan "information wants to be free" is about free speech, it has more in common with free beer. Techtopians support Web 2.0, free software, radical transparency, openness, and universal access.

Techtopians believe Microsoft is evil because Microsoft wants to be paid for its software and generally doesn't participate in open source projects. Techtopians believe that most music and movie companies are evil because they want to be paid for their creations and they expect others to obtain their permission for derivative uses. Techtopians believe that broadband companies are evil because they want to be paid for the bandwidth they provide. To techtopians, anyone who opposes free peer-to-peer sharing is evil. In fact, anyone who tries to limit techtopians' online activities for commercial purposes is bad.

However, techtopians are confronted with a major obstacle. The vast majority of people do not think that paying for software or information is evil. They may not like to pay, but they understand that people who create applications and information for a living have the right to be compensated. People who are forced to work without compensation are slaves to those who benefit from their work.

Slaves also have no privacy. Google dresses up its relentless assault on privacy—Google calls it "transparency"—as both ethical and good business practice. Eric Schmidt said during an earnings call, "We've taken a position from a religious and business perspective that the world is better off if you take the information you're producing and make it searchable."[588]

If "Don't Be Evil" means sharing with others, then why doesn't Google have a customer service department that users can reach when they have a question or problem? Some pundits have noticed that customer service isn't one of Google's priorities because customer service does not scale efficiently. That may be true, but it doesn't excuse a large and highly profitable company from showing respect for others by providing good service.

Google's high-tech peers—companies including Microsoft, Apple, eBay, and Amazon—all have customer service departments. These companies understand that the way to show respect for customers is to allocate the resources needed to provide good service. They also understand that meeting their commitments is a matter of principle (doing what you promised) and not just efficiency (how convenient and cost-effective it is for your business).

If you ask people how businesses can best live up to the "Don't Be Evil" motto, many will ignore the hyperbole and talk about basic values: being honest, obeying the law, and showing respect for users, employees, and the public.

Google shows disrespect for users by treating the security of their data as a low priority. Google weighs security in terms of its own interests rather than users' interests.

Google shows disrespect for its employees by colluding with other companies to limit the solicitation of employees for other job opportunities. Google and five other companies (Adobe, Apple, Intel, Intuit, and Pixar) agreed to stop conspiring to restrict employees' career options only after the Department of Justice launched an antitrust investigation.[589] Google has also been accused of getting employees to sign non-compete agreements and then laying them off.[590]

Google shows disrespect for the public by refusing to release Equal Employment Opportunity (EEO) data, claiming that information about the percentage of women and minorities hired is a "trade secret."[591] Yet Google is anxious to let everyone know that it hires graduates of elite universities.

Google shows disrespect for the rule of law. Google has been sued—at considerable expense and risk—by diverse content industries for copyright infringement. Google assiduously avoids asking for permission to use and even profit from others' intellectual property.

Google suggests that such suits are simply a fact of life for large, innovative companies. However, Google isn't just the target of fishing expeditions; Google has settled such suits for large sums of money.

We've catalogued a host of misdeeds. Google agreed to pay groups representing authors and publishers $125 million for digitizing books without permission; the settlement was amended in response to DOJ objections to make Google pay ongoing royalties. Google is being sued for $1 billion by Viacom for distributing copyrighted material without permission via YouTube. Google paid Yahoo! 2.7 million common shares of stock (worth $250 million at the time and twice that shortly after) to settle a patent lawsuit. Google is being sued by Apple, Oracle, Microsoft, and others for patent infringement. Google has also been accused of copyright infringement by Agence France Presse (AFP) and the Associated Press (AP). Google has been sued by companies including Rosetta Stone for trademark infringement.[592] Google has been accused of aiding and abetting websites trafficking in pirated movies and music.

Clearly, there are many industry groups, companies, and individuals who believe that Google does not live up to its "Don't Be Evil" motto.

Many of these misdeeds can be traced to Google's techtopian philosophy. Google does not believe it should be necessary to obtain the permission of copyright holders to copy and search their content. Google does believe, however, that the interpretation of "fair use" should be expanded to allow greater sharing.

There are many other examples that show Google does not live up to its "Don't Be Evil" motto. Google brokers information and ads without disclosing conflicts of interest. Google CEO Eric Schmidt served on Apple's board of directors, claiming Google did not compete with Apple.[593] When the FTC threatened to investigate possible competitive conflicts of interest,

Schmidt resigned from Apple's board.[594] Google has since introduced products that compete with Apple's products.

Google has been the focus of antitrust investigations, in both the U.S. and Europe, several times in recent years. These investigations were not based on mere allegations. Actions were taken or threatened when investigators found concrete evidence that Google had violated antitrust laws (such as with the planned Google-Yahoo! advertising deal in 2008).

Google's "Don't Be Evil" motto does not mean that Google subscribes to a higher standard of ethics. It means that Google subscribes to a different standard of ethics—a standard that values sharing and convenience over private intellectual property and respect for others.

* * *

Google implores others to operate in an open manner and help protect the environment. But Google exempts itself whenever it suits its interests.

For example, Google's founders bought a Boeing 767 passenger jet for private use. It is certainly their prerogative to do so. However, they obtained landing rights at Moffett Field, a NASA facility normally closed to private planes, through a backroom deal. And though Larry Page and Sergey Brin are fervent proponents of renewable energy, their private Boeing 767 gives them an extraordinarily large carbon footprint.[595]

It's hard to imagine a more egregious example of the U.S. Government bestowing favors on an individual company. Moffett Field is owned by the American public. If NASA decided to make it available for private use, then NASA should have publicly announced the new policy and invited bids for landing rights to ensure the best return for American taxpayers.

When the *New York Times* inquired about the deal, Google said that it was a personal matter.[596] However, the use of government property is always a public matter. Though Google was granted special treatment, there has been no comment from the NASA Office of Inspector General.

* * *

There is also evidence of unethical behavior from the operations side of Google's business.

A key component of Google's search service is the distributed PC network that it uses to index the entire Web. Google has a number of data centers (the exact number is a company secret), each of which houses row upon row of rack mounted PCs. To keep its costs as low as possible, Google bought the servers from RackSaver.com and used the free Linux operating system (OS). The data centers are interconnected, creating the equivalent of a massive supercomputer with total redundancy.

Growing its business after the dot-com bust, Google obtained bargains for data center space and telecommunications bandwidth. Warehouses were rented to house stacked PCs with enormous power and cooling requirements. By all accounts, Google convinced desperate warehouse owners to provide free electricity. Many of the warehouse owners were unprepared for the huge electricity bills.[597] As Eric Schmidt joked, "All our data centers have gone bankrupt. Because we use so much power and we negotiate such low rates."[598]

The bankrupted warehouse owners were left with two choices. They could negotiate new deals that barely covered their costs, permitting them to at least hold on to their properties. Or they could bail out, taking whatever Google offered for their warehouses.

Meanwhile, Google took advantage of tough times in another business. During the Internet gold rush, the telecommunications industry built far more fiber optic capacity than was needed. In this case, there was no need to deceive anyone. Fiber owners were desperate to rent as much of their unused capacity as possible. Google not only knows how to leverage others' intellectual property, Google knows how to leverage others' distress.

Google also made secret deals for data centers with local officials in places such as Lenoir, North Carolina.[599] Tommy Tomlinson, A columnist with the Charlotte Observer, called the agreement "unarmed robbery."[600]

In exchange for building a $600 million data center estimated to produce 200 jobs over five years, Google received perquisites expected to save the company more than \$250 million, including an 80% discount on real estate taxes and an exemption for sales taxes on electricity use.

Tomlinson attributed the lopsided deal to the simple fact that "public officials did the public's business in private."[601] Google had the best negotiators money could buy, and it showed: "it appears our local boys got schooled like a church-leaguer guarding Michael Jordan."[602] Tomlinson also came to the disheartening realization that the 200 jobs would not be filled by locals; Google hires mostly engineers and computer scientists—not laid-off furniture makers.

Google has the right to keep its plans confidential and the right to seek the best deals available. But local governments are supposed to serve local citizens. Backroom deals take local citizens out of the loop, raising concerns about the quality and appropriateness of the deals.

* * *

Does Google have good values?

A business can have good values and behave ethically without promising to make the world a better place. As Milton Friedman said, "There is one and only one social responsibility of business—to use its resources and engage in activities designed to increase its profits so long as it stays within the rules of the game, which is to say, engages in open and free competition without deception or fraud."[603]

In other words, an ethical business is honest and treats everyone with whom it interacts with respect. Google, in contrast, is like the political activist who wants to save the world but is rude to the relatively small number of people that he or she sees every day.

Google is not the pillar of morality that it pretends to be. Most of the people who are aware of Google's ignominious rap sheet consider Google to be unethical or (at best) ethically challenged.

Why has Google made morality so central to the Google brand? By creating an aura of moral superiority, and establishing a pattern of acting without permission, Google hopes to escape ethical scrutiny and impose its political ideology on others.

Now it's time to examine that ideology.

Chapter Ten

The Digital Road to Serfdom

Google has a hidden, radical agenda: *Googleism.*

Googleism, like many other "isms," is a utopian political ideology. Its goal is to create an ideal society.

Googleism promises to change the world by making information free of charge and accessible to all. While there is nothing wrong with wanting to make the world a better place—it's one reason why Google's supporters are so passionate—it becomes problematic when proponents use force or deception to achieve their objectives.

The overwhelming majority of people want to improve the world. If you have to pressure or trick people to accept your solution, then it must not be the solution they would choose. When examined more closely, Google's utopia turns out to be what most people would consider a dystopia.

The American economist Milton Friedman challenged the assumption that individuals and organizations with political goals do more for humanity. "Is it really true that political self-interest is nobler somehow than economic self-interest?"[604]

Googleism is based on the following radical ideas:

Innovation without permission: If you are developing innovative solutions, then you shouldn't need others' permission to use their property or violate their privacy. This "permissionless" approach is fundamentally opposed to individualism (which recognizes that every person has certain inviolable rights) and democracy (which grants every person a say in matters that affect them).

Information should be free: The digital, online world creates a fresh opportunity to abolish private property. Radicals want to establish an "information commons" based on the "economics of abundance." Opponents call it a "something for nothing" entitlement that destroys striving, competition, and choice.

Publicacy: Everyone should have equal access to information. This Web 2.0 ideal seeks to create a more egalitarian Internet by replacing user privacy, private property, and data security with radical forms of openness, transparency, and accessibility.

Technological determinism: If it's technically possible, then it should be done, because inevitably it will be done. This principle is destructive because it places the development and application of technology above all other values.

Google knows best: Google is trustworthy and morally superior because it is the only company guided by its "Don't be evil" motto. This principle is destructive because it establishes a double standard that exempts Google from the laws, rules, norms, and standards of accountability that apply to everyone else.

The sum of these beliefs, Googleism, tells us that in an information-based society, authority and power should not come from ordinary people but from an engineering elite—Google's *central planners* of technology and innovation. The technology is too sophisticated and complex to be managed by non-experts. For example, Google customizes search results for the user's location and does not permit users to turn off the feature.[605]

Letting experts run everything works better in theory than it does in practice. In 1944, Austrian economist Friedrich A. Hayek published *The Road to Serfdom,* a book debunking centralized planning. In what soon became a classic, Hayek demonstrated that centralized economic planning by experts cannot create prosperity and inevitably leads to tyranny. Hayek also showed that socialism and fascism are just variations on the same theme.

The crux of Hayek's argument was that while people can be persuaded to embrace an economic system based on top-down, expert planning, experience shows that individualism, limited government, and free markets are much more productive. There is simply no way that "experts" can possess the knowledge that is distributed throughout the market and expressed by constantly changing price signals.

Or as Milton Friedman put it: "...the record of history is absolutely crystal clear... there is no alternative way, so far discovered, of improving the lot of the ordinary people that can hold a candle to the productive activities that are unleashed by a free enterprise system."[606]

It's ironic that Google prefers the central planning model over the self-organizing model because in many ways Hayek's thinking anticipated the Internet's success. Hayek showed that a self-organized economy was more flexible and responsive than a centrally managed economy. Likewise, the Internet succeeded by using a decentralized, user-driven model (in which intelligence is distributed among users and Web sites) instead of a telephone switch model (in which intelligence is concentrated in one location).

Now one company—Google—is attempting to centralize the collection, storage, and use of information. Just as economic collectivism leads to serfdom (in which the many serve the few), information collectivism leads to a type of serfdom in which Internet users receive only the knowledge, privacy, property, and security allotted to them by the ruling elite.

No doubt Google and its supporters will deny that Hayek's arguments are applicable to Google's vision and strategy. Hayek was talking about government—which by definition is a monopoly—while Google is simply one of many private companies. However, we've seen that Google has created a Googleopoly by dominating search and search advertising and extending its reach to every major type of digital content and every major digital hardware platform. Googleopoly is a virtual world government, organizing all of the world's information, translating between the world's languages, adjudicating place names and borders on digital maps, determining which Web sites are found, and deciding what forms of speech should be protected and what forms of speech should be censored.

To wit, Google wants to be the Internet's feudal lord, giving Internet users free products and services in exchange for unrestricted access to, and use of, their information.

The analogy with serfdom works in other ways. Google advocates a larger and more powerful federal government, protecting Google's rights and serving Google's interests but otherwise not interfering in Google's business.

For example, Google supports regulating broadband service providers much like telephone utilities are regulated under Title II of the Communications Act.[607] Google supports transforming the nation's electricity grid into a smart grid so that Google can access real-time usage and pricing information.[608] Google is also involved in the government's push to create electronic medical records, offering Google Health as "a single place to organize and store your health information online."[609]

Google envisions the Internet as a place where all of the world's information is freely accessible to everyone. As Google's Vint Cerf said, "Google represents the idea that all things should be egalitarian... and accessibility to everyone is the underlying principle."[610]

However, Google's egalitarian utopia is already beginning to devolve into a dystopia. In George Orwell's political allegory *Animal Farm*, what started as "All animals are equal" quickly deteriorated into "All animals are equal, but some animals are more equal than others." The most ominous evidence that Google is creating an information tyranny is that Google's leaders believe they are exempt from the rules and practices that they urge others to follow. Consequently, a basic tenet of Googleism seems to be: all Internet users are equal, but some Internet users are more equal than others.

Until now, no one has critically examined how and why Google wants to change the world. Is Google's agenda constructive or destructive? Would most people support Google's agenda if they knew more about it?

Google has an amazing ability to change the subject without people noticing. When anyone challenges its agenda, Google retreats behind a technology shield. Technology has produced and enabled so many good things over the last few decades—how could anyone oppose technology? A question about the propriety of Google's agenda is treated as an attack on technology.

Technology is merely a tool; it is neither inherently good nor inherently bad. What matters are the intentions and the results achieved by those developing and promoting technology. Google has done a masterful job portraying technology as inherently beneficial and, in the process, obscuring its destructive political agenda.

Google has the right to convince others that its vision for the future is best. Unfortunately, rather than promoting Googleism in the arena of ideas, Google tries to impose Googleism on others without their knowledge.

People flock to Google's products and services because they are useful and free of charge. But most people also understand that you don't get something for nothing—there's always a price. Google gives away products and services in order to gather and monetize information about users.

Google sees Internet users as sheep to be herded and sheared.

* * *

What inspired Google's utopian vision?

A good place to start is the philosophy of Harvard Law School professor Lawrence Lessig. Lessig founded the "free culture movement" to oppose what he and others see as unnecessarily restrictive copyright, trademark, and patent laws. Lessig (through his advocacy) and Google (through its actions) promote the idea that there should be greater freedom to use and redistribute others' creative works via the Web and other digital media.

Underlying this philosophy is Lessig's belief that "code is law." Lessig argues that the architectures of cyberspace regulate our lives much as laws passed by Congress regulate our lives. The former is "West Coast Code" while the latter is "East Coast Code."[611]

Equating computer code to laws passed by Congress leads Lessig to some rather odd conclusions. One obvious implication is that we, the people, should have more of a say in the architectures of cyberspace. Specifically, we must look at West Coast Code and ask, "Whose interests does it serve and at what price?" Lessig worries, for example, about code that mainly serves the interests of copyright holders.

Lessig tells us that there are two types of code. "Open code" is publicly shared, while "closed code" is privately owned. Then Lessig points out that "Secret laws are not law." From there he draws the dubious conclusion that proprietary code is bad in the same way that secret laws are bad.

Lessig founded the Creative Commons, "a nonprofit organization that increases sharing and improves collaboration."[612] Creative Commons provides free legal tools for content developers who want to share their creations. Critics question whether Creative Commons' legal tools are necessary. According to Hungarian intellectual property expert Péter Benjamin Tóth, copyright holders are already free to retain, sell, or grant rights as they see fit.[613] Andrew Keen goes further, calling Lessig an "intellectual property communist."[614]

Novelist William Gibson echoed some of Lessig's ideas in a *New York Times* op-ed: "In a world characterized by technologically driven change, we necessarily legislate after the fact, perpetually scrambling to catch up, while the core architectures of the future, increasingly, are erected by entities like Google."[615]

However, Gibson is not sure he is comfortable with such a world. First he quotes Eric Schmidt: "I actually think most people don't want Google to answer their questions... They want Google to tell them what they should be doing next." Then Gibson asks himself, "Do we really desire Google to tell us what we should be doing next?" Finally, he answers his own question: "I believe that we do, though with some rather complicated qualifiers."

Author of *What Would Google Do?* Jeff Jarvis has no qualms at all. Having given the second half of his book the hopeful title "If Google Ruled the World,"[616] Jarvis buys the Google myth lock, stock, and barrel.

Google and Lessig apparently believe that cyberspace offers us a second chance to abolish private property—except for their own, of course. Gibson doesn't mind living under an information dictator—as long as it's a benevolent dictator. Jarvis is absolutely enthralled by the prospect.

* * *

Google's top executives don't see their company as a business. They see it as an organization spearheading a political movement.

Google's goal is not making money—it's changing the world. As Google chairman Eric Schmidt told author Ken Auletta during an on-stage interview, "The goal of the company is not to monetize anything... The goal is to change the world—and monetization is a technique to do that."[617]

A year later, Schmidt was even more adamant. "Google pays very well. Google is clearly a growth company, by any metric. And people at Google don't work for those reasons at Google... We don't want them to come to Google for those reasons. We want them to come to Google to change the world."[618]

Schmidt isn't just adding a dash of philosophy to Google's corporate mission. The recipe was clearly spelled out in the Founders' 2004 IPO letter:

> *Google is not a conventional company. We do not intend to become one... Our goal is to develop services that significantly improve the lives of as many people as possible... We also believed that searching and organizing all the world's information was an unusually important task that should be carried out by a company that is trustworthy and interested in the public good. We believe a well functioning society should have abundant, free and unbiased access to high quality information... We aspire to make Google an institution that makes the world a better place.*[619]

This thinking lurks behind each and every Google product. For example, when Google introduced the Chrome operating system, Eric Schmidt remarked, "You don't change the world incrementally."[620]

Schmidt even believes that trampling over peoples' privacy serves a noble cause: "Google will reveal how everybody lives and thinks and speaks and looks and that is beneficial to world peace."[621]

It gets worse. Eric Schmidt brags that Google is redefining what we consider creepy. "There is what I call the creepy line. The Google policy on a lot of things is to get right up to the creepy line and not cross it. I would argue that implanting something in your brain is beyond the creepy line—at least for the moment, until the technology gets better... As far as I know, we do not have a medical lab working on implants. As far as I know. I will check after this."[622]

Google isn't a business. Google is a self-appointed shadow government, and Googleism is its political ideology.

* * *

Google's mission, "to organize the world's information and make it universally accessible and useful," is extremely political.

Google's mission may sound altruistic, but it takes much more than it gives. It deprives users of their privacy; individuals and organizations of their intellectual property rights; markets of fair competition; and individuals, organizations, and governments of their sovereignty. And it's all for the selfish purpose of concentrating control over information in Google's hands.

Google's mission is also destructive. By expropriating private, confidential, and secret information, Google destroys safety, security, and freedom. And by making information and content freely available, Google denies individuals fair compensation for their intellectual and artistic creations, destroying their livelihoods.

Larry Page, Sergey Brin, and Eric Schmidt have repeatedly said that monetization is a technique for changing the world. Google doesn't want everyone's private information just to sell advertising. Google doesn't want to organize everyone's intellectual property just to sell advertising. Google doesn't want to organize government information just to sell advertising.

Google craves the ability to influence people. Google wants to decide what information and content people find, view, and use. Google wants to acquire the power concomitant with a virtual world government.

Google routinely and instinctively frames issues and opponents in political terms. For example, when Oracle sued Google for patent infringement in August of 2010, Google's spokesperson said:

> We are disappointed Oracle has chosen to attack both Google and the open-source Java community with this baseless lawsuit. The open-source Java community goes beyond any one corporation and works every day to make the web a better place. We will strongly defend open-source standards and will continue to work with the industry to develop the Android platform.[623]

Likewise, Google frames its company as the antithesis of evil, implying that most companies (particularly Google's competitors) are evil. Google portrays its engineers as innocent idealists who only want what's good for users, implying that other firms really only care about money. And like a populist politician, Google casts its company as championing the interests of ordinary people: "This is a future for the average person, not just the elite."[624]

Another key element of Google's political frame is portraying Google as benign. If the traditional news and music industries are being destroyed, then it's because the Internet is a disruptive technology. In other words, it's the "creative destruction" identified by Austrian economist Joseph Schumpeter as the automatic consequence of business innovation.

If Google's activities were limited to developing innovative solutions for the free market, then it would be fair to characterize what it is doing as creative destruction. However, Google is doing much more. Google is chipping away at the foundation of our information society: intellectual property rights.

It's not "creative destruction," the incidental destruction of old ways, it is "destructive creation," the purposeful destruction of traditional products, industries, and practices to make way for Google's advertising-centric model and techtopian society.

In short, Google is trying to change our economic system.

Google depicts itself as the champion of neutrality, openness, and freedom of speech—implying that other companies are against these virtues. Google projects this image by following George Lakoff's prescription[625]— using and emphasizing the right choice of words and metaphors. For example, when Eric Schmidt compared Google's mobile strategy to Apple's mobile strategy, he said, "Apple's core strategy is closedness" and shamelessly added, "With Apple's model—which works extremely well, as I know as a former Apple board member—you have to use their development tools, their platform, their software, their hardware."[626]

And how does Schmidt describe Google's approach? "Google's core strategy is openness... Ours is a fundamentally open [strategy]. Open internet. Open web. It's how we fundamentally drive everything."[627]

There is just one problem with Schmidt's portrayal of Google: It's not true. Google's search engine is closed. Google's AdWords auction system is closed. Though Google's Android device operating system is open in some ways, it's closed in others. For example, Android phones come packaged with closed-source Google applications. More disturbingly, a joint report by researchers at Duke University, Penn State University, and Intel Labs found that, "While some mobile phone operating systems allow users to control applications' access to sensitive information, such as location sensors, camera images, and contact lists, users lack visibility into how [Android] applications use their private data."[628]

Google claims to be a staunch supporter of competition. Google insists that it operates in a highly competitive environment in which "competition is one click away." However, both the Department of Justice and the Federal Trade Commission have found that Google dominates key markets.

Google wants us to believe that it courageously confronted the Chinese government over freedom of speech. However, this issue erupted around the time that Google's network and password system were hacked. Google spun an event that revealed how vulnerable its network is into something completely different: how Google stood up to Chinese censorship and publicly humiliated China. It was probably the biggest and most public foreign policy row ever between a company and a foreign government. In fact, Google responded like a virtual nation pursuing an independent foreign policy.

Google also used the Chinese hacking incident to tout its transparency, claiming that it had been "far more transparent about the intrusions than any of the more than two dozen other companies that were compromised, the vast majority of which have not acknowledged the attacks."[629] However, Google's overall transparency record is poor. Though Google issues a "Transparency Report" concerning government requests for information, it only discloses the number of requests from each country. Google does not report what information it collects and what it does with that information.[630]

Google is political on every level. Google not only promotes its radical agenda; Google lobbies government agencies, cuts deals with local officials, and courts federal politicians. Google even offers a free product suite called Political Campaign Toolkit.[631]

In an article titled "Google Goes to Washington with Own Brand of Lobbying," the *Wall Street Journal* illuminated Google's blatant foray into gifting politicians:

> *Google's newly hired team leader for political sales, Peter Greenberger, explained how attendees could use online ads and other services from Google to help their candidates win. One Google product could provide details about people who visited a campaign's Web site, such as the approximate area where they lived, Mr. Greenberger explained. "Tremendously valuable info," he said, adding, "It's free. Did I mention it's free? It's free."*

> *Free in the sense that Google isn't charging money for the service. But the Internet giant is ultimately hoping for something in return: greater influence in the nation's capital.*[632]

Google has encouraged the White House to use YouTube to get its messages out. Google even set up a special YouTube channel for the White House.[633] The White House responded almost immediately by exempting

YouTube from federal online privacy rules; Google was allowed to use persistent cookies to track users visiting White House pages featuring embedded YouTube videos.[634] That ignited a torrent of criticism from privacy advocates, forcing the White House to partially reverse its decision; only users who clicked on the YouTube videos would be tracked.[635]

Google also offered members of the House and Senate their own YouTube channels.[636] A Google company blog post added "...and if your elected representative doesn't have a YouTube channel yet, give them a call or an e-mail and encourage them to get started."[637]

Political pundits have complained for decades about a revolving door between business and government. Google's top Government Affairs official, Andrew McLaughlin, left the firm to become deputy chief technology officer for the Obama Administration.[638] His job involved overseeing many of the policy issues Google cares about most. Consumer groups complained that there was an obvious conflict of interest and demanded that the appointment be cancelled.[639] The complaint wasn't that McLaughlin had worked for Google; the complaint was that he moved directly from being Google's top government affairs executive to a position in which he could help implement Google's ideas and policies. McLaughlin was later reprimanded[640] for a serious breach of ethics; when some of his private emails were accidentally made public they showed that he continued to discuss policy issues with Google contacts.[641]

Potential conflicts of interest arise when government agencies purchase Adwords ads at taxpayer expense. For example, the U.S. Department of Health and Human Services (HHS) purchased ads directing users to HealthCare.gov, a website promoting the Patient Protection and Affordable Care Act. These advertisements appear at the top of the results page whenever users search for "Obamacare" or phrases such as "Obamacare pros and cons."[642] However, the term "Obamacare" is primarily used by opponents of the Act. Given AdWords' opaque operation, there is no way to be certain that Google isn't pulling levers to ensure favorable placement of the HHS ads.

Google not only provides political candidates with free campaign management tools; Google donates AdWords advertising to an array of causes. Specifically, Google has awarded more than $270 million worth of AdWords advertising to 4,000 organizations.[643] Google sponsors the Alliance for Youth Movements, a group that supports "digital activists" working on behalf of causes that are never clearly identified.[644] Google also recruited Jared Cohen from the State Department to run Google Ideas—what Cohen describes as a "think/do tank."[645] Cohen explains, "There are things the private sector can do that the U.S. government can't do" such as getting together two hundred engineers to build something.

Given Google's opaque operations, there is no way to be certain that Google isn't pulling levers to promote and even begin implementing specific policies.

By now alarm bells should be going off. Google has unprecedented power to determine what information gets found. Google is also creating strong ties to the political echelon, providing campaign management and message distribution tools, while working both sides of the business-government revolving door.

* * *

Google wants to influence our democratic institutions and processes—while claiming to be neutral.

Google's executives and employees have the right to hold and promote political views. However, it's unethical (and perhaps even illegal) to promote specific parties and positions while claiming to operate an unbiased, neutral, and apolitical search service. As we've seen, Google executives and employees have demonstrated a clear preference for one political party. They are anything but neutral. Yet they have more power than any other organization to filter the information accessed by the public.

If the implication that Google might try to sway the public seems far-fetched, consider this. In 2006, Eric Schmidt told a group of British politicians that "within five years" general elections would be changed forever by "truth predictor" software.[646] He added that, "We [at Google] are not in charge of truth but we might be able to give a probability."[647]

Four years later, Google continues to think along similar lines—except that its ambitions have soared. During an interview with *Atlantic* editor James Bennet, Schmidt said:

> *We're at a point now in technology where we really can change the entire political discourse if we want to. Typical example would be that everybody here has a mobile phone. In fact, you have more than one. The fact of the matter is that in Washington, and I've been part of this for years, people write lots of reports about things. But they never test them. But with the mobile phone you could just ask. You could measure everything. And you might be surprised at to what people actually do versus what they say they do—one of the first rules of the Internet. So it seems to me that you could completely change the way that government works and the way the discussion works.*[648]

Here is Google saying, in essence, that the job of fact-checking—traditionally handled by journalists, editorialists, and the Federal Election Commission (regarding campaign finances)—would be better handled by Google.

Google already has the power to rank news and commentary. While denying that it wants to determine what is and what is not true, Google proposes to add fact-checking (based on probability) to its repertoire. There is a very fine line between censoring, on the one hand, and using fact-checking and ranking tools to promote your views, on the other.

In fact, Google has already introduced a product that combines fact-checking with ranking. Google Instant displays search results as you type your search terms. This enables Google to send you the results it wants you to see before you finish entering your query. Google has also blacklisted hundreds of words for Google Instant—words that Google doesn't want suggested to you.[649]

If you point out that suggesting some search terms and blacklisting others is a form of bias, then Google responds with evasive circular logic. Google would never be biased, the company insists, because that would undermine trust in Google.

One fact cannot be denied: Google has acquired unprecedented expertise concerning how to influence people. Google understands the importance of search and search ranking better than anyone. Google knows when you click on a link and when you don't click on a link. Google has spent years collecting tracking data for hundreds of millions of Internet users. Google has entered the political campaign business, and it is reasonable to conclude that Google has acquired expertise in selling political candidates, parties, and issues.

Google is the inventor of political search advertising and is dangerously equipped to engage in political campaigning. What makes it dangerous is that Google knows more about scientifically and effectively influencing large numbers of people than anyone else in history.

The point was concretely demonstrated by the brilliant and seminal social network research produced by Paul Adams, Google's Senior User Experience Researcher.[650] Adams' research[651] shows that Google has a tremendous grasp of social networking—a better grasp even than Facebook. The point was driven home after Adam's presentation was made public; Facebook went into all-hands-on-deck crisis mode for three months to fix several strategic weaknesses exposed by Adams.[652]

The biggest of these flaws was that Facebook forced people to put all of their friends in one large bucket when, as Adams deftly showed, most people have several distinct groups of "friends" (childhood friends, college friends, business friends, and so forth) that for good reasons they don't want to mix together.

It's telling that Google understood this point but Facebook, the leader in social networking, did not. After all, Google possesses much more of the world's information, and that includes a great deal of private information such as preferences, intentions, secrets, and those with whom the secrets are shared. No doubt Google studies and analyzes this data. When Google casually disclosed a better understanding of Facebook's audience and business opportunity, Facebook wisely took emergency action.

It bears repeating: Google knows more about influencing people than any individual or company in history.

For example, Google understands that there are only a few people who are essential to influencing any given person. As Adams explained in his presentation, the average Facebook user has 130 "friends" but only interacts regularly with four to six of them. And 80% of a person's Skype phone calls are placed to just two people.

Google also understands how people influence each other online. There are two key factors. First, you need to know what the target's social network looks like. Second, you need to know what the target's past experience has been. No one knows as much about individuals' online experiences as Google.

Google's interest in all of this is hardly academic. Near the end of his presentation, Adams concludes, "we need to design things to support these interactions: buy clothes, buy cars, choose bank, choose job, donate money, and vote."[653] Google has publicly touted[654] its ability to influence politics:

> *Google sees itself as a force in a political race that could hinge on making the best of Web and other tools, Google VP-Global Communications Elliot Schrage said Thurs[day] at the Politics Online conference in Washington.*

> *Candidates are starting to see the Web's power. Schrage said: "Already candidates and campaigns are spending tens of thousands on AdWords campaigns alone." Google is trying to "make services easier to use" through a "special sales and political team dedicated to helping political camps," he said.[655]*

* * *

What does it all mean?

Google possesses well documented political biases. Google is a highly political company that is actively working to change the world. Google has even threatened, "we really can change the entire political discourse if we want to."[656] And it's no idle threat: Google is accumulating the information and power to do just that.

As Fox News correspondent Brit Hume reported, Google banned Republican Senator Susan Collins's ads against Moveon.org based on a company policy with no legal basis and that is only selectively enforced.[657] Google claimed the action wasn't political—that it simply prohibits ads that use trademarked names without permission.[658] But as Hume reported, Google routinely allows advocacy ads that mention trademarked names such as Wal-Mart, Exxon Mobil, and Blackwater USA.

Even if Google's claim that its algorithms are unbiased were true, others could manipulate the search process for political ends. For example, the *Daily Kos* encouraged its readers to work together to drive up the search rankings of articles it considers damaging to Republican candidates. Chris Bowers, campaign director for the *Daily Kos*, said, "This is a more general education project on SEO, with the 2010 elections as a teaching moment."[659] Even if Google does not directly support or oppose specific candidates, Google can sit back and selectively permit others to do the job for them.[660]

Elections are often very close and therefore vulnerable to subtle manipulation. For example, the 2000 presidential election came down to about 300 contested votes in Florida. Political insiders will tell you that elections are often determined by a small percentage of "swing" counties or precincts.

Google has a tremendous amount of personal information about millions of voters and possesses the ability to analyze and use that information to get out the vote and push people's political hot buttons.

In fact, there is evidence that Google is already doing this. Google's mission is to "change the world," and that must ultimately involve political institutions and processes. Google brags that it can influence political campaigns. Google has even developed a tool for tracking election predictions.[661] And Google has threatened even bigger changes. All of this is facilitated by Google's secretive and unaccountable operations.

For example, Google is partnering with the Pew Center for the States to provide technology solutions for state and local election offices.[662] This includes using Google Maps to direct voters to their local polling places. That sounds helpful, but a study by Aristotle, Inc. of 12 key states estimated that Google directed more than 700,000 households to the wrong polling place in the November 2010 elections.[663] If government comes to rely on one company to provide access to information about elections, then it creates opportunities for that company to influence election outcomes whether by design or by accident. Do we really want to take the risk?

In a blog post titled "Brave New Google," author Nicholas Carr recounts Eric Schmidt's comments about how Google can tell you what you should be doing next. Carr concludes (sarcastically), "I hope Google will also be able to tell me the best candidate to vote for in elections. I find that such a burden."[664]

It would be naïve to think that Google would never exercise its power to "nudge" the political process behind the scenes. Professors Richard H. Thaler and Cass R. Sunstein have even written a book, *Nudge: Improving Decisions About Health, Wealth, and Happiness*, that explains how "choice environments" can be designed to "make it easier for people to choose what is best for themselves…"[665]

Professor Thaler, it turns out, is a friend of Google Chief Economist Hal Varian.[666]

* * *

Google's ideology, Googleism, was inspired by several of cyberspace's most controversial philosophers.

Googleism is built around a set of core beliefs. One of the most important is "innovation without permission." That may sound like a harmless endorsement of entrepreneurial zeal, but in Google's hands it's much more.

For example, in a joint blog post Google CEO Eric Schmidt and Verizon President and CEO Lowell McAdam defined "innovation without permission" as the freedom to use the network and develop applications without advance permission.[667] The implication is that property rights must never be allowed to impede innovation.

A blog post by Vint Cerf, Google Vice President and Chief Internet Evangelist, is even more blatant. Cerf defines "innovation without permission" as not having to "seek permission from carriers or pay special fees."[668] In other words, if you use a disproportionate share of a carrier's capacity, then you shouldn't have to pay extra. In testimony before the United States Senate Committee on the Judiciary, Cerf specifically referred to "traditional cable and telephony systems" as obstacles to innovation.[669]

A post on Google's *European Public Policy Blog* takes the idea further. Google engineering director Rian Liebenberg introduces the notion of an "innovation without permission" culture—a culture in which all barriers to innovation are removed.[670] It's also a culture that Liebenberg believes should be enshrined in law.

These ideas spring from common sources. Richard Stallman, a self-described "software freedom activist" and president of the Free Software Foundation, is the father of the "innovation without permission" ideology. Stallman pioneered the free software movement; invented "GNU," a non-proprietary alternative to the UNIX operating system; and introduced "copyleft," a minimalist form of copyright designed to ensure that free software always remains free—even when it is enhanced.

The better-known Linux operating system, pioneered by Linus Torvalds, was essentially an offshoot of Stallman's GNU free software. To the chagrin of Stallman, the Linux project rebranded "free software" as "open source software," positioning it as a respectable alternative to Microsoft's proprietary operating system.

Google's commitment to free software is real if somewhat one-sided. When Oracle sued Google for infringing Java software patents acquired from Sun Microsystems, Google wrapped itself in the open-source Java community. The Free Software Foundation also jumped to Google's defense.[671]

In fact, Google's "innovation without permission" slogan was largely inspired by the Free Software Foundation's definition of free software: "Free software is a matter of the users' freedom to run, copy, distribute, study, change and improve the software... Being free to do these things means (among other things) that you do not have to ask or pay for permission."[672]

In *Free Software, Free Society*,[673] a collection of Stallman's essays published in 2002, he explains:

> *It follows that society should not have owners for programs.*[674]

> *...I am working to build a system where people are free to decide their own actions; in particular, free to help their neighbors, and free to alter and improve the tools that they use in their daily lives. A system based on voluntary cooperation and on decentralization.*[675]

> *For those who believe that owners are more important than anyone else, this paper is simply irrelevant... But why would a large number of Americans accept a premise that elevates certain people above everyone else? Partly because of the belief that this premise is part of the legal traditions of American society. Some people feel that doubting the premise means challenging the basis of society.*[676]

> *...We are not required to agree with the Constitution or the Supreme Court. (At one time, they both condoned slavery.)*[677]

Stallman believes that software and digital content ownership rights are a form of inequality that is "unethical" and "antisocial" because they impede the advance of knowledge, the creativity of individuals, and the creativity of society at large.

The broader ideology behind "innovation without permission" was articulated in 2003 by Eben Moglen, Professor of Law at Columbia

University and former general counsel for the Free Software Foundation, in his "The dotCommunist Manifesto":

> *Creators of knowledge, technology, and culture discover that they no longer require the structure of production based on ownership and the structure of distribution based on coercion of payment. Association, and its anarchist model of propertyless production, makes possible the creation of free software, through which creators gain control of the technology of further production. The network itself, freed of the control of broadcasters and other bandwidth owners, becomes the locus of a new system of distribution, based on association among peers without hierarchical control, which replaces the coercive system of distribution for all music, video, and other soft goods.*[678]

> *Protecting the ownership of ideas requires the suppression of free technology, which means the suppression of free speech.*[679]

> *We are committed to the struggle for free speech, free knowledge, and free technology.*

> *By these and other means, we commit ourselves to the revolution that liberates the human mind. In overthrowing the system of private property in ideas, we bring into existence a truly just society, in which the free development of each is the condition for the free development of all.*[680]

However, the person deserving the most credit for bringing "innovation without permission" into mainstream use is Lawrence Lessig, author of several books advocating common ownership of intellectual property.[681] Lessig also serves on the board of directors of the Free Software Foundation and is a recipient of the organization's Freedom Award.

It's no surprise that Lessig and Google have a close relationship. During a speech at Google, Lessig bragged that nearly all of the lawyers he trains end up working for Google.[682]

Lessig was first to promote the idea of an Internet commons, or "dot.commons." In his book *The Future of Ideas—The Fate of the Commons in a Connected World*, Lessig defines the dot.commons as "…a resource for decentralized innovation. They create the opportunity for individuals to draw upon resources without connections, permission or access granted by others. They are environments that commit to being open."[683]

Lessig's book *Free Culture* spawned a free culture movement that spread to 30 colleges and universities. The following is an excerpt from the Students for Free Culture's utopian "Free Culture Manifesto":

> *The mission of the Free Culture movement is to build a bottom-up, participatory structure to society and culture, rather than a top-down, closed, proprietary structure. Through the democratizing power of digital technology and the Internet, we can place the tools of creation and distribution, communication and collaboration, teaching and learning into the hands of the common person—and with a truly active, connected, informed citizenry, injustice and oppression will slowly but surely vanish from the earth.*
>
> *…The future is in our hands; we must build a technological and cultural movement to defend the digital commons.*[684]

Tim O'Reilly, who coined the term "Web 2.0," has also influenced Google's thinking. His article "What Is Web 2.0" turned out to be a veritable roadmap of Google's strategy.[685]

O'Reilly fervently believes that transparency is more important than privacy. For example, when Google was criticized for scanning Gmail messages, O'Reilly rushed to Google's defense, citing nine reasons why the critics were wrong—one of which was, "Google has a history of providing tasteful, unobtrusive, useful advertising."[686]

When Consumer Watchdog released a humorous video animation in which Google's chairman Eric Schmidt is shown handing out free goodies from an ice cream truck in order to acquire full body scans of children,[687] O'Reilly again leaped to Google's defense, insisting that tracking and profiling are acceptable because Google provides "real value in exchange for the data."[688]

George Lakoff, the Left's political wordsmith, is one of Google's favorite spin doctors. Google's popularization and politicization of words and phrases such as "Don't Be Evil," "[make] the world a better place," and "open" are straight out of Lakoff's playbook.

Another inspiration for Google's anti-capitalist, counter-cultural ideology is the annual Burning Man festival in northern Nevada. Google's founders and Eric Schmidt were for a long time regular attendees. According to Wikipedia, participants describe Burning Man as an "experiment in community, radical self-expression, and radical self-reliance."[689] The event gets its name from the ritual burning of an effigy of a man at its conclusion. According to the organizers, the event is governed by ten principles[690]:

> *Radical Inclusion*: Anyone may participate.
> *Gifting*: Participants should exchange gifts rather than cash.
> *Decommodification* [sic]: No commercial "exploitation" allowed.
> *Radical Self-reliance*: Participants should rely on "inner resources."
> *Radical Self-expression*: As determined by the individual or group.
> *Communal Effort*: Creative cooperation and collaboration.
> *Civic Responsibility*: Assume responsibility for public welfare.
> *Leave No Trace*: Participants must clean up after themselves.
> *Participation*: A radical participatory ethic.
> *Immediacy*: Overcome barriers to recognizing your inner self.

Burning Man clearly rejects many aspects of mainstream American society and draws on utopian ideals such as communalism, socialism, and environmentalism. And it has had a genuine impact on Google: the founders' first doodle of the Google brand[691] used the Burning Man symbol (a stickman) in the second "o" of Google.[692] Reportedly, Eric Schmidt's past attendance at Burning Man made the founders more comfortable in hiring him.

* * *

Googlenomics is an important specialty within Googleism.

One of the leading philosophers of Googlenomics is Hal Varian, Google's chief economist. Varian co-authored *Information Rules: A Strategic Guide to the Network Economy* along with University of California at Berkeley professor Carl Shapiro.[693] The book is widely read by both business managers and students of economics. Published in 1998, *Information Rules* describes opportunities for locking in customers and exploiting network effects. The book also anticipates antitrust complaints and maps out a defense strategy.

Another Googlenomics visionary is Yale University professor Yochai Benkler, author of *The Wealth of Networks: How Social Production Transforms Markets and Freedom*.[694] Benkler apparently imagines his book as the modern equivalent of Adam Smith's classic, *The Wealth of Nations*.

Benkler credits Eben Moglen, Lawrence Lessig, and Richard Stallman with pioneering key ideas in his book. Above all, Benkler is an enthusiastic proponent of the establishment of an online "information commons" and its impact on social relations:

> *Its central question is whether there will or will not, be a core common infrastructure that is governed as a commons and therefore available to anyone who wishes to participate in the networked information environment outside the market-based, proprietary framework.*[695]

> *It will likely result in a significant redistribution of wealth, and no less importantly, power, from previously dominant firms and business models, to a mixture of individuals and social groups...*[696]

We have the opportunity to change the way we create and exchange information, knowledge and culture. By doing so, we can make the twenty-first century one that offers individuals greater autonomy, political communities greater democracy, and societies greater opportunities for self-reflection and human connection. We can remove some of the transactional barriers to material opportunity, and improve the state of human development everywhere. Perhaps these changes will be the foundation of a true transformation toward more liberal and egalitarian societies.[697]

Chris Anderson, editor of *Wired* magazine and author of *The Long Tail: Why the Future of Business is Selling Less of More*[698] and *Free: The Future of a Radical Price,*[699] provides a more accessible explanation of Googlenomics. Anderson's interpretation of Stewart Brand's maxim, "Information wants to be free," is this: with digital technology the cost per bit gets closer and closer to zero. He sees Google as a leading force for "the economics of abundance" made possible by the low incremental cost of processing, storage, and bandwidth.[700]

At a Google-hosted book signing in Washington, DC in July of 2010, Anderson cited Google Chief Economist Hal Varian as the person who "taught me everything I know about free." Anderson also called Google "...the citadel of free" and "...the poster child of making money around free."[701]

Googlenomics is not just another word for Google's business model. It's a carefully thought out system for, above all, changing social relations. As Chris Anderson trumpets, "free" is a radical pricing scheme. But it's more than that—it's a key component of the "free culture" movement.

* * *

Google sees Internet technology, in its hands, as a once-in-a-lifetime opportunity to remake society. Google and its techtopian allies are pushing for a society in which:

o   Openness, transparency and free-sharing replace privacy, secrecy, and property;

o   People work together for the common good rather than working as individuals or corporations for their own benefit;

o   Products and services based on shared information, the wisdom of crowds, openness, mash-ups, and universal access are preferred over products and services based on the profit motive and private ownership;

o   The traditional economics of scarce resources is replaced by the economics of abundant information, processing power, storage, and bandwidth; and

o   The Internet is governed by computer code created by elite engineers and scientists rather than traditional laws and market forces.

Googleism, like many other "isms," is based on the false idea that we can build more prosperous, egalitarian, and happy societies through greater planning and control.

Googleism assumes that technology should rule society rather than assuming that society should rule technology. Consequently, the technological elite should be granted increasing power while people, companies, and national governments surrender their sovereignty. Once the technological elite are firmly in power, society can be operated like a machine with a central control panel.

However, as F. A. Hayek showed, central planning is a dangerous illusion. It may appeal to engineers, but it doesn't lead to greater efficiency.

It may promise to relieve people of economic want, but it must first relieve them of the freedom to control their own lives.

If you take away people's online privacy and intellectual property rights, then you end up with digital serfs.

Part III

Where Is Google Leading Us?

Chapter Eleven

Where Is Google Leading Us?

This is a wake-up call for everyone concerned about the future of the Internet.

The Internet succeeded beyond all expectations as a self-organized and unregulated network. The original vision was quite modest: to interconnect the world's otherwise incompatible computer networks. But the idea quickly evolved into something far more earthshaking: the World Wide Web.

We have been so busy celebrating the Web's success that we have overlooked its dangers. The same technology that empowers citizens can also empower entities bent on controlling them. And though the Internet has been largely self-organized and unregulated, there's no guarantee that it will remain so.

Utopian views of the Web are counterbalanced by its dystopian reality. Consumers may enjoy more information and more choices, but they are also being digitally fingerprinted,[702] tracked, and profiled. The Web grants everyone anonymity, including scammers, spammers, stalkers, WikiLeakers, and terrorists. Perversely, the Web shields the bad guys while it exposes consumers to powerful new threats.

In many ways, the future of the Internet is being decided right now: what we tolerate today could become tomorrow's time-honored practice. If users allow companies to track and profile them year after year, then it will be assumed that they do not oppose the practice. If the definition of "fair use" is expanded to allow users to read entire chapters of books, then it will be assumed that the copyright holders do not object. And if the courts do not correctly apply constitutional and legal principles to the Internet because the laws were written in pre-Internet days, then over time their incorrect decisions will acquire the authority of legal precedent.

With its unsurpassable lead in information access (search) and e-commerce (search advertising), Google is imposing its solutions while most of the world is just coming to realize the nature and magnitude of the problem.

* * *

Google wants to reorder your world.

Google is the most ambitious corporation in history. The Internet has already revolutionized the way we work and play. Google wants to take the next big step—a world-scale step. Google wants to influence what we think and do.

Google's data mining engineers understand better than anyone else that the Internet can be a powerful instrument for transforming our economy, culture, and society. And only they have the googol-scale infrastructure and megalomaniacal vision to pull it off.

We've seen that Google does not respect others' privacy, intellectual property rights, or online security. We've seen that Google believes it is exempt from many rules and laws. And we've seen that Google is a global monopolist with an irresponsible corporate culture.

However, the situation is even worse than we feared, because the whole is greater than the sum of the parts. When you add all of Google's violations, conflicts of interest, and misrepresentations together, a pattern emerges. Google has a radical agenda to change the world in ways that most people would oppose if only they knew enough about it. Google is leading us to an upside-down world in which users are systematically dispossessed through publicacy, "what's yours is mine," and unearned trust.

Google wants to use the Internet to fulfill a dream we thought was finally abandoned—the dream of a collectivist society, a planned economy, and one world government.

* * *

Google is the leader of a techtopian movement that wants to change the Internet.

Techtopians understand that until now every utopian scheme has failed. But that was in the physical world. Armed with new tactics designed specifically for cyberspace, techtopians hope to achieve online what could never be achieved offline.

Where do the techtopians' beliefs, as described in the last chapter, actually lead?

By advocating publicacy and an information commons, techtopians seek to abolish privacy and private intellectual property. By urging people to work together for the common good, techtopians hope to discourage people from striving as individuals and private enterprises for their own good. By touting products and services based on sharing and openness, techtopians diminish opportunities for individual creativity, unconventional thinking, and the quest for excellence. By emphasizing radical free business models, techtopians are trying to replace traditional business models based on the sale of finite goods and services. And by promoting the idea that the online world should be governed by the computer code produced by elite engineers and scientists, techtopians are attempting to circumvent the laws passed by Congress.

Most Internet users have not even heard of the techtopians' *free culture movement*. Unfortunately, what you don't know can hurt you. In fact, many aspects of the free culture movement sound appealing: free products and services (you can't beat the price), increased freedom to copy and redistribute copyrighted content (get it from a friend), open systems ("open" sounds better than "closed"), and sharing (yours is mine).

However, while Google's political agenda starts with the free culture movement, it doesn't end there.

* * *

Google's goals are bigger than the free culture movement's goals.

The free culture movement appeals to Google because the movement's goals complement Google's mission "to organize the world's information and make it universally accessible and useful." The less privacy there is, the more information there is for Google to organize. The more sharing there is, the more content there is for Google to organize. And so on.

But why stop there?

If all information—news, books, music, video, people, and behavior— can be reduced to 1s and 0s, then who is best qualified to collect, analyze, and apply information? Data mining engineers are the logical choice for running the Internet. The happy coincidence is that Google was founded and is run by data mining engineers.

Unfortunately (from Google's perspective), a great deal of content languishes in analog format. Though much progress has been made in digitizing everything, there is plenty of work left to do. However, most analog content is owned by people who are stuck in the analog era.

Google considers digitization a prerequisite to creating a better world. Once everything has been reduced to 1s and 0s, Google's engineers believe, it is possible to come up with mathematically precise solutions to every problem—provided that your computer network is large enough to collect, store, and process sufficient data.

However, that won't come about overnight.

Consequently, Google's plan is to get there in stages. We know what the first two stages are because the first is well underway and the second is starting to unfold. Our understanding of the subsequent stages is based on clues provided by Google plus the natural evolution of its ideas.

In the first stage, *online anarchism*, the main task is to break down the existing order by convincing everyone that it shouldn't be necessary to pay or obtain permission to use others' property. The first stage seeks to prove that, contrary to Milton Friedman, there is a free lunch for those willing to snatch it from its owner's hands.

The resulting "permissionless" society is merely a stepping stone to the next stage. Under *online collectivism*, privacy, confidentiality, and intellectual property are treated as obstacles to egalitarian information access and sharing. Everyone is urged to put the common good above self-interest. Like all egalitarian societies, however, it turns out that some people are more equal than others, and in this case it's the data mining engineers who enjoy the greatest privileges.

The combination of an engineering elite, collectivism, and advanced technology leads inexorably to a *centrally planned* Internet. Competition and diversity are eliminated as sources of inefficiency. Nothing is left to chance—everything is managed and controlled using algorithms and filters. It is what F. A. Hayek might have called, "the digital road to serfdom."

The increased centralization leads to a single information bottleneck, the *Google-programmed* Internet. Everything we find, learn, feel, desire, and buy is influenced by Google's algorithms, hard-coded preferences, and arbitrary scoring system. Google's search engine decides who wins and who loses.

At the end of the line comes the *unaccountable* Internet in which Google's power is off the charts and trust is by necessity blind. Google becomes the exclusive and omniscient editor, observer, distributor, revenue collector, and decision maker. There are no checks and balances. There is no individualism, free-market competition, or security. The tyranny that grew from stage to stage is now absolute. Google's data mining engineers not only run the Internet, they run the world.

* * *

Thankfully, things don't always go according to plan.

Google will encounter bumps in the road. The bumps will determine whether we end up where Google wants us to go or are diverted to a different place. For those who don't want an Internet run by and for data mining engineers, these bumps in the road could be their best and last hope for a different outcome:

Tougher privacy laws: Support is growing for laws or rules that protect citizens' privacy by allowing individuals to choose how much of their information is collected and shared. Contrary to what some say, most

Americans care deeply about privacy. Congress will eventually pass privacy legislation.

Legal victories for intellectual property (IP) owners: You can fool most of the people most of the time about things that don't affect them directly, but you can't fool people who see their creations being shared without their permission. Google will increasingly lose IP cases or be forced to settle out of court.

If the *Viacom v. Google* (YouTube) case goes all the way to the U.S. Supreme Court, that body will likely decide in favor of Viacom. In an analogous case, the Supreme Court ruled unanimously against Grokster, saying, "one who distributes a device with the object of promoting its use to infringe copyright, as shown by clear expression or other affirmative steps taken to foster infringement, is liable for the resulting acts of infringement by third parties."[703]

Security disasters: Google has become too big not to fail. It's only a matter of time before Google experiences the data security equivalent of September 11, 2001. Thinking you are smarter than everyone else only increases the risk. Long Term Capital Management (LTCM) and Enron were said to be the smartest in their fields, and they failed in spectacular fashion.

The Chinese hacking incident was merely a precursor to something worse. A WikiLeaks-like release of sensitive information possessed by Google could be an international disaster.

Antitrust suits: The U.S. Department of Justice and/or the European Union are likely to file antitrust charges against Google for abusing its monopoly power.

Sovereignty clashes: Google has appointed itself Supreme Information Authority. But not everyone will go along. Individuals, competitors, and governments will increasingly defend their sovereignty against Google's systematic encroachment.

Continuing conflicts of interest: Google's foray into "contextual discovery," Google's name for pushing ads to mobile users based on knowledge of their location, conflicts with Google's claim to provide unbiased access to information.[704] Simply put, there is no way to reconcile promising to never feed users biased search results with a new line of business that pushes information to users that they did not request.

* * *

Just as most Internet users do not realize the extent to which they are being tracked, most Internet users do not realize that they are being led somewhere that they do not want to go. It's late, but not too late. The steps that must be taken to protect privacy, property, and competition are—as we'll see in the next chapter—really quite simple and modest.

Chapter Twelve

What Should We Do About It?

Is there a way to safeguard user privacy, strengthen intellectual property rights, protect data security, and restore fair competition to online markets?

Fortunately, the answer is "yes."

For starters, we need to wake up and recognize the problem; demand transparency and accountability; institute checks and balances; and make Google obey laws, regulations, and rules.

But there's one more thing we must do: recognize and defeat Google's radical agenda. All utopian schemes eventually end in failure. However, the longer they last, the more damage they cause. Now is the time for everyone who understands the importance of *individualism*, the *rule of law,* and *property rights* to step forward.

The challenge is to fix what's wrong without undermining what's right. Google does things that are destructive, but it also delivers real value to users, advertisers, and Web publishers. It's important to stop Google's destructive actions while resisting the temptation to penalize Google for its outstanding business success.

* * *

The solution involves a mix of pressure from the public and industry, and limited government action. It is preferable to have Internet users, Web publishers, and online advertisers prevail on Google to respect privacy and property and behave in a more transparent and accountable fashion. In other cases, the solution is to enforce existing laws or (in the case of privacy) draft new laws.

Recommendations:

Insist That Google Follow the Golden Rule: We should subject Google to the most universal of ethical tests: does it treat others the way it expects to be treated?

Unfortunately, Google doesn't even come close to passing the Golden Rule test. A core principle of Google's ideology, Googleism, is that Google knows what's best for everyone. If you really believe you are smarter than everyone else, then it is easy to convince yourself that you should be exempt from laws and rules that constrain those who are not as smart and innovative.

Google urges others to be transparent and open. If Google were equally transparent and open, many problems would disappear.

Google zealously guards its intellectual property. If Google showed comparable respect for others' intellectual property, then many problems would disappear.

Enforce Existing Laws and Rules: Google's monopoly power stems largely from lax law enforcement. The authorities have failed to understand the centrality of search, network effects, and the first mover advantage.

The Department of Justice and the European Union should pursue anti-monopolization cases to block Google from extending its search advertising monopoly, prevent Google from locking up all of the major information silos, and stop Google from destroying competition with its predatory, radical free strategy.

Google is in stop-us-if-you-can mode. The antitrust authorities' goals should not be to punish Google, but to preserve a competitive marketplace and halt the continuing predatory concentration of control over information in one company's hands.

Failure to constrain Google through antitrust enforcement today could lead to intrusive and burdensome regulation of the digital economy tomorrow. That would be the worst of all possible worlds. Put another way, if we fail to prevent Big Brother Inc. (Google) from monopolizing control over information, then we might one day find ourselves ruled by something like the Big Brother in George Orwell's novel *Nineteen Eighty-Four*.

The DOJ has done the right thing by blocking the proposed Google-Yahoo! ad agreement and opposing the original Google Books settlement.

The FTC has not done as well. The FTC was asleep at the switch when it approved the Google-DoubleClick merger, giving Google permission to buy rather than compete for the roughly one-third of user, advertiser, and publisher relationships that Google did not already control. The FTC also approved Google's acquisition of AdMob despite "serious antitrust concerns," effectively granting Google an extension of its search advertising monopoly to the mobile market.

Seek Redress from the Appropriate Authorities: The individuals, companies, and organizations who believe that Google has acted illegally in harming them should seek redress in the courts. There is strength in numbers, and those harmed should make it increasingly hard for the authorities to ignore Google's pattern of misbehavior on multiple levels.

Prevent Google from Manipulating Markets: Given Google's near perfect market information in online advertising markets, and Google's detailed profiles (often containing financial information) of people, companies, and transactions, the SEC, Commodity Future Trading Commission (CFTC), and foreign financial regulators should closely monitor Google's use of this uniquely comprehensive inside information. Specifically, Google should be required to implement meaningful internal controls and submit to third party audits.

As the world's dominant information market maker using the de facto online currency of keywords and their derivatives—by way of opaque search algorithms, ad auctions, and mysterious quality scores—Google should be subjected to the same legal obligations, accountability, responsibilities, internal controls, and audits that any other market-maker is subjected to in order to ensure that Google is not abusing its monopoly broker position to self-deal, front-run customers, skim proceeds, discriminate against competitors, or blacklist information that it doesn't like.

Google has more serious hidden conflicts of interest than any company in history, and it would be naïve to think it is immune to temptation.

Prevent Google from Tampering with Elections: Google is in the influence peddling business. Google enables advertisers to target users based on private information available to Google through its search engine, free products and services, and other Web surveillance mechanisms. Google also sells online advertising to political candidates, campaigns, and parties.

Put all of this together and you have a company with the unique ability to influence elections, policymaking, and even legal decisions.

Governments need to better understand the many ways that Google is able to influence voters and government agencies. Google even influences those who do not rely on Google's search services, because Google influences many of the people and sources that they do rely on.

Elections and referendums are often won by those who do the best job influencing the hard-to-identify undecided voters. Google's extensive and unauthorized profiling of users is essentially extensive and unauthorized profiling of voters. Independent oversight—with representation of the major political parties—is needed to ensure that Google is not clandestinely influencing elections. Given Google's radical agenda, its ability to influence elections and elected officials may be the single most destructive power that Google possesses.

Pass Privacy Legislation: U.S. consumers clearly want Do Not Track rules modeled after the popular and largely effective Do Not Call rules. Several polls show that citizens overwhelmingly demand the right to opt out of online tracking for behavioral profiling.

Do Not Track rules could be easily implemented by requiring browsers to indicate the user's Do Not Track preference in packet headers and require those who gather and use tracking information to honor each user's preference.[705]

Congress also needs to address the prevailing finders-keepers-losers-weepers standard: the quiet understanding that companies are free to sell or make public in a derivative form the private digital information that they collect. More specifically, Congress should replace the patchwork of pre-Internet privacy laws by passing comprehensive online privacy legislation that is consumer-centric and company- and technology-neutral.

My testimony in June of 2009 on "The Potential Privacy Implications of Behavioral Advertising"[706] before a Joint House Subcommittee explained that technological developments have dramatically altered online privacy. During the Web's early years, privacy was not a big problem because the industry was fragmented. Now, thanks to business consolidation and more sophisticated tracking technology, online privacy has become almost nonexistent. Most consumers are unaware of the growing risks and mistakenly believe they have more control over their private data than they do.

Pressure Google to Upgrade to Enterprise-Level Security: A major security breach at Google could be catastrophic. Google should not be limping along on consumer-grade security. Multiple layers of security backed by best security practices are needed. Google has too much sensitive data about too many people.

Oppose Google's Radical Agenda: Google's radical vision of a single source for accessing the world's information, a single database for storing the world's information, and a single algorithm for ranking the world's information is a threat to the sovereignty of individuals, organizations, societies, and even governments.

The first step is to oppose acts and schemes that threaten private intellectual property. The second step is to recognize that privacy is essential to individual liberty and must be safeguarded as well. History warns that when citizens are deprived of privacy, tyranny often follows.

A single worldwide repository of information controlled from a digital Tower of Babel can only have a homogenizing effect on culture. Bland universal standards will replace diversity of thought, belief, and heritage.

Google's vision of universal information access on a global scale is the precursor to a single world government. When Google knows more about a country's population, leaders, political institutions, and economy than anyone else, national sovereignty is threatened. If governments outsource collecting, storing, and applying information to Google, then they will soon find that for all intents and purposes they are working for Google.

The solution is simple. If Google Inc. were transparent and accountable, respected other people's privacy and property rights, and obeyed all laws as their framers intended, then Google would not be an untrustworthy and destructive company.

Conclusion

The Tyranny of Central Planning

Google's mission statement should frighten people.

The only way a single entity could "organize the world's information and make it universally accessible and useful" would be for it to collect and store all private and public information. That would require ubiquitous surveillance, with all information considered in the public domain and access controlled by a single company.

Amazingly, few people have questioned the appropriateness of Google's mission. In theory, a single source for all information would be convenient and useful. In practice, it means appointing one entity the world's supreme editor and information gatekeeper and abolishing privacy.

Contrary to what Google says, it's a very good thing that the world's information is scattered among diverse repositories, that not all information is universally accessible, and that a great deal of information and content is private property. A society in which one entity controls access to all information is a totalitarian society.

In fact, there are disturbing parallels between Google's mission and the goals of the now defunct Soviet Union.

The Soviet Union's founders believed that a centrally planned economy would produce more quality goods and services than an economy based on free-market competition. They also believed that a centrally planned economy would lead to a more just society. And they believed that for the benefits of central planning to be fully realized, it would have to be done on a worldwide basis. They were tragically wrong on all three counts.

What we learned from the Soviet experiment is that central planning leads to brutality, tyranny, injustice, incompetence, and poverty. Societies based on individual freedom, competition, checks and balances, sovereignty and diversity are more productive because they give individual citizens a reasonable shot at realizing their full potential.

Unfortunately, supporters of utopian political systems don't give up easily. To techtopians, the Soviet Union failed not because central planning was a bad idea, but because the Soviets did not possess the technology needed to make it work. With today's computers and Internet, central planners can collect and store far more data, and they can instantly transmit commands to any location.

However, the techtopians are badly mistaken. Google's search engine, computer network, and tentacles reaching every major hardware platform, type of content, and corner of the Web will only exacerbate the tyranny of central planning. The data mining engineer's belief in reducing everything to binary data and algorithmic control can only create a more inhumane system.

Google's mission is flat-out wrong, both pragmatically and ethically.

* * *

The scale of Google's ambition raises a giant red flag.

Though Google is only twelve years old, it is the most powerful company in the world. From the very start, Google's founders' wanted to do something bigger than anyone had ever done. They chose the largest number ever named, the googol, as the source of their brand name. In doing so, they knew exactly what they were doing and why: "The name reflects the immense amount of information that exists and the scope of Google's mission."[707]

Google's founders' true genius, however, was envisioning the Internet as one enormous mathematical puzzle. They alone recognized that everything on the Internet is represented as bits that can be collected, stored, organized, and analyzed. They alone acted on this profound insight.

Ever since then, Google's leaders have taunted us about the extent of their ambition. Yet almost no one has taken their remarks seriously. Co-founder Sergey Brin said, "The perfect search engine would be like the mind of God."[708] Chairman Eric Schmidt bragged, "Our model is just better. Based on that we should have 100% share."[709] Google executive Amit Singhal boasted that Google is "the biggest kingmaker on this earth."[710] And Google executive Marissa Mayer declared, "We are trying to build a virtual mirror of the world at all times."[711]

So there you have it. Google believes its search engine, once perfected, would rival the mind of the Creator. Google doesn't just aim for 100% market share, Google believes it deserves 100% market share. Who if not Google should select the kings from among the subjects? And Google is a virtual mirror of the entire world.

Google has been touting its superhuman aspirations for years:

o   Google's mission is to achieve *omniscience*;
o   Google has an *omnivorous* appetite for data and market share;
o   Google seeks *omnipresence* on the Web and beyond;
o   Google's repertoire of products and information types is *omnifarious*; and
o   Google is scaling its infrastructure, databases, and software to achieve *omnipotence*.

When you add it all up, Google's ambitions are totalitarian. Google doesn't just want to organize *some* of the world's information. Nor does it propose to merely *help* organize the world's information. Google wants it all. And if Google gets it all, there will be no room left for privacy, private intellectual property, or competition.

Google has warned us, and we have no one to blame but ourselves if things go awry. Google aspires to be "…an institution that makes the world a better place."[712] Not a company with conventional business goals but an institution pursuing radical social goals.

* * *

Google's first goal is to destroy the existing order.

Step back and look at what Google is doing. There are some inescapable conclusions.

Google is knowingly and purposely destroying privacy (through massive online tracking), intellectual property (by skirting property laws), competition (by dumping free products on the market), and individual competitors (by suddenly pulling the rug out from under AdWords customers).

Google admits that it sometimes hides what it is doing. For example, Eric Schmidt stated that for Google Chrome "it was important that our strategic aspirations be relatively under the radar."[713] It's perfectly reasonable for companies to keep their product plans confidential. But Schmidt wasn't talking about product or business plans—he was talking about radical aspirations. Google's reason for introducing a free Web browser wasn't to sell anything—it was to better spy on users.

To achieve its destructive goals, Google depends on assumed acquiescence. Google knows that if people do not complain sufficiently about loss of privacy, then Google can claim that it has the tacit consent of users. The longer Google gets away with providing access to copyrighted content without permission, the harder it will be to stop Google. The more market power Google accrues from these activities, the more negotiating leverage Google attains. That, in a nutshell, has been Google's strategy for Google Books, YouTube, Google News, and other products.

Google cloaks its destructive practices in Clayton Christensen's[714] notion of "disruptive innovation." However, Christensen is referring to the natural disruption that occurs in the free market when a better product or service comes along. Google, in contrast, uses words such as "disruptive" to excuse abuses of power. For example, Google dumps free goods and services in strategic markets to destroy competitors and potential competitors. And Google devalues intellectual property by systematically infringing (or enabling others to infringe) copyrights, trademarks, and patents.

Google often destroys in subtle but effective ways. Google exploits the uncertainty and confusion created by the growth of digital and online technologies. Does fair use allow users to upload and share copyrighted videos in five-minute segments? Is it OK to host copyrighted videos as long as you have a process for reviewing complaints and eventually taking them down? The longer Google gets away with such practices, the harder they are to stop. As they say, possession is nine-tenths of the law.

With its search and search advertising monopoly, Google can destroy online products and services that depend on transaction or subscription-based business models. Google can destroy much of the proprietary software market with its cloud computing solutions. And Google is rapidly gaining share in the mobile market—squeezing out for-sale operating systems—with its free, monopoly-subsidized Android operating system and applications.

Google also has an unintentional destructive side: data security. More and more businesses rely on Google despite the fact that Google represents a single point of failure. Most of the Internet would be hurt if Google were hit by a "zero-day threat"—what Byron Acohido describes as "a hazard so new that no viable protection against it yet exists."[715] Google's extreme centralization invites attacks from spammers, malware pushers, identity thieves, saboteurs, and WikiLeaks copycats.

In fact, Google has offered support for WikiLeaks, Julian Assange's simultaneous assault on national security, privacy, and intellectual property rights. When asked about WikiLeaks, Eric Schmidt said: "Has Google looked at the appropriateness of indexing WikiLeaks? The answer is yes, and we decided to continue because it's legal."[716] In other words, Google is indexing and making accessible stolen content. The claim that it is "legal" does not make it right.

Given such behavior, it's worth taking another look at the symbolism invoked by Google's founders at the Googleplex. The B-52 bomber chair suggests that the Google chairman's job is to nuke the competition. The T-Rex mascot suggests that Google's founders see their company as a terrifying predator.

* * *

Google is well along in its mad quest to centralize control of information.

Google has indexed more than one trillion Web pages. Google has profiled more than one billion users. Google has developed the algorithms, computer infrastructure, databases, and monetization schemes to continue centralizing control at an accelerating rate.

Google's algorithms are the control levers in Google's central planning system. Algorithms are essentially computer programs that solve problems using math and logic. To make its algorithms work, Google must first reduce everything it observes online—people, users, advertisers, publishers, developers, data, and content—to streams of 1s and 0s. Then Google determines the general outcomes that it wants its automated system to produce.

Google's data mining engineers treat even human behavior as binary data. However, quantifying everything involves an enormous number of assumptions—many of which are subjective because they require estimates or best guesses. That means that what starts as something vague or uncertain, such as human choice, ends up as something that appears precise and certain. The mechanistic approach justifies the totalitarian system by first dehumanizing people.

Google treats human behavior as probabilistic. Doing so enables Google to compute answers to tough questions. But the computations often depend on the assumption that all people and groups of people think and act alike. Google's algorithms see the world as a massive regression toward the mean. For many queries, that is fantastically effective. For others, it is merely a best guess.

Google is the ultimate central planner because Google must anticipate answering every possible query. Google has learned to preplan the handling of different situations, such as handling searches using misspelled keywords.

Google has already developed tools to plan activities such as e-commerce and online education. The utility of these tools will increase as

Google acquires more information from the users of its free products. For example, Google offers politicians free tools for planning political campaigns. As Google collects voter, district, and state political preference metadata from various tools, it acquires the ability—even if it does not use it today—to influence political campaigns and election results.

Google begins the planning process by ranking Web pages, setting filters, and making other decisions. When Google says that its search engine is unbiased, Google really means that the decisions about how to rank Web pages were made in advance so the process could be automated.

In other words, Google is trying to organize the Internet around the centralization of information and preplanned processes. The more Google succeeds at this, the greater Google's ability to achieve further success. As a Googler might say, rinse and repeat.

A central plan requires central planners. However, techtopians believe that even planning can be automated. If that's true, more and more power will be concentrated in the hands of fewer and fewer Google technocrats. Ultimately, the Internet could be run by a central committee much as the Soviet Union was run by a central committee.

* * *

George Orwell foresaw that the centralization of information could be used by the few to oppress the many.

For over a century, individualists have warned that technology could one day be used to spy on citizens, bombard the public with continuous and ubiquitous propaganda, manipulate individuals in subtle ways, and ultimately strip people of their humanity.

In George Orwell's dystopian novel *Nineteen Eighty-Four*, Big Brother and his ruling clique use two-way "telescreens" to spy on, brainwash, and control the people.[717]

Writing in the 1940s, Orwell envisioned the telescreen as a combination television and video camera (with microphone). The telescreen broadcasts non-stop propaganda into the homes of the middle and upper classes as well as into public places. And the telescreen permits the Thought Police to eavesdrop on individual citizens.

What Orwell didn't know is that a more powerful tool would emerge in the 1990s: Internet-connected computers. While telescreens allow human operators to watch and listen, the World Wide Web can be used to automatically collect data on millions of users. The telescreen's human operators are prone to error and fatigue. An Internet-connected PC, in contrast, can gather data 24/7 without getting tired and without making mistakes.

Internet-connected PCs represent a more advanced, accurate, and subtle technology—technology that people willingly use for work and enthusiastically use for play. Though most seem unaware, the new technology quietly records users' every keystroke, mouse click, and thought, and influences them in ways that are subtle yet effective.

The Internet is a much more powerful tool for controlling the populace. The Internet can be used to track all citizens at all times—often in ways that most citizens don't realize. The Internet's reach can be extended to other devices such as mobile phones and televisions. Detailed profiles of every citizen can be created over time. And the Internet can be used to influence people in subtle (and therefore more effective) ways.

Certainly Google does not have the power of the government to control every aspect of people's lives, to arrest and execute dissenters, or to wage never-ending wars.

However, Google does have the power to track and profile individuals, influence groups of people and society as a whole, and offer tools and information to government in exchange for special treatment and privileges. In the wrong hands, the information Google possesses could be used to blackmail, silence, or destroy dissidents and political opponents.

Google is assembling the building blocks for a telescreen more powerful than anything Orwell imagined. With its Android operating system, Google is extending its reach beyond Internet PCs in homes, schools, and offices to mobile phones, televisions, and other devices. With a variety of platforms, Google will be able to follow you everywhere. Using artificial intelligence,

Google will know your next move before you do. Using neuroscience and Lakoffian linguistics,[718] Google will be able to influence enough voters to determine the outcome of close election races.

Google also resembles the ruling elite in another one of George Orwell's novels, *Animal Farm*.[719] Like the pigs who gain control of Mr. Jones's farm, Google has a double standard; there is one set of rules for Google and another set of rules for everyone else. Google is highly secretive, zealously guards its intellectual property, and treats even charitable endeavors as profit centers. But Google treats everyone else quite differently: Google violates users' privacy, redistributes others' intellectual property, and insinuates that other businesses are greedy and unethical.

Google disguises its double standard using Googlespeak, Google's additions to what Orwell called "Newspeak" in *Nineteen Eighty-Four*. Googlespeak makes generous use of words and phrases including: transparency, openness, neutrality, universal, equal access, free speech, and disruptive. In most cases, these words mean one thing when applied to others and the exact opposite when applied to Google.

There are more ominous parallels between Google and *Nineteen Eighty-Four*. Eric Schmidt publicly admitted that Google's ability to spy on people achieves what Orwell feared most: "We know where you are. We know where you've been. We can more or less know what you're thinking about."[720]

Google has even learned how to enlist users to spy on themselves: "There's such an overwhelming amount of information now, we can search where you are, see what you're looking at if you take a picture with your camera. One way to think about this is, we're trying to make people better people, literally give them better ideas—augmenting their experience. Think of it as augmented humanity."[721] Are there any limits to Google's surveillance ambitions and powers? "We can suggest what you should do next, what you care about. Imagine: We know where you are, we know what you like."[722]

Schmidt is so excited about the opportunities to control people he can barely contain his enthusiasm: "I actually think most people don't want

Google to answer their questions. They want Google to tell them what they should be doing next."[723]

Naturally, Schmidt admires totalitarian societies. Schmidt told *Atlantic* editor James Bennet, "China can best be understood as a large, well-run business… And China has roughly the following objectives: It wants to maximize its cash flow, becoming the creditor, if you will, the bank of the world. And second it wants to maximize both its internal demand as well as export demand. And the entire country seems to be organized around that principle."[724]

George Orwell's technological forecast was about as good as it gets. But his real genius was in understanding people and their foibles.

Orwell anticipated that in the future totalitarians would use technology to exercise immense power. He knew, specifically, that the ruling clique would employ electronic surveillance to gather information about citizens. He realized that the ruling clique would want to monopolize and manipulate the information presented to citizens for the purpose of mind control. He appreciated the power of words to mislead, and would have recognized phrases such as, "Don't Be Evil" and, "make the world a better place" as newspeak.

Google's unbiased search algorithm would probably remind Orwell of the Ministry of Truth. Google's search filters would probably remind him of memory holes. And Google's frequent references to transparency and openness would probably remind him of doublethink.

Most important, Orwell would have recognized the Google Rule: *Whoever controls others' information, rules.*

* * *

We have reached a critical juncture in the battle for cyberspace. The decisions we make today will define the Internet of tomorrow.

It's a battle between individualism and collectivism, between free-market competition and Googleopoly, and between sovereignty and serfdom. It's a battle to determine how information gets found. It's a battle to determine how companies win and lose. It's a battle to determine whether search and search advertising are tools for empowering businesses and users—or tools for controlling them.

It's also a battle to place adequate checks and balances on Google's power. Will there be many information gatekeepers and e-commerce toll collectors or will there be few? The fewer gatekeepers and toll collectors, the more power each accrues. If one gatekeeper/toll collector is allowed to dominate, it will acquire absolute power—and the absolute corruption that inevitably accompanies it.

Google's mission to organize the world's information is wrong. Google wants information to be "free" so that Google does not have to pay for it. However, by centralizing and devaluing information, Google undermines individual freedom, free-market competition, and local sovereignty. Google may pave the way with free products and services, but it is still a road to serfdom.

* * *

Google misleads us.

Google began life as an information servant, but it is turning into the world's information master. The company that started by working for users—helping them quickly find the information they want—soon discovered how to make users work for it, generating behavioral data that Google gathers, hoards, analyzes, studies, monetizes, and exploits to acquire ever more power.

Google is now arguably the most powerful influencer in history. Using advanced technology and ingenious anti-corporate PR ("Don't Be Evil"), Google disguises what it is doing in a way that would deserve our admiration were it not so dishonest.

Consider, for example, Google Instant. Google has evolved its core search service from answering our questions to instantly presenting the information that Google wants us to find as we type in the first few letters of a query. Google pretends that Google Instant only saves us time and keystrokes. What Google Instant actually does is distract and divert us as Google wishes.

Google's "contextual discovery"[725] business takes influencing to the next level, leveraging the information Google already possesses about us, including our exact location at any moment, to send us search results we did not request. *Contextual discovery saves us the trouble of thinking for ourselves.*

Google's priority email service[726] is another example of how Google is evolving influencing into controlling. With Priority Mailbox, Google reads your emails and listens to your voicemails, applies everything else they know about you, and then *tells you what you should do next.*

The overarching pattern is clear. Google knows the best answer for you before you even know the question. It's no exaggeration to say the goal of Google's central planners is to *tell you what to read, what to watch, what to think, and what to do.* Google executives have said as much on multiple occasions.

Actions speak louder than words. Google dispenses soaring rhetoric about serving users, but Google's actions are all about influencing and controlling users. Absolute power corrupts absolutely.

Forewarned is forearmed: Google's real mission is to remake the world in its own image through hidden influence, manipulation, and central planning. And Google's immense unaccountable power is so destructive precisely because Google is shockingly political, unethical, and untrustworthy.

The Google Code

(A satirical look at Google's guiding principles)

I. The Google Rule: *Whoever controls others' information rules*

II. Google's Golden Rule: *Treat others as Google does not want to be treated*

III. Google's Moral Relativism: *Implying that others are evil makes Google look ethical*

IV. Google's Moral Compass: *"Evil is whatever Sergey says is evil."* – Eric Schmidt

V. Google's Code of Ethics: *"The Google policy on a lot of things is to get right up to the creepy line and not cross it."* – Eric Schmidt

VI. Google's Rule of Thumb: *If it doesn't scale, it can't be monopolized*

VII. Google's Law of Free: *"A sucker is born every minute."*

VIII. Google's Law of Privacy: *Profiling is in the eye of the beholder*

IX. Google's Law of Property: *All good things come to those who take them*

X. Google's Law of Innovation: *If at first you don't succeed, buy whoever did*

Bibliography

Acohido, Byron. *Zero Day Threat: The Shocking Truth of How Banks and Credit Bureaus Help Cyber Crooks Steal Your Money and Identity.* New York: Union Square Press, 1 April 2008.

Anderson, Chris. *Free: The Future of a Radical Price.* New York: Hyperion, 7 July 2009.

Anderson, Chris. *The Long Tail: Why the Future of Business is Selling Less of More.* New York: Hyperion, 11 July 2006

Asimov, Isaac. *The Foundation Trilogy.* New York: Doubleday, 1 October 1983.

Auletta, Ken. *Googled: The End of the World As We Know It.* London: Penguin Press HC, November 2009.

Battelle, John. *The Search: How Google and Its Rivals Rewrote the Rules of Business and Transformed Our Culture.* New York: Portfolio Trade, 2005, 2006.

Benkler, Yochai. *The Wealth of Networks: How Social Production Transforms Markets and Freedom.* New Haven, CT: Yale University Press, 23 October 2007.

Brandt, Richard L. *Inside Larry and Sergey's Brain.* London: Portfolio Press, 17 September 2009.

Carr, Nicholas. *The Big Switch: Rewiring the World, from Edison to Google.* New York: W. W. Norton & Company, 17 January 2008.

Carr, Nicholas. *The Shallows: How the Internet Is Changing the Way We Think, Read and Remember.* London: Atlantic Books, 1 Sep 2010.

Chester, Jeff. *Digital Destiny: New Media and the Future of Democracy.* New York: New Press, 8 January 2007.

Conti, Greg. *Googling Security: How Much Does Google Know About You?* London: Addison-Wesley Professional, 20 October 2008.

DeLong, James V. "Google the Destroyer," *TCS Daily*, 7 January 2008, http://www.ideasinactiontv.com/tcs_daily/2008/01/google-the-destroyer.html

Friedman, Milton. *Free to Choose: A Personal Statement.* New York: Mariner Books, 26 November 1990.

Girard, Bernard. *The Google Way: How One Company Is Revolutionizing Management As We Know It.* San Francisco: No Starch Press, 1 April 2009.

Hayek, Frederick. *The Road to Serfdom.* London: Routledge, 17 May 2001.

Huxley, Aldous. *Brave New World.* New York: Harper Perennial Modern Classics, 17 October 2006.

Jeanneney, Jean-Noël. *Google and the Myth of Universal Knowledge.* Chicago: University of Chicago Press, 1 November 2006.

Keen, Andrew. *The Cult of the Amateur.* New York: Bantam Dell Publishing Group, 5 June 2007.

Lakoff, George. *Don't Think of an Elephant!: Know Your Values and Frame the Debate--The Essential Guide for Progressives.* White River Junction, VT: Chelsea Green Publishing, 15 September 2004.

Lessig, Lawrence. *code 2.0.* Seattle: CreateSpace, 30 December 2009.

Lessig, Lawrence. *Free Culture: The Nature and Future of Creativity*. New York: Penguin Books, 22 February 2005.

Lessig, Lawrence. *Remix: Making Art and Commerce Thrive in the Hybrid Economy.* New York: Penguin Press HC, 16 October 2008.

Lessig, Lawrence. *The Future of Ideas: The Fate of the Commons in a Connected World.* New York: Vintage Books, 22 October 2002.

Lowe, Janet. *Google Speaks: Secrets of the World's Greatest Billionaire Entrepreneurs, Sergey Brin and Larry Page.* Hoboken, NJ: Wiley Press, 4 May 2009.

McLeod, Kembrew and Lessig, Lawrence. *Freedom of Expression: Resistance and Repression in the Age of Intellectual Property.* Minneapolis, MN: University of Minnesota Press, 8 March 2007.

Orwell, George. *Animal Farm.* New York: Plume Publishing, 1 June 1996.

Orwell, George. *Nineteen Eighty-Four.* New York: Plume Publishing, 6 May 2003.

Spector, Robert. *Amazon.com: Get Big Fast.* New York: Harper Paperbacks, 22 January 2002.

Stross, Randall. *Planet Google: One Company's Audacious Plan to Organize Everything We Know.* New York: Free Press, 18 September 2008.

Thaler, Richard H. *Nudge.* New Haven, CT: Yale University Press, 2008.

Vise, David A. *The Google Story.* New York: Delacorte Press, 22 November 2005.

Zittrain, Jonathan. *The Future of the Internet—And How to Stop It.* New Haven, CT: Yale University Press, 14 April 2008.

Additional Resources

http://precursorblog.com/

http://googlemonitor.com/

http://googleopoly.net/

Acknowledgements

First, I want to thank my wife Sara for her unwavering love, encouragement, support, wisdom, patience, and belief in me, and my son Adam and daughter Grace for their love, encouragement, ideas, and candor. I am grateful to my family for their patience during the long hours it took me to fulfill the dream of writing this book. My family is a true blessing. Special thanks to my father Sherrill Cleland, who encouraged me intellectually and provided me with life experiences that helped me "see the world whole." Very special thanks to my late mother Betty Cleland, who I miss so much, who remains the most courageous person that I have ever known, and who taught me to stand up for what I believe is right. I hope and trust I honor my father and mother with this book.

This book would never have been written without the initiative and foresight of my wise and skilled publisher, editor and co-author, Ira Brodsky, who more than anyone is responsible for getting my ideas and story into book form; thank you Ira. Thanks to my very able assistant, Barbara Lochen, for her many important contributions; and thanks to artist Miguel De Angel for making the concept of a T-Rex in sheep's clothing come to life.

I would be remiss if I did not give special thanks to Jim Delong, a leading property rights defender with the Convergence Law Institute, who inspired the organizing theme of this book with his insightful 2007 piece "*Google the Destroyer.*" Michael Boland of Dome Advisors deserves credit for inspiring the chapter "Digital Road to Serfdom" by urging me to study Friedrich Von Hayek's classic, *The Road to Serfdom,* a few years back. I am indebted to Adam Thierer of the Mercatus Center for helping me decipher and understand the roots of the "information commons" ideology and identify the intellectual leaders of this nascent but rapidly growing techtopian-socialist movement. I have also learned from the wisdom of James Gattuso of the Heritage Foundation and Randy May of the Free State Foundation.

I also admire and want to thank Harry Markopolos, the investigator who diligently and persistently presented evidence to the U.S. Government that Bernie Madoff was committing fraud, for being such a courageous example to me in standing up for what he knew was right, and for blazing a trail for this book by writing: *"No One Would Listen: A True Financial Thriller."*

I would also like to acknowledge and thank others who contributed to my professional development. I am especially grateful to my former Precursor Group partner and good friend Bill Whyman for his brilliant analytical mind and deep knowledge; he has taught me more than anyone about the tech sector, the Internet, and software. Thanks to my late friend, John Wilkie, long-time *Wall Street Journal* antitrust reporter, who shared a deep interest in Google antitrust issues, and who is sorely missed by many.

Thanks to my former bosses Secretary of State James A. Baker III, Bob Zoellick, Janet Mullins, Peter Madigan, John F.W. Rogers, and Jill Kent, who were instrumental in helping me develop the professional skills and confidence needed to identify and analyze Google's destructive impact on the world.

Thanks to the late Congresswoman Barbara Jordan, my "Political Values & Ethics" professor, who taught me to focus on the critical clash between freedom and equality in political ideologies. Thanks also to my Kalamazoo College political science faculty advisor, Don Flesche, for his encouragement. And thanks to my WRA teachers: Tom Demong, who taught me writing, and Ms. Anne Chapman, who encouraged my conceptual thinking.

Lastly, I apologize to anyone that I may have overlooked; please forgive me and thank you for your help.

Scott Cleland
March 2011

Notes

[1] "What If Google and Bing Waged a Search War and Nobody Noticed?" Kevin Ryan, September 16, 2010, *Advertising Age*, http://adage.com/digitalnext/post?article_id=145916

[2] "Top 10 Reasons to Work at Google," "Uniting the world, one user at a time. People in every country and every language use our products. As such we think, act, and work globally – just our little contribution to making the world a better place." http://www.google.com/intl/en/jobs/lifeatgoogle/toptenreasons/

[3] "Google's Tar Pit," Joshua Green, December 2007, *The Atlantic*, http://www.theatlantic.com/magazine/archive/2007/12/google-8217-s-tar-pit/6420/

[4] "How Good (or Not Evil) Is Google?" David Carr, June 21, 2009, *New York Times*, http://www.nytimes.com/2009/06/22/business/media/22carr.html?_r=1

[5] "Quick profile," Corporate information, "Google's mission is to organize the world's information and make it universally accessible and useful." http://www.google.com/corporate/facts.html

[6] "Code of conduct: conclusion," Google investor relations, "Google aspires to be a different kind of company." http://investor.google.com/corporate/code-of-conduct.html#VIII

[7] David A. Vise and Mark Malseed, *The Google Story* (New York: Delacorte Press, 2005), p. 47.

[8] http://investor.google.com/corporate/code-of-conduct.html

[9] (Vise & Malseed, 2005) p. 174

[10] See my "Testimony Before the Senate Judiciary Subcommittee On Antitrust," September 27, 2007, http://googleopoly.net/cleland_testimony_092707.pdf (written testimony); http://googleopoly.net/senate_charts.pdf (presentation charts)

[11] "We knew the web was big," Jesse Alpert & Nissan Hajaj, Software Engineers, Web Search Infrastructure Team, July 25, 2008, *Official Google Blog*, "We've known it for a long time: the web is big. The first Google index in 1998 already had 26 million pages, and by 2000 the Google index reached the one billion mark. Over the last eight years, we've seen a lot of big numbers about how much content is really out there. Recently, even our search engineers stopped in awe about just how big the web is these days -- when our systems that process links on the web to find new content hit a milestone: 1 trillion (as in 1,000,000,000,000) unique URLs on the web at once!" http://googleblog.blogspot.com/2008/07/we-knew-web-was-big.html

[12] "The Anatomy of a Large-Scale Hypertextual Web Search Engine," Sergey Brin and Lawrence Page, 1998, http://infolab.stanford.edu/~backrub/google.html

[13] (Battelle, 2005) p. 116, by that time GoTo.com had changed its name to Overture.

[14] "Searches Per Day," Danny Sullivan, *Search Engine Watch*, Apr 20, 2006, http://searchenginewatch.com/2156461

[15] Viacom's Statement of Undisputed Facts in Support of its Motion for Partial Summary Judgment on Liability and Inapplicability of the Digital Millennium Copyright Act Safe Harbor Defense, paragraph [SUF] 38, March 18, 2010, http://googlemonitor.com/wp-content/uploads/2010/03/Viacom-Statement-of-Undisputed-Facts-PUBLIC-VERSION.pdf

[16] (Conti, 2009), p. 226

[17] "Google wants your phonemes," Juan Carlos Perez, October 23, 2007, *InfoWorld*, http://www.infoworld.com/t/data-management/google-wants-your-phonemes-539

[18] "Google Seduces With Utility," David Carr, November 23, 2008, *New York Times*, "If Google owns me, it's probably because I am in favor of what works. ..."I'm glad to hear it," said Eric E. Schmidt, the chief executive of Google, who was in New York last week. "We want a little bit of Google in many parts of your life."" http://www.nytimes.com/2008/11/24/business/media/24carr.html?_r=2

[19] "From the height of this place," Jonathan Rosenberg, SVP, Product Management, February 16, 2009, *The Official Google Blog*, "We won't (and shouldn't) try to stop the faceless scribes of drivel, but we can move them to the back row of the arena." http://googleblog.blogspot.com/2009/02/from-height-of-this-place.html

[20] "Google, Yahoo, others work to make search engines better at scanning the Web," Brian Palmer, May 25, 2010, *The Washington Post*, http://www.washingtonpost.com/wp-dyn/content/article/2010/05/24/AR2010052402609.html

[21] "Groups magnify chances of Google hits," Richard Waters, July 12, 2010, *Financial Times*, http://www.ft.com/cms/s/0/ec7cb18c-8dda-11df-9153-00144feab49a,dwp_uuid=8783d24a-8a9e-11df-bd2e-00144feab49a.html

[22] "Google Uses Searches to Track Flu's Spread," Miguel Helft, November 11, 2008, *New York Times*, "There is a new common symptom of the flu, in addition to the usual aches, coughs, fevers and sore throats. Turns out a lot of ailing Americans enter phrases like "flu symptoms" into Google and other search engines before they call their doctors. ...That simple act, multiplied across millions of keyboards in homes around the country, has given rise to a new early warning system for fast-spreading flu outbreaks, called Google Flu Trends. ..."We know it matches very, very well in the way flu developed in the last year," said Dr. Larry Brilliant, executive director of Google.org. Dr. Finelli of the C.D.C. and Dr. Brilliant both cautioned that the data needed to be monitored to ensure that the correlation with flu activity remained valid." http://www.nytimes.com/2008/11/12/technology/internet/12flu.html

[23] "Sniffly Surfing: Google Unveils Flu-Bug Tracker," Robert A. Guth, November 12, 2008, *Wall Street Journal*, "The Google group examined flu-related keywords over five years, noting times when searches of those terms surged. It then compared those times to CDC records and found a strong correlation between when people searched flu keywords and when people have had flu-like symptoms. It spent the past year testing new search results against data from the CDC, tweaking its software to make its results more accurate, Google executives said.

The Flu Trends site displays results of its analysis in a five-tier scale of flu activity ranging from "minimal" to "intense," with a middle point of "moderate." The site includes CDC flu prevention messages, a flu vaccination locator and links to flu-related news items. ...Still, some consumers question how helpful the new Google health service will be for them. Tony Deen, a 22-year-old recent college grad in San Francisco, says he hasn't had the flu since he was a kid and uses health Web sites only when he has a medical problem. "It's not like I can flee the city if the flu is coming," Mr. Deen says. But "it might convince me to get a flu shot if people are getting sick."
http://online.wsj.com/article/SB122644309498518615.html

[24] "Top 5 moments from Eric Schmidt's talk in Abu Dhabi," Jon Fortt, March 11, 2010, *Fortune*/CNN Money, "...Just moments after he skillfully parried the "scary Google" crowd, Schmidt fanned the flames a little, "One day we had a conversation where we figured we could just try to predict the stock market," he said. "And then we decided it was illegal. So we stopped doing that"..."
http://tech.fortune.cnn.com/2010/03/11/top-five-moments-from-eric-schmidts-talk-in-abu-dhabi/

[25] "Big Brother Google?" Esther Dyson, December 19, 2008, *Project Syndicate*,
http://www.project-syndicate.org/commentary/dyson3/English

[26] "Google Seduces With Utility," David Carr, November 23, 2008, *New York Times*, "Mission accomplished, at least on my desktop, but I asked Mr. Schmidt if I shouldn't be worried that I am putting all of my digital eggs in one multicolored, goofy-lettered basket. ..."That depends on what you think of our company and our values," he said. "Do you believe we have good values?""
http://www.nytimes.com/2008/11/24/business/media/24carr.html?_r=2

[27] "Google's approach to competition," Adam Kovacevich, Senior Manager, Global Communications and Public Affairs, May 8, 2009, *Google Public Policy Blog*, "Google's six principles of competition and openness:
1. Help other businesses be more competitive.
2. Make it easy for users to change.
3. Open is better than closed.
4. Competition is just one click away.
5. Advertisers pay what a click is worth to them.
6. Advertisers have many choices in a dynamic market."
http://googlepublicpolicy.blogspot.com/2009/05/googles-approach-to-competition.html

[28] "Google, Caffeine and the future of search," Matt Warman, June 17, 2010, *UK Telegraph*, http://www.telegraph.co.uk/technology/google/7833590/Google-Caffeine-and-the-future-of-search.html

[29] "Google Wins Key Copyright Ruling," Sam Schechner and Jessica E. Vascellaro, June 22, 2010, *The Wall Street Journal*,
http://online.wsj.com/article/SB10001424052748704629804575325191988055312.html?mod=WSJ_hpp_LEFTWhatsNewsCollection

[30] "A Race to the Bottom: Privacy Ranking of Internet Service Companies," September 6, 2007, *Privacy International*, http://www.privacyinternational.org/article.shtml?cmd[347]=x-347-553961 Also see Interim Rankings document at: http://www.privacyinternational.org/issues/internet/interimrankings.pdf

[31] "Google CEO On Privacy," (video), December 7, 2009, *Huffington Post*, "CNBC's Mario Bartiromo asked CEO Schmidt in her December 3, 2009 interview: "People are treating Google like their most trusted friend. Should they?" ...Schmidt tells Baritoromo: "If you have something that you don't want anyone to know, maybe you shouldn't be doing it in the first place."" http://www.huffingtonpost.com/2009/12/07/google-ceo-on-privacy-if_n_383105.html

[32] "Google and the Search for the Future," Holman W. Jenkins, Jr., August 14, 2010, *Wall Street Journal*, http://online.wsj.com/article/SB10001424052748704901104575423294099527212.html

[33] "Eric Schmidt: If you don't like Street View, move house," Shane Richmond, October 26, 2010, *UK Telegraph*, http://blogs.telegraph.co.uk/technology/shanerichmond/100005899/eric-schmidt-if-you-dont-like-street-view-move-house/

[34] "Google's Eric Schmidt: You can trust us with your data," Shane Richmond, July 1, 2010, *UK Telegraph*, http://www.telegraph.co.uk/technology/google/7864223/Googles-Eric-Schmidt-You-can-trust-us-with-your-data.html

[35] http://www.google.com/corporate/privacy_principles.html

[36] http://www.google.com/history/intl/en/privacy.html

[37] "Privacy Principles," http://www.google.com/corporate/privacy_principles.html

[38] "Google's Business Model: YOU Are the Product," Mike Elgan, February 5, 2009, *Internet.com*, http://itmanagement.earthweb.com/columns/executive_tech/article.php/3801006/Googles-Business-Model-YOU-Are-the-Product.htm

[39] "Why no one cares about privacy anymore," Declan McCullagh, March 12, 2010, *CNET News*, http://news.cnet.com/8301-13578_3-20000336-38.html

[40] "Facebook's Zuckerberg Says The Age of Privacy is Over," Marshall Kirkpatrick, January 9, 2010, *ReadWriteWeb*, http://www.readwriteweb.com/archives/facebooks_zuckerberg_says_the_age_of_privacy_is_ov.php

[41] "The Blind Eye to Privacy Law Arbitrage by Google -- Broadly Threatens Respect for Privacy," Testimony of Scott Cleland, President, Precursor LLC Before the House Energy & Commerce, Subcommittee on telecommunications and the Internet, July 17, 2008, http://www.netcompetition.org/Written_Testimony_House_Privacy_071707.pdf

[42] "Consumer Reports Poll: Americans Extremely Concerned About Internet Privacy," September 25, 2008, http://www.consumersunion.org/pub/core_telecom_and_utilities/006189.html

[43] "Americans Reject Tailored Advertising and Three Activities that Enable It," Joseph Turow, University of Pennsylvania - Annenberg School for Communication; Jennifer King, UC Berkeley School of Information; Berkeley Center for Law & Technology; Chris Jay Hoofnagle, University of California, Berkeley - School of Law, Berkeley Center for Law & Technology; Amy Bleakley, Annenberg Public Policy Center; Michael Hennessy, Annenberg Public Policy Center, September 29, 2009, *Social Science Research Network*, http://papers.ssrn.com/sol3/papers.cfm?abstract_id=1478214

[44] "Results from June 4-7 Nationwide Poll," June 7, 2010, Zogby International, http://www.precursorblog.com/files/pdf/topline-report-key-findings.pdf

[45] "Consumer Advocates Seek a 'Do-Not-Track' List," Louise Story, October 31, 2007, *New York Times*, http://www.nytimes.com/2007/10/31/technology/31cnd-privacy.html

[46] "Innovation: Google may know your desires before you do," Paul Marks, July 16, 2010, *New Scientist*, http://www.newscientist.com/article/dn19186-innovation-google-may-know-your-desires-before-you-do.html

[47] "Google and the Search for the Future," Holman W. Jenkins, Jr., August 14, 2010, *Wall Street Journal*, http://online.wsj.com/article/SB10001424052748704901104575423294099527212.html

[48] http://desktop.google.com/support/linux/bin/answer.py?hl=en&answer=63220

[49] "Google security vulnerabilties stack up," Dan Goodin, June 3, 2007, UK *Register*, http://www.theregister.co.uk/2007/06/03/google_vulns_stack_up/

[50] "Google Android apps found to be sharing data," September 30, 2010, *BBC Technology Blog*, http://www.bbc.co.uk/news/technology-11443111

[51] "Google Responds To Android Privacy Report," Nick Saint, October 1, 2010, *San Francisco Chronicle*, http://www.sfgate.com/cgi-bin/article.cgi?f=/g/a/2010/10/01/businessinsider-google-responds-to-android-privacy-report-we-consistently-advise-users-to-only-install-apps-they-trust-2010-10.DTL

[52] "Schmidt: Google gets 'right up to the creepy line'," Sara Jerome, October 10, 2010, *The Hill*, http://thehill.com/blogs/hillicon-valley/technology/122121-schmidt-google-gets-right-up-to-the-creepy-line

[53] "Where you Point Your Mouse May Influence Google Search Rankings, Advertisement Placement, and Oneboxes," Bill Slawski, July 13, 2010, *SEO by the Sea blog*, http://www.seobythesea.com/?p=4024

[54] Google's goal: to organise your daily life," Caroline Daniel and Maija Palmer, May 22, 2007, *Financial Times*, ""We are very early in the total information we have within Google. The algorithms will get better and we will get better at

personalisation. ..."The goal is to enable Google users to be able to ask the question such as 'What shall I do tomorrow?' and 'What job shall I take?'""
http://www.ft.com/cms/s/2/c3e49548-088e-11dc-b11e-000b5df10621.html

[55] http://www.google-watch.org/bigbro.html

[56] "Google as Big Brother," http://www.google-watch.org/bigbro.html

[57] "Gmail Selling Access to Key Words in Your Account to the Highest Bidder," July 6 2010, *MyFoxChicago.com*,
http://www.myfoxchicago.com/dpp/news/special_report/google-email-gmail-ads-20100706

[58] http://www.consumerwatchdog.org/corporateering/corpact6/

[59] (Vise and Malseed, 2005) p. 155

[60] (Vise and Malseed, 2005) p. 156

[61] Battelle, The Search: *How Google and Its Rivals Rewrote the Rules of Business and Transformed Our Culture* (New York: Portfolio Trade, 2005), p. 195.

[62] (Vise and Malseed, 2005) p. 156

[63] (Vise and Malseed, 2005) p. 157. The Privacy Rights Clearinghouse and 30 other groups signed a public letter to Google. The groups urged Google to be more explicit about its policies and practices.

[64] Randall Stross, *Planet Google: One Company's Audacious Plan to Organize Everything We Know* (New York: Free Press, 2008), p. 161. Google's Gmail team debated whether to include a delete button. Paul Buchheit argued that with Gmail's search capabilities and Google's immense storage it would be easier for users to retain all e-mail messages.

[65] (Battelle, 2005) p. 199

[66] (Stross, 2008) p. 162. Google employees were deluged with requests from family, friends, and strangers for a Gmail delete button.

[67] (Vise and Malseed, 2005) pp. 160-163.

[68] Greg Conti, *Googling Security: How Much Does Google Know About You?* (London: Addison-Wesley Professional, 2009)

[69] (Vise and Malseed, 2005) p. 160. Larry Page concluded the advertising feature wasn't a mistake, but the way the service was rolled out was wrong.

[70] http://www.google.com/privacy.html

[71] "We provide such information to our subsidiaries, affiliated companies or other trusted businesses or persons for the purpose of processing personal information on our behalf. We require that these parties agree to process such information based on our instructions and in compliance with this Privacy Policy and any other appropriate confidentiality and security measures."
http://www.google.com/privacypolicy.html

[72] (Stross, 2008) p. 64. Google has stated that only a small number of its employees have access to users' e-mail. However, only the e-mail of certain categories of users is placed off limits: "...any public figure, any employee at a particular company, or any acquaintance." Noting that these categories do not include strangers, Stross asked "Does this forbid recreational reading of e-mail messages of strangers?"

[73] http://www.consumerwatchdog.org/corporateering/corpact6/

[74] http://www.consumerwatchdog.org/corporateering/corpact6/

[75] (Stross, 2008) p. 132. Keyhole's main innovation was downloading adjacent images in the background so that the user could move seamlessly between images.

[76] "Individuals need protection from Google," Robert Halfon, October 28, 2010, *UK Telegraph*, http://www.telegraph.co.uk/technology/google/8090486/Individuals-need-protection-from-Google.html

[77] "Google Forgets to Erase Out Detailed Shots of White House," August 19, 2005, *Ryan Hemelaar's Tech Blog*, http://ryanhemelaar.blogsome.com/2005/08/19/google-forgets-to-erase-out-detailed-shots-of-white-house/

[78] "Google's Street View Captures Dead Bodies in Brazil," David Murphy, October 2, 2010, *PC Magazine*, http://www.pcmag.com/article2/0,2817,2370128,00.asp

[79] "Rare photo puts Google operations on view," Mike Aldax, July 7, 2008, *The Examiner*, http://www.sfexaminer.com/local/rare-photo-puts-google-operations-view

[80] "Google balances privacy, reach," Elinor Mills, July 14, 2005, *CNET News*, http://news.cnet.com/Google-balances-privacy,-reach/2100-1032_3-5787483.html

[81] The UK Guardian, "Google Earth used to target Israel," Clancy Chassay and Bobbie Johnson, October 25, 2007, *UK Guardian*, Google's official response when asked by *The Guardian* about terrorists use of Google Earth: "Google has engaged, and will continue to engage, in substantive dialogue with recognised security experts and relevant agencies worldwide."
http://www.guardian.co.uk/technology/2007/oct/25/google.israel

[82] (Stross, 2008) p. 150. Mills also found information on Schmidt's net worth, fund raising activities, and hobbies. As punishment, Google informed CNET that it would not respond to any questions or requests from CNET reporters for one year. However, after two months Google restored its normal working relationship with CNET.

[83] "Google 'burglar's charter' street cameras given the all clear by privacy watchdog," David Derbyshire and Arthur Martin, July 31, 2008, *Mail Online*, http://www.dailymail.co.uk/sciencetech/article-1031861/Google-burglars-charter-street-cameras-given-clear-privacy-watchdog.html

[84] "Privacy Laws Trip Up Google's Expansion in Parts of Europe,' Kevin O'Brien, November 18, 2008, *New York Times*, http://www.nytimes.com/2008/11/18/technology/18google.html?_r=1&pagewanted=print

[85] "Japanese seek to scrap Google's Street View," December 19, 2008, *AFP*, "A group of Japanese journalists, professors and lawyers demanded Friday that the US Internet search giant Google scrap its "Street View" service in Japan, saying it violates people's privacy."
http://www.google.com/hostednews/afp/article/ALeqM5hHtzamj64sVKodOrfGjs5UZ4MwCw

[86] "Google Earth used to target Israel," Clancy Chassay and Bobbie Johnson, October 25, 2007, *The Guardian*, http://www.guardian.co.uk/technology/2007/oct/25/google.israel

[87] "Terrorists 'use Google maps to hit UK troops'," Thomas Harding, January 13, 2007, *UK Telegraph*, http://www.telegraph.co.uk/news/worldnews/1539401/Terrorists-use-Google-maps-to-hit-UK-troops.html

[88] "Google Earth lays bare UK's nuclear defences," Karl Flinders, March 2, 2009, *Computer Weekly.com*, http://www.computerweekly.com/Articles/2009/03/02/235080/Google-Earth-lays-bare-UK39s-nuclear-defences.htm

[89] "Google Earth, IPhone trouble Israeli security chief," November 1, 2010, *Reuters*, http://www.alertnet.org/thenews/newsdesk/LDE6A00J0.htm

[90] "Google Earth map marks Temple Mount Palestinian," Aaron Klein, January 16, 2007, *WorldNetDaily.com*, http://www.wnd.com/?pageId=39701

[91] "Google Street View logs Wi-Fi networks, Mac addresses," Andrew Orlowski, April 22, 2010 , *The Register*, "Google's roving Street View spycam may blur your face, but it's got your number. The Street View service is under fire in Germany for scanning private WLAN networks, and recording users' unique Mac (Media Access Control) addresses, as the car trundles along. ...Germany's Federal Commissioner for Data Protection Peter Schaar says he's "horrified" by the discovery. ..."I am appalled... I call upon Google to delete previously unlawfully collected personal data on the wireless network immediately and stop the rides for Street View," according to German broadcaster ARD." http://www.theregister.co.uk/2010/04/22/google_streetview_logs_wlans/

[92] "Google finally admits that its Street View cars DID take emails and passwords from computers," Vanessa Allen, October 28, 2010, UK *Daily Mail*, http://www.dailymail.co.uk/sciencetech/article-1323310/Google-admits-Street-View-cars-DID-emails-passwords-computers.html

[93] http://precursorblog.com/content/google-wi-spy-was-intentional-plan-beat-skyhook-wireless

[94] "Copy of Google's submission today to several national data protection authorities on vehicle-based collection of wifi [sic] data for use in Google location based services," http://docs.google.com/viewer?a=v&q=cache:p_muyvYJ9s4J:www.google.com/googleblogs/pdfs/google_submission_dpas_wifi_collection.pdf+google+collects+Wi-Fi+access+point+information+for+user+location+determination&hl=en&gl=us&pid=bl&srcid=ADGEESjEN98-MbHJNx98s_dxdjb-oiw_osxpTZFkrKRYkBSX_zYZ3I1ipQGiM5hFzO4LfzkhG0snp3gD4Ad84DeRPr6hsA7UD_TrN37EVx6XVXtg3OZ7Kuykw8_QqvpV8SDs6Ap_rpXR&sig=AHIEtbR7u1s44d4MI-8RGzYE4EEBHpTeug

[95] "Google admits wi-fi data collection blunder," Maggie Shiels, May 15, 2010, *BBC News*, "The issue came to light after German authorities asked to audit the data the

company's Street View cars gathered as they took photos viewed on Google maps. ...Google said during a review it found it had "been mistakenly collecting samples of payload data from open networks"."
http://news.bbc.co.uk/2/hi/technology/8684110.stm

[96] "Google Street View accused of Congress 'snooping'," Maggie Shiels. July 9, 2010, *BBC News*, http://news.bbc.co.uk/2/hi/technology/8802741.stm

[97] "Eric Schmidt says Google should not be prosecuted for wi-fi records," Murad Ahmed, May 18, 2010, *Sunday Times*, "Eric Schmidt said that the company had not authorised the activity of its Street View cars, which have been collecting snippets of people's online activities, broadcast over unprotected home and business wi-fi networks. ...He said that the company should not face prosecution over the incident, saying that nobody had been harmed by the gathering of people's information. "No harm, no foul," he said. ...Speaking at Google's Zeitgeist conference at the Grove Hotel in Hertfordshire, Mr Schmidt said that the greater damage had been done to the company's reputation rather than to individuals themselves. ..."A relatively small of data was collected and this was not authorised," he said. "We stopped driving immediately. There appears to be no use of data. It's sitting on a hard drive." He added: "We will not delete [the collected data] until ordered to do so."" http://www.timesonline.co.uk/tol/news/uk/article7130067.ece

[98] "Google chief: Only miscreants worry about net privacy,' Cade Metz, December 7, 2009, *The Register*,
http://www.theregister.co.uk/2009/12/07/schmidt_on_privacy/

[99] "Tracking Friends the Google Way," Katherine Boehret February 3, 2009, *Wall Street Journal*, http://solution.allthingsd.com/20090203/tracking-friends-the-google-way/

[100] http://www.google.com/support/mobile/bin/answer.py?answer=136640

[101] "Tracking Friends the Google Way," Katherine Boehret, February 3, 2009, *Wall Street Journal*, "Usability issues aside, location-based services like Latitude can be just plain creepy, especially when a Big Brother like Google is tracking your whereabouts. So Google incorporated easy-to-change privacy settings so that locations can be automatically detected, manually entered or completely hidden from other people. Or people can sign out of Latitude altogether."
http://solution.allthingsd.com/20090203/tracking-friends-the-google-way/

[102] "Google mobile privacy policy," December 14, 2010,
http://www.google.com/mobile/privacy.html

[103] "EXCLUSIVE: Google Takes a Stand for Location Privacy, Along with Loopt," Kevin Bankston, March 4, 2009, *Electronic Frontier Foundation*,
http://www.eff.org/deeplinks/2009/03/exclusive-google-takes-stand-location-privacy-alon

[104] "Google Latitude to Cops: 'I Don't Remember'," Ryan Singel, March 5, 2009, *Wired*, http://www.wired.com/epicenter/2009/03/googles-latitud/

[105] "Google Latitude, now with Location History & Alerts," Chris Lambert, Software Engineer, November 10, 2009, *Google Mobile Blog*,

http://googlemobile.blogspot.com/2009/11/google-latitude-now-with-location.html

[106] "Insecurity in Open Source," Ben Chelf, October 6, 2006, *BusinessWeek*, http://www.businessweek.com/technology/content/oct2006/tc20061006_394140.htm?campaign_id=bier_tco.g3a.rss1007

[107] "11.1 You retain copyright and any other rights you already hold in Content which you submit, post or display on or through, the Services. By submitting, posting or displaying the content you give Google a perpetual, irrevocable, worldwide, royalty-free, and non-exclusive license to reproduce, adapt, modify, translate, publish, publicly perform, publicly display and distribute any Content which you submit, post or display on or through, the Services. This license is for the sole purpose of enabling Google to display, distribute and promote the Services and may be revoked for certain Services as defined in the Additional Terms of those Services." http://www.google.com/accounts/TOS?hl=en

[108] http://www.consumersunion.org/pub/core_telecom_and_utilities/006189.html

[109] "Don't expect to peer into Google cloud services security," Tim Greene, October 07, 2010, *Network World*, http://www.networkworld.com/news/2010/100710-google-cloud-security.html

[110] "Google CEO Eric Schmidt Talks Future, Economic Trouble," Nicholas Kolakowski, March 4, 2009, *eWeek.com*, "And cloud computing is coming, Schmidt said. ..."Cloud computing is one of those changes that's going to happen regardless of whether companies that are participating in the ecosystem allow it, because the technology will make it happen," he elaborated. ...This is ultimately good for Google: With everybody online, "you can get a lot of information about user behavior that you can mine or build interesting products for."" http://www.eweek.com/c/a/Search-Engines/Google-CEO-Eric-Schmidt-Talks-Future-Economic-Trouble/

[111] (Conti, 2009) pp. 82-84

[112] "Google Analytics Usage Statistics," BuiltWith (technology usage statistics website), as of July 2010, http://trends.builtwith.com/analytics/Google-Analytics

[113] (Conti, 2009) pp. 222-225

[114] (Conti, 2009) pp. 212-215

[115] (Conti, 2009) pp. 216-217

[116] "Microsoft: Google Chrome doesn't respect your privacy," Emil Protalinski, March 2010, *ARS Technica*, http://arstechnica.com/microsoft/news/2010/03/microsoft-google-chrome-doesn-your-privacy-microsoft-google-chrome-doesnt-respect-your-privacy.ars

[117] (Conti, 2009) p. 226-7. Conti explains that when a website embeds a YouTube video on one of its pages it normally does not host the video. The code provided by YouTube simply pulls a movie object from Google's servers each time the page is loaded by a user's browser.

[118] "Court orders YouTube to give Viacom video logs," Anick Jesdanun, July 3, 2008, *Associated Press*, http://www.usatoday.com/tech/news/techpolicy/2008-07-03-google-video-logs_N.htm

[119] "Google Told to Turn Over User Data of YouTube," Miguel Helft, July 4, 2008, *New York Times*, http://www.nytimes.com/2008/07/04/technology/04youtube.html?_r=1

[120] "Video Privacy Protection Act," Electronic Privacy Information Center, http://epic.org/privacy/vppa/

[121] (Conti, 2009) p. 99. The searches of five different AOL users are presented in five separate tables.

[122] (Conti, 2009) p. 80. Conti quotes Google at length (his emphasis): "You can choose to stop storing your web activity in Web History either temporarily or permanently, or remove items, as described in Web History Help. If you remove items, they will be removed from the service and will not be used to improve your search experience. *As is common practice in the industry, Google also maintains a separate logs system for auditing purposes and to help us improve the quality of our services for users.* For example, we use this information to audit our ads systems, understand which features are most popular to [sic] users, improve the quality of our search results, and help us combat vulnerabilities such as denial of service attacks."

[123] (Battelle, 2005) p.9. Battelle suggests that search could lead to the creation of something like Hal, the conversational but ultimately devious computer depicted in the movie *2001: A Space Odyssey*.

[124] (Conti, 2009)

[125] "Google CEO Eric Schmidt's Most Controversial Quotes About Privacy, Catharine Smith First, November 4, 2010, *The Huffington Post*, http://www.huffingtonpost.com/2010/11/04/google-ceo-eric-schmidt-privacy_n_776924.html#s170433

[126] "Microsoft to alter Windows Vista," Stephen Labaton, June 20, 2007, *New York Times*, http://www.nytimes.com/2007/06/20/technology/20soft.html?ref=technology

[127] http://desktop.google.com/support/linux/bin/answer.py?hl=en&answer=63220

[128] http://desktop.google.com/support/bin/answer.py?hl=en&answer=32889

[129] "Google Desktop 3 criticized," Elinor Mills, February 10, 2006, *CNET News*, http://news.cnet.com/Google-Desktop-3-criticized/2100-1032_3-6038197.html

[130] "Google Desktop Privacy Policy," November 2008, "If you cancel your Google Account or uninstall Google Desktop, the files indexed in the Search Across Computers feature will no longer be accessible through Google Desktop and may remain on our servers for up to 10 days before being deleted." http://desktop.google.com/en/privacypolicy.html

[131] "Google Desktop Tracked: the Aftermath," Rixstep.com, "As a condition of downloading and using the Software, you agree to the terms of the Google Pack Privacy Policy at http://pack.google.com/intl/en/policy_info.html, which may be

updated from time to time and without notice."
http://rixstep.com/2/20070621,05.shtml

[132] "Google can sort digital photos on face value," Jefferson Graham, September 17, 2008, *USA Today*,
"If the human brain sees a million images per day and can instantly identify them, why couldn't software do that, too? Making such a thing a reality has been the longtime goal of German-born physicist Hartmut Neven, whose facial-recognition software firm was purchased by Google in 2006, with the stated goal of bringing his vision to digital photography. ...Neven joined forces with Google's Picasa photo editing and management software team, spending two years developing a tool that could bring photo facial recognition to the masses."
http://www.usatoday.com/tech/products/2008-09-16-picasa-google_N.htm

[133] "Google's goal: to organise your daily life," Caroline Daniel and Maija Palmer, May 22, 2007, *Financial Times*, http://www.ft.com/cms/s/2/c3e49548-088e-11dc-b11e-000b5df10621.html

[134] https://www.google.com/accounts/ServiceLogin?hl=en&continue=http://www.google.com/history&nui=1&service=hist

[135] "Google's latest power grab," Danny Sullivan, April 2007, *Advertising Age*,
"Millions have installed the Google Toolbar, which includes a PageRank meter that rates sites' popularity on a scale of zero to 10. To work, that meter has to report to Google which page is being viewed. That means Google sees every site some toolbar users are visiting. ...Until last week, the meter was switched off by default. Now Google pushes a version with the meter enabled and encourages surfers who already have the toolbar to flip the switch. The enticement? Doing so allows those surfers to view a log of all their web visits. In addition, that web history will influence how pages rank in the search results they see."
http://adage.com/digital/article?article_id=116394

[136] "Plugging privacy leaks," Hiawatha Bray, July 10, 2010, *The Boston Globe*,
http://www.boston.com/business/technology/articles/2010/07/10/plugging_privacy_leaks/

[137] "Google Toolbar," http://en.wikipedia.org/wiki/Google_Toolbar

[138] "The Skinny on Google TV and Why It Will Make Google Fat Money," Clint Boulton, June 16, 2010, *eWeek Google Watch*,
http://googlewatch.eweek.com/content/google_tv/the_skinny_on_google_tv_and_why_it_will_make_google_fat_money.html

[139] "Google seeks clearer path to state data," Miguel Helft, April 30, 2007, *New York Times*, http://www.nytimes.com/2007/04/30/technology/30data.html?_r=1

[140] "Google to enlist NSA to help it ward off cyberattacks," Ellen Nakashima, February 4, 2010, *New York Times*, http://www.washingtonpost.com/wp-dyn/content/article/2010/02/03/AR2010020304057.html?hpid=topnews

[141] "WARNING: Google Buzz Has A Huge Privacy Flaw," Nicholas Carlson. February 10, 2010, *Business Insider*, The author points out that this privacy flaw could allow a wife to see that her husband has been chatting with an old girlfriend or a boss could

tell that an employee has been exchanging e-mails with executives at a competitor.
http://www.businessinsider.com/warning-google-buzz-has-a-huge-privacy-flaw-2010-2

[142] "Outraged Blogger Is Automatically Being Followed By Her Abusive Ex-Husband On Google Buzz," Nick Saint, February 12, 2010, *Business Insider*,
http://www.businessinsider.com/outraged-blogger-is-automatically-being-followed-by-her-abusive-ex-husband-on-google-buzz-2010-2

[143] "Farewell, GOOG-411," David Pogue, October 14, 2010, *New York Times*,
http://pogue.blogs.nytimes.com/2010/10/14/farewell-goog-411/

[144] http://www.google.com/goog411/ In the demonstration video, the caller is not warned that the call is being recorded.

[145] "The content in Google Apps belongs to Google," Joshua Greenbaum, August 28, 2007, *ZDNet Blog*, http://blogs.zdnet.com/Greenbaum/?p=130

[146] "Stopping Google," Drake Bennett, June 22, 2008, *Boston.com*,
http://www.boston.com/bostonglobe/ideas/articles/2008/06/22/stopping_google/?page=2

[147] "Google Search Uncovers Los Rios Student Data," abstract of article from March 7, 2007 issue of *Sacramento Bee*,
http://www.adamdodge.com/esi/google_search_uncovers_los_rios_student_data

[148] "77% of Google users don't know it records personal data," Andrew Orlowski, January 24, 2006, *The Register*,
http://www.theregister.co.uk/2006/01/24/google_privacy_poll/

[149] "Exhaustive Google Product List,
http://spreadsheets.google.com/pub?key=ty_BGDs9hnuBMRvj3AFeB2g&output=html

[150] https://www.23andme.com/about/corporate/

[151] http://mrl.nyu.edu/~dhowe/trackmenot/

[152] http://www.scroogle.org/cgi-bin/scraper.htm

[153] "Google Dashboard Is Small Step For User Control, Consumer Watchdog Says," John M. Simpson, November 5, 2009, *Consumer Watchdog*,
http://www.consumerwatchdog.org/corporateering/articles/?storyId=30797

[154] "Google CEO Discusses Economy," November 5, 2009, *BNET*,
http://findarticles.com/p/articles/mi_8077/is_20091105/ai_n50964590/pg_8/?tag=content;col1

[155] "Google's Eric Schmidt: You can trust us with your data," Shane Richmond, July 1, 2010, *UK Telegraph*, "Google, Schmidt says, is kept in check by its customers and by the competition: "All of our testing indicates that the vast majority of people are perfectly happy with our policy. And this message is the message that nobody wants to hear so let me say it again: the reality is we make decisions based on what the average user tells us and we do check. And the reason that you should trust us is that if we were to violate that trust people would move immediately to someone else. We're very non-sticky so we have a very high interest in maintaining the trust of those users.""

http://www.telegraph.co.uk/technology/google/7864223/Googles-Eric-Schmidt-You-can-trust-us-with-your-data.html

[156] "S#*! Your Google CEO Says," Natasha Tiku, September 16, 2010, *Daily Intel*, http://nymag.com/daily/intel/2010/09/shit_schmidt_says.html

[157] "Google's Vint Cerf on the Future of Journalism, David Needle, May 19, 2009, *InternetNews.com*, http://www.internetnews.com/webcontent/article.php/3820976

[158] "Advertising Week 2010: Google, Facebook, Others Talk Privacy, Ken Bruno, September 28, 2010, *Forbes*, http://blogs.forbes.com/marketshare/2010/09/28/advertising-week-2010-google-facebook-others-talk-privacy/

[159] "Letter from the Founders: 'An Owners' Manual' for Google Shareholders," Form S-1 Registration Statement, April 29, 2004, http://www.sec.gov/Archives/edgar/data/1288776/000119312504073639/ds1.htm

[160] "Google 2.4% Rate Shows How $60 Billion Lost to Tax Loopholes," Jesse Drucker, October 21, 2010, *Bloomberg News*, http://www.bloomberg.com/news/2010-10-21/google-2-4-rate-shows-how-60-billion-u-s-revenue-lost-to-tax-loopholes.html

[161] Ken Auletta, *Googled: The End of the World As We Know It* (London: Penguin Press HC, 2009), p. 39, "One, Winograd said, they snuck onto the loading dock where new Stanford computers were delivered and "borrowed" them to expand their computing power."

[162] (Auletta, 2009) p.39. "Some years later, Page confessed that their embryonic search engine in 1997 hogged so much computer capacity that "we caused the whole Stanford network to go down.""

[163] (Auletta, 2009) p.42. Brin acquired that particular skill by reading *The MIT Guide to Lock Picking*.

[164] (Battelle, 2005) pp.104-118

[165] (Vise & Malseed, 2005) "If they [Sergey and Larry] could conquer the sophisticated venture capitalists on Sand Hill Road, why couldn't they sell ads themselves and keep 100 cents of every dollar, rather than share the proceeds with Overture?" p.88.

[166] (Battelle, 2005) The Story of Bill Gross, GoTo.com, and Overture is told in detail, pp. 96-121.

[167] (Battelle, 2005) pp.107-108

[168] US Patent 6269361, Abstract: A system and method for enabling information providers using a computer network such as the Internet to influence a position for a search listing within a search result list generated by an Internet search engine. The system and method of the present invention provides a database having accounts for the network information providers. Each account contains contact and billing information for a network information provider. In addition, each account contains at least one search listing having at least three components: a description, a search term comprising one or more keywords, and a bid amount. The network information provider may add, delete, or modify a search listing after logging into

his or her account via an authentication process. The network information provider influences a position for a search listing in the provider's account by first selecting a search term relevant to the content of the web site or other information source to be listed. The network information provider enters the search term and the description into a search listing. The network information provider influences the position for a search listing through a continuous online competitive bidding process. The bidding process occurs when the network information provider enters a new bid amount, which is preferably a money amount, for a search listing. The system and method of the present invention then compares this bid amount with all other bid amounts for the same search term, and generates a rank value for all search listings having that search term. The rank value generated by the bidding process determines where the network information providers listing will appear on the search results list page that is generated in response to a query of the search term by a searcher located at a client computer on the computer network. A higher bid by a network information provider will result in a higher rank value and a more advantageous placement.

[169] (Battelle, 2005) pp. 226-227.

[170] "Google, Yahoo bury the legal hatchet," Stefanie Olsen, August 9, 2004, *CNET News*, http://news.cnet.com/Google,-Yahoo-bury-the-legal-hatchet/2100-1024_3-5302421.html

[171] (Battelle, 2005) pp. 180-185.

[172] (Battelle, 2005) p. 182. "Rammelt pointed to the case of Oceana, an environmental organization that purchased the keywords "cruise ships" and then displayed ads that directed consumers to a Web site eviscerating the cruise industry for anti-environmental practices."

[173] (Battelle, 2005) pp.184-185.

[174] (Vise and Malseed, 2005)

[175] (Vise and Malseed, 2005) P. 225.

[176] (Vise and Malseed, 2005) P. 226.

[177] "EU court rules that Adwords do not infringe trademark laws," Jennifer Baker, July 08, 2010 , *IDG News Service*, https://www.networkworld.com/news/2010/070810-eu-court-rules-that-adwords.html?hpg1=bn

[178] "Google changes trademark ad policy in Europe," Leila Abboud and Kate Holton, August 4, 2010, *Reuters*, http://www.reuters.com/article/idUSTRE6732G320100804

[179] "Small firms back Rosetta Stone in Google trademark abuse lawsuit," Byron Acohido, November 3, 2010, *USA Today*, http://content.usatoday.com/communities/technologylive/post/2010/11/small-firms-back-rosetta-stone-in-google-trademark-abuse-lawsuit/1

[180] "Agence France-Presse, Google settle copyright dispute," Caroline McCarthy, April 6, 2007, *CNET News*, http://news.cnet.com/Agence-France-Presse%2C-Google-settle-copyright-dispute/2100-1030_3-6174008.html

[181] http://investor.google.com/corporate/code-of-conduct.html

[182] http://investor.google.com/corporate/code-of-conduct.html#VII

[183] http://investor.google.com/corporate/code-of-conduct.html#V

[184] (Stross, 2008) pp. 96-97

[185] "Google and its enemies," Jonathan V. Last, December 10, 2007, *Weekly Standard*, http://www.weeklystandard.com/Content/Public/Articles/000/000/014/431afruv.asp

[186] "Publishers sue Google over scanning plans," Hillel Italie, Associated Press, October 19, 2005, *USA Today*, http://www.usatoday.com/tech/news/techpolicy/business/2005-10-19-google-publishers-email_x.htm

[187] "Statement of Interest of the United States of America," p. 4, US Department of Justice, February 4, 2010, http://thepublicindex.org/docs/amended_settlement/usa.pdf

[188] "Statement of Interest of the United States of America," US Department of Justice, February 4, 2010, "Good intentions of members of a price-fixing combination are no legal justification for lessening price competition." (p. 18); "Google retains its upstream monopoly" and "The reseller clause cannot create new competitors to Google." (p. 22) http://thepublicindex.org/docs/amended_settlement/usa.pdf

[189] "Statement of Interest of the United States of America," p. 9, US Department of Justice, February 4, 2010, http://thepublicindex.org/docs/amended_settlement/usa.pdf

[190] "Statement of Interest of the United States of America," p. 11, US Department of Justice, February 4, 2010, http://thepublicindex.org/docs/amended_settlement/usa.pdf

[191] "Some Libraries Shun Google in Book Battle," Curt Nickisch, April 22, 2008, *NPR*, http://www.npr.org/templates/story/story.php?storyId=89850150

[192] Jean-Noël Jeanneney, *Google and the Myth of Universal Knowledge* (Chicago: University of Chicago Press, 2006).

[193] "The GBS Makes for Angry Neighbors," May 10, 2010, *The Open Book Alliance*, http://www.openbookalliance.org/2010/05/the-gbs-makes-for-angry-neighbors/

[194] Viacom's Statement of Undisputed Facts in Support of its Motion for Partial Summary Judgment on Liability and Inapplicability of the Digital Millennium Copyright Act Safe Harbor Defense is supported by fellow plaintiffs Comedy Partners, Country Music Television, Inc., Paramount Pictures Corporation, and Black Entertainment Television, LLC.

[195] Viacom's Statement of Undisputed Facts, paragraph [SUF] 85, March 18, 2010, http://googlemonitor.com/wp-content/uploads/2010/03/Viacom-Statement-of-Undisputed-Facts-PUBLIC-VERSION.pdf

[196] Ibid, SUF 50

[197] Ibid, SUF 60

[198] Ibid, SUF 44

[199] Ibid, SUF 40

[200] Ibid, SUF 55

[201] Ibid, SUF 47

[202] Ibid, SUF 38

[203] SUF 158, SUF 159, http://googlemonitor.com/wp-content/uploads/2010/03/Viacom-Statement-of-Undisputed-Facts-PUBLIC-VERSION.pdf

[204] SUF 162, http://googlemonitor.com/wp-content/uploads/2010/03/Viacom-Statement-of-Undisputed-Facts-PUBLIC-VERSION.pdf

[205] Ibid SUF 164

[206] Ibid SUF 199

[207] "Viacom Files Federal Copyright Infringement Complaint Against YouTube And Google," Viacom press release, March 13, 2007, http://www.viacom.com/news/pages/newstext.aspx?rid=1009865

[208] "Viacom Int'l Inc. et. al. v. YouTube, Inc. et. al. No. 07 Civ. 2103 (LLS)," letter to the Honorable Louis L. Stanton, March 1, 2010, Shearman and Sterling LLP counsel for Viacom, http://googlemonitor.com/wp-content/uploads/2010/03/baskinmarch1courtltr.pdf

[209] http://en.wikipedia.org/wiki/MGM_Studios,_Inc._v._Grokster,_Ltd.

[210] Ibid, paragraph [SUF]161, "On June 8, 2006, Google senior vice president Jonathan Rosenberg, Google Senior Vice President of Product Management, emailed Google CEO Eric Schmidt and Google co-founders Larry Page and Sergey Brin a Google Video presentation that stated the following: "Pressure premium content providers to change their model towards free[;] Adopt 'or else' stance re prosecution of copyright infringement elsewhere[;] Set up 'play first, deal later' around 'hot content.'" The presentation also stated that "[w]e may be able to coax or force access to viral premium content," noting that Google Video could "Threaten a change in copyright policy" and "use threat to get deal sign-up.""

[211] Ibid SUF 216

[212] "Some Media Companies Choose to Profit From Pirated YouTube Clips," Brian Stelter, August 15, 2008, *New York Times*, http://www.nytimes.com/2008/08/16/technology/16tube.html?_r=2&scp=1&sq=now%20playing%20on%20outube&st=cse&oref=slogin

[213] "YouTube Surpasses 100 Million U.S. Viewers for the First Time," press release, March 4, 2009, *ComScore*, http://www.comscore.com/Press_Events/Press_Releases/2008/06/US_Online_Video_Usage

[214] "Germany Is the Last Holdout in YouTube's European Music Quest," Kevin O'Brien, October 17, 2010, *New York Times*, http://www.nytimes.com/2010/10/18/technology/18euroyoutube.html?pagewanted=1&_r=2&sq=Google&st=nyt&scp=11

[215] "Google Wins Key Copyright Ruling," Sam Schechner and Jessica E. Vascellaro, June 22, 2010, *Wall Street Journal*,

http://online.wsj.com/article/SB10001424052748704629804575325191988055312
.html?mod=WSJ_hpp_LEFTWhatsNewsCollection

[216] "Media firms say Google benefitted from film piracy," Matthew Karnitschnig and Julia Angwin, February 12, 2007, *Wall Street Journal*, http://online.wsj.com/article/SB117125197567105533.html?mod=home_whats_ne ws_us

[217] "Google's mismanagement of the Android Market," Jon Lech Johansen, June 27, 2010, *nanocr.eu blog*, http://nanocr.eu/2010/06/27/googles-mismanagement-of-the-android-market/

[218] "News from the Goolag: As Evil as They Wanna Be: Does Google Adsense drive piracy?," Chris Castle, July 26, 2010, *Music • Technology • Policy blog*, http://musictechpolicy.wordpress.com/2010/07/26/news-from-the-goolag-as-evil-as-they-wanna-be-does-google-adsense-drive-piracy/

[219] "Big media wants more piracy busting from Google," Greg Sandoval, October 13, 2010, *CNET News*, http://news.cnet.com/8301-31001_3-20019411-261.html

[220] "Who Profits from Online Piracy?" Ellen Seidler, June 9, 2010, PopUpPirates, http://popuppirates.wordpress.com/

[221] "Use Their Work Free? Some Artists Say No to Google," Andrew Adam Newman, June 14, 2009, *The New York Times*, http://www.nytimes.com/2009/06/15/business/media/15illo.html?_r=1

[222] Ibid.

[223] "Patent Litigation Weekly: Skyhook Takes a Shot at Google," Joe Mullin, September 20, 2010, Corporate Counsel, http://www.law.com/jsp/cc/PubArticleCC.jsp?id=1202472220685&Patent_Litigatio n_Weekly_Skyhook_Takes_a_Shot_at_Google

[224] "Google CEO Eric Schmidt won't resign from Apple despite threats of anti-trust lawsuit," Angsuman Chakraborty, May 8, 2009, *Simple Thoughts blog*, http://blog.taragana.com/index.php/archive/google-ceo-schmidt-has-no-plans-to-resign-from-apple-board-despite-ftc-inquiry/

[225] "Google Music Will Soon Battle Apple's iTunes," Mike Schuster, June 15, 2010, *Minyanville*, http://www.minyanville.com/businessmarkets/articles/google-music-apple-itunes-itunes-store/6/15/2010/id/28763?page=full

[226] "Google's AdMob takeover to spark mobile ad M&A wave," Christoph Steitz and Nicola Leske, December 4, 2009, *Reuters*, http://www.reuters.com/article/idUSTRE5B31MO20091204

[227] "Apple sues HTC for patent infringement," Nancy Weil, March 2, 2010, *ComputerWorld*, http://www.computerworld.com/s/article/9164258/Apple_sues_HTC_for_patent_i nfringement

[228] "Oracle sues Google over Java in Android Legal clash of the titans," Dan Goodin, August 13, 2010, *UK Register*, "The patents in the case are 6,125,447, "Protection domains to provide security in a computer system"; 6,192,476, "Controlling access to a resource"; 5,966,702, "Method and apparatus for pre-processing and packaging

class files"; 7,426,720, "System and method for dynamic preloading of classes through memory space cloning of a master runtime system process"; RE38,104, "Method and apparatus for resolving data references in generated code"; 6,910,205, "Interpreting functions utilizing a hybrid of virtual and native machine instructions"; and 6,061,520, "Method and system for performing static initialization."" http://www.theregister.co.uk/2010/08/13/oracle_sues_google/

[229] "Why Oracle, not Sun, sued Google over Java," Stephen Shankland, August 13, 2010, CNET News, "Responding to a request for comment, a Google spokesperson said: "We are disappointed Oracle has chosen to attack both Google and the open-source Java community with this baseless lawsuit. The open-source Java community goes beyond any one corporation and works every day to make the Web a better place. We will strongly defend open-source standards and will continue to work with the industry to develop the Android platform."" http://news.cnet.com/8301-30685_3-20013549-264.html

[230] "Complaint for Patent and Copyright infringement: Demand for Jury Trial," Oracle America, Inc., August 12, 2010, "On information and belief, Google has been aware of Sun's patent portfolio, including the patents at issue, since the middle of this decade, when Google hired certain former Sun Java engineers.

15. On information and belief, Google has purposefully, actively, and voluntarily distributed Android and related applications, devices, platforms, and services with the expectation that they will be purchased, used, or licensed by consumers in the Northern District of California. Android has been and continues to be purchased, used, and licensed by consumers in the Northern District of California. Google has thus committed acts of patent infringement within the State of California and, particularly, within the Northern District of California. By purposefully and voluntarily distributing one or more of its infringing products and services, Google has injured Oracle America and is thus liable to Oracle America for infringement of the patents at issue in this litigation pursuant to 35 U.S.C. § 271." http://regmedia.co.uk/2010/08/13/oracle_complaint_against_google.pdf

[231] Google pits the law against its open source designs," Dana Blankenhorn, September 7, 2010, ZDNet, http://www.zdnet.com/blog/open-source/google-pits-the-law-against-its-open-source-designs/7282?alertspromo=&tag=nl.rSINGLE

[232] "Why Oracle, not Sun, sued Google over Java," Stephen Shankland, August 13, 2010, CNET News, http://news.cnet.com/8301-30685_3-20013549-264.html

[233] "Complaint for Patent Infringement," Skyhook Wireless, Inc., September 15, 2010, "Infringement of United States Patent No. 7,414,988," "Infringement of United States Patent No. 7,433,694," "Infringement of United States Patent No. 7,474,897," and "Infringement of United States Patent No. 7,305,245," http://docs.justia.com/cases/federal/district-courts/massachusetts/madce/1:2010cv11571/131440/1/

[234] "Patent Litigation Weekly: Skyhook Takes a Shot at Google," Joe Mullin, September 20, 2010, Corporate Counsel,

http://www.law.com/jsp/cc/PubArticleCC.jsp?id=1202472220685&Patent_Litigatio n_Weekly_Skyhook_Takes_a_Shot_at_Google

[235] "Complaint and Jury Demand," Skyhook Wireless, Inc., September 15, 2010,

[236] "Patent Litigation Weekly: Skyhook Takes a Shot at Google," Joe Mullin, September 20, 2010, Corporate Counsel, http://www.law.com/jsp/cc/PubArticleCC.jsp?id=1202472220685&Patent_Litigatio n_Weekly_Skyhook_Takes_a_Shot_at_Google

[237] "Maslow's hierarchy of needs," Wikipedia, http://en.wikipedia.org/wiki/Maslow%27s_hierarchy_of_needs

[238] "Our Philosophy: Ten things we know to be true,"
1. Focus on the user and all else will follow.
2. It's best to do one thing really, really well.
3. Fast is better than slow.
4. Democracy on the web works.
5. You don't need to be at your desk to need an answer.
6. You can make money without doing evil.
7. There's always more information out there.
8. The need for information crosses all borders.
9. You can be serious without a suit.
10. Great just isn't good enough.
http://www.google.com/intl/en/corporate/tenthings.html

[239] "Google security and product safety," http://www.google.com/intl/en/corporate/security.html

[240] "Google shock for Los Rios," Match 7, 2007, *Sacramento Bee*, http://callcenterinfo.tmcnet.com/news/2007/03/07/2400543.htm

[241] http://googlemonitor.com/wp-content/uploads/2010/06/Google%27s_Total_Information_Awareness.pdf In the aftermath of the September 11, 2001 terrorist attacks, Admiral John Poindexter, former National Security Advisor to President Reagan, proposed that the U.S. intelligence apparatus apply all available surveillance and information technology assets to tracking terrorists. There was a public outcry against Total Information Awareness; such a system would monitor all citizens all of the time. Congress officially defunded the program in 2003. It is ironic and frightening that Google, a private corporation, has in ten short years effectively achieved Total Information Awareness.

[242] "Privacy guardians warn multinationals to respect laws," April 20, 2010, Office of the Privacy Commissioner of Canada, http://www.priv.gc.ca/media/nr-c/2010/nr-c_100420_e.cfm

[243] "BITS; Google, Privacy And California," Saul Hansell, June 2, 2008, *New York Times*, A California statute requires companies to put a link to their privacy policy on their home page. A Google spokesman said "By having a link to our privacy policy one click from our home page [i.e., on their about page], and because the privacy policy is easily found by using the search box on the home page, we comply

with this statute.''
http://query.nytimes.com/gst/fullpage.html?res=9906E4D9143BF931A35755C0A96
E9C8B63
[244] "Google TV's Dark Side," Lance Ulanoff, October 7, 2010, *PC Magazine*,
http://www.pcmag.com/article2/0,2817,2370379,00.asp
[245] "Second Google Desktop Attack Possible, Researchers Say," Robert McMillan,
CIO.com,
http://www.cio.com/article/29018/Second_Google_Desktop_Attack_Possible_Rese
archers_Say
[246] "Corporate data slips out via Google calendar," Robert McMillan, *About.com*,
http://pcworld.about.com/od/privacy/Corporate-data-slips-out-via-G.htm
[247] "Hackers target Google Gadgets," Jordan Robertson, Associated Press, *USA
Today*, http://www.usatoday.com/tech/news/computersecurity/2008-08-07-
hackers-google_N.htm?csp=34
[248] "Security Bug Opens Google Buzz to Hackers," Robert McMillan, *The New York
Times*, http://www.nytimes.com/external/idg/2010/02/16/16idg-security-bug-
opens-google-buzz-to-hackers-49739.html
[249] "Google Safe Browsing Feature Could Compromise Privacy," Kelly Jackson
Higgins, *DarkReading*,
http://www.darkreading.com/security/privacy/showArticle.jhtml?articleID=218800
199
[250] "Goolag makes Google Hacking a snap," Robert McMillan, February 22, 2008,
NetworkWorld.com, http://www.networkworld.com/news/2008/022208-goolag-
makes-google-hacking-a.html
[251] "Sinister take on search engine optimization," Joseph Menn, July 12, 2010,
Financial Times, http://www.ft.com/cms/s/0/f130298e-8dda-11df-9153-
00144feab49a,dwp_uuid=8783d24a-8a9e-11df-bd2e-00144feab49a.html
[252] "It's every man for himself," Jack Schofield, October 1, 2008, *UK Guardian*,
http://www.guardian.co.uk/technology/2008/oct/02/interviews.internet
[253] "How Google Works," David F. Carr, July 6, 2006, *Baseline*, "To cope with these
demands, Page and Brin developed a virtual file system that treated the hard drives
on multiple computers as one big pool of storage. They called it BigFiles. Rather
than save a file to a particular computer, they would save it to BigFiles, which in
turn would locate an available chunk of disk space on one of the computers in the
server cluster and give the file to that computer to store, while keeping track of
which files were stored on which computer. This was the start of what essentially
became a distributed computing software infrastructure that runs on top of Linux."
http://www.baselinemag.com/c/a/Infrastructure/How-Google-Works-1/3/
[254] "Bigtable: A Distributed Storage System for Structured Data," Fay Chang, Jeffrey
Dean, Sanjay Ghemawat, Wilson C. Hsieh, Deborah A. Wallach, Mike Burrows,
Tushar Chandra, Andrew Fikes, and Robert E. Gruber, November, 2006, Google
Research Publications, http://labs.google.com/papers/bigtable.html

[255] "Let's make the Web faster," Google code, http://code.google.com/speed/articles/

[256] "Google public DNS," http://code.google.com/speed/public-dns/

[257] "The biggest threat to open source in 2009," Dana Blankenhorn, January 1, 2009, *ZDnet*, http://www.zdnet.com/blog/open-source/the-biggest-threat-to-open-source-in-2009/3244

[258] "Google searchers could end up with a new type of bug," Byron Acohido and Jon Swartz, March 31, 2008, *USA Today*, http://www.usatoday.com/money/industries/technology/2008-03-31-javascript-hackers_N.htm

[259] "Hackers infiltrate search engines, social networks," Jon Swartz, April 8, 2008, *USA Today*, http://www.usatoday.com/tech/news/computersecurity/2008-04-08-tech-hack_N.htm?loc=interstitialskip

[260] "How to avoid getting hook," Ian Fette, April 29, 2008, *Official Google blog*, http://googleblog.blogspot.com/2008/04/how-to-avoid-getting-hooked.html

[261] "GrandCentral Offline: If You Wanna Be A Phone Company, You Can't Go Dead," Michael Arrington, April 13, 2008, *TechCrunch*, http://techcrunch.com/2008/04/13/if-you-wanna-be-a-phone-company-you-cant-go-dead/

[262] "Gmail can be used as "Spam Bazooka," Garett Rogers, May 9, 2008, *ZDNet blog*, http://blogs.zdnet.com/Google/?p=1036

[263] (Conti, 2009) p. 164

[264] "Sign into multiple Google accounts at once," Garett Rogers, August 3, 2010, *Googling Google, ZDNet blog*, http://www.zdnet.com/blog/google/sign-into-multiple-google-accounts-at-once/2340

[265] "Google testing multiple account sign in," Christopher Dawson, August 3, 2010, *Googling Google, ZDNet blog*, http://www.zdnet.com/blog/google/google-testing-multiple-account-sign-in/2336

[266] "Google Security Chief by Day, TV Magician 'Eran Raven' by Night," Ryan Tate, January 4, 2010, *ValleyWag*, http://valleywag.gawker.com/5439749/google-security-chief-by-day-tv-magician-eran-raven-by-night

[267] "Google to defend the cloud at RSA Conference," Neil Roiter, April 17, 2009, *Information Security*, http://searchsecurity.techtarget.com/news/interview/0,289202,sid14_gci1354119,00.html

[268] "Cloud computing providers debate compliance, security and transparency," Alexander B. Howard, April 30, 2009, *SearchCompliance.com*, http://searchcompliance.techtarget.com/news/article/0,289142,sid195_gci1355241,00.html

[269] "Hack uses Google Street View data to stalk its victims," Dan Goodin, August 3, 2010, *UK Register*, http://www.theregister.co.uk/2010/08/03/google_street_view_hack/

[270] "Android's Serious Piracy Problem Costs Developers Big Money," Jay Yarow, August 2, 2010, *Business Insider*, http://www.businessinsider.com/android-piracy-2010-8#ixzz0wz8MFY2V

[271] "A new approach to China," David Drummond, SVP, Corporate Development and Chief Legal Officer, January 12, 2010, *Official Google Blog*, http://googleblog.blogspot.com/2010/01/new-approach-to-china.html

[272] "Google attack puts spotlight on China's 'red' hackers," Melanie Lee and Lucy Hornby, January 19, 2010, *Reuters*, http://www.nationalpost.com/news/story.html?id=2463144

[273] "Google threatens Pull Out of China - Focus befell on Cyber Security," January 14, 2010, *International Reporter*, http://internationalreporter.com/News-5463/google-threatens-pull-out-of-china-focus-befell-on-cyber-security.html

[274] "Researchers Call Google Hackers 'Amateurs'," Andy Greenberg, March 2, 2010, *Forbes*, "But follow Google's hackers down their rabbit hole, as one group of cybersecurity researchers says it has done, and a portrait of those digital intruders emerges that conflicts with their "superhacker" image." http://www.forbes.com/2010/03/02/damballa-hackers-botnets-technology-security-google.html?feed=rss_home

[275] "WikiLeaks: Google attacks ordered by Li Changchun," Dan Sabbagh, December 5, 2010, *UK Guardian*, "Li Changchun, China's fifth most powerful man, was named by US diplomats as the alleged orchestrator of hacker attacks on Google's email systems last winter. ...A member of China's ruling politburo, he is the individual in charge of propaganda and censorship and the man behind the 'great firewall of China'." http://www.guardian.co.uk/world/2010/dec/05/the-us-embassy-cables-china

[276] "Cyberattack on Google Said to Hit Password System," John Markoff, April 19, 2010, *New York Times*, "Ever since Google disclosed in January that Internet intruders had stolen information from its computers, the exact nature and extent of the theft has been a closely guarded company secret. But a person with direct knowledge of the investigation now says that the losses included one of Google's crown jewels, a password system that controls access by millions of users worldwide to almost all of the company's Web services, including e-mail and business applications. ...The program, code named Gaia for the Greek goddess of the earth, was attacked in a lightning raid taking less than two days last December, the person said. Described publicly only once at a technical conference four years ago, the software is intended to enable users and employees to sign in with their password just once to operate a range of services." http://www.nytimes.com/2010/04/20/technology/20google.html?_r=1&ref=technology

[277] "Cyberattack on Google Said to Hit Password System," John Markoff, April 19, 2010, *New York Times*, "The theft began with an instant message sent to a Google employee in China who was using Microsoft's Messenger program, according to the person with knowledge of the internal inquiry, who spoke on the condition that he

not be identified. ...By clicking on a link and connecting to a "poisoned" Web site, the employee inadvertently permitted the intruders to gain access to his (or her) personal computer and then to the computers of a critical group of software developers at Google's headquarters in Mountain View, Calif. Ultimately, the intruders were able to gain control of a software repository used by the development team."
http://www.nytimes.com/2010/04/20/technology/20google.html?_r=1&ref=techn ology

[278] "Google to end censorship in China over cyber attacks," Tania Branigan, January 13, 2010, *The Guardian*,
http://www.guardian.co.uk/technology/2010/jan/12/google-china-ends-censorship

[279] "Microsoft Security Fightback Includes SUS Overhaul," Ryan Naraine, October 10, 2003, Internet News, http://www.internetnews.com/dev-news/article.php/3090281/Microsoft-Security-Fightback-Includes-SUS-Overhaul.htm

[280] "Google to enlist NSA to help it ward off cyberattacks," Ellen Nakashima, February 4, 2010, *The Washington Post*, "Under an agreement that is still being finalized, the National Security Agency would help Google analyze a major corporate espionage attack that the firm said originated in China and targeted its computer networks, according to cybersecurity experts familiar with the matter. The objective is to better defend Google -- and its users -- from future attack."
http://www.washingtonpost.com/wp-dyn/content/article/2010/02/03/AR2010020304057.html?wpisrc=nl_tech

[281] "White House, Google violate lobbying pledge," Timothy P. Carney, June 25, 2010, *Examiner*, "Consumer Watchdog, a liberal nonprofit, used FOIA to obtain e-mails between White House Deputy Chief Technology Officer Andrew McLaughlin and his former colleagues at Google. McLaughlin was Google's head of global public policy and government affairs, up until he joined the White House. ... The topic of net neutrality -- where the Obama administration and Google share a pro-regulation position that would profit Google -- appears repeatedly in McLaughlin-Google e-mails." http://www.washingtonexaminer.com/opinion/columns/White-House_-Google-violate-lobbying-pledge-97103794.html

[282] Jeff Jarvis, *What Would Google Do?* (New York: HarperBusiness, 2009) p. 210.

[283] "Google's Computing Power Refines Translation Tool," Miguel Helft, March 8, 2010, *New York Times*, "The network of data centers that it built for Web searches may now be, when lashed together, the world's largest computer. Google is using that machine to push the limits on translation technology. Last month, for example, it said it was working to combine its translation tool with image analysis, allowing a person to, say, take a cellphone photo of a menu in German and get an instant English translation."
http://www.nytimes.com/2010/03/09/technology/09translate.html

[284] "Remarks on Internet freedom, Hillary Rodham Clinton, Secretary of State, The Newseum, Washington, DC, January 21, 2010, U.S. Department of State website, http://www.state.gov/secretary/rm/2010/01/135519.htm

[285] "Google Wants U.S. to Weigh WTO Challenge to China Censorship," Mark Drajem, March 02, 2010, *Bloomberg BusinessWeek*, http://www.businessweek.com/news/2010-03-02/google-wants-u-s-to-weigh-wto-challenge-to-china-censorship.html

[286] "Google chief: Only miscreants worry about net privacy," Cade Metz, December 7, 2009, *Register*, http://www.theregister.co.uk/2009/12/07/schmidt_on_privacy/

[287] "How Google dominates the Web," October 19th, 2010, *Royal Pingdom blog*, http://royal.pingdom.com/2010/10/19/how-google-dominates-the-web/

[288] "When Google Runs Your Life," Quentin Hardy, December 28, 2009, *Forbes* Magazine, http://www.forbes.com/forbes/2009/1228/technology-google-apps-gmail-bing.html

[289] "Google: Don't fear us," Joseph N. DiStefano, March 1, 2010, *Philly.com*, http://www.philly.com/philly/business/Google_Dont_be_afraid_of_us.html

[290] "Google, Caffeine and the future of search," Matt Warman, July 17, 2010, *UK Telegraph*, http://www.telegraph.co.uk/technology/google/7833590/Google-Caffeine-and-the-future-of-search.html

[291] http://googleopoly.net/Googleopoly_VI_Presentation.pdf

[292] "The Great Disruption," Jeremy Philips, November 4, 2009, *Wall Street Journal*, http://online.wsj.com/article/SB10001424052748703932904574510493674064458.html

[293] Author Nicholas Carr deserves credit for coining the term "Googleopoly." See his blog post of April 16, 2007: http://www.roughtype.com/archives/2007/04/googleopoly.php

[294] "The Great Disruption," Jeremy Philips, November 4, 2009, *Wall Street Journal*, http://online.wsj.com/article/SB10001424052748703932904574510493674064458.html

[295] "Yahoo! Inc. and Google Inc. Abandon Their Advertising Agreement, November 5, 2008, Department of Justice press release, http://www.justice.gov/opa/pr/2008/November/08-at-981.html

[296] "Hogan's Litvack Discusses Google/Yahoo," Nate Raymond, December 2, 2008, *The AM Law Daily*, http://amlawdaily.typepad.com/amlawdaily/2008/12/hogans-litvack.html

[297] "Yahoo! Inc. and Google Inc. Abandon Their Advertising Agreement," Department of Justice press release, November 5, 2008, http://www.justice.gov/opa/pr/2008/November/08-at-981.html

[298] "Antitrust Pick Varney Saw Google as Next Microsoft," James Rowley, February 17, 2009, *Bloomberg*, http://www.bloomberg.com/apps/news?pid=newsarchive&sid=aG9B5.J3Bl1w

[299] "Google becoming "giant monopoly" - German minister," Dave Graham and Klaus-Peter Senger, January 9, 2010, *Reuters*, http://www.reuters.com/article/idUSTRE6081F820100109

[300] http://www.google-watch.org/

[301] "The Big Question: Is Google gaining a monopoly on the world's information?" Stephen Foley, February 19, 2010, *UK Independent*, http://www.independent.co.uk/news/business/analysis-and-features/the-big-question-is-google-gaining-a-monopoly-on-the-worlds-information-1903996.html

[302] "WSJ publisher calls Google 'digital vampire'," Matthew Flamm, June 24, 2009, *Crain's New York Business*, http://www.crainsnewyork.com/article/20090624/FREE/906249985

[303] "comScore Releases March 2010 U.S. Search Engine Rankings," comScore press release, April 12, 2010, http://comscore.com/layout/set/popup/Press_Events/Press_Releases/2010/4/com Score_Releases_March_2010_U.S._Search_Engine_Rankings

[304] "Google received 70 percent of U.S. searches," Experian Hitwise press release, April 7, 2010, http://www.hitwise.com/us/press-center/press-releases/google-searches-mar-10/

[305] http://precursorblog.com/content/why-googles-search-ad-monopoly-understated

[306] "Google's Market Share in Your Country," March 13, 2009, Google Operating System blog, http://googlesystem.blogspot.com/2009/03/googles-market-share-in-your-country.html

[307] "comScore Releases March 2008 European Search Rankings," May 7, 2008, comScore estimated that Google sites handled 79.2% of all European searches, http://www.comscore.com/Press_Events/Press_Releases/2008/05/Top_European_Search_Engines

[308] http://precursorblog.com/content/googles-us-revenue-share-increases-938-2q10-googles-eu-revenue-share-even-higher

[309] http://precursorblog.com/content/googles-us-revenue-share-increases-938-2q10-googles-eu-revenue-share-even-higher

[310] "Regulator Defends Yahoo Japan Deal," Daisuke Wakabayashi, July 29, 2010, *Wall Street Journal*, http://online.wsj.com/article/SB10001424052748703940904575394854222773696.html?mod=WSJ_Tech_LEFTTopNews

[311] http://precursorblog.com/content/japan-powered-google The deal was later approved by Japan's antitrust authorities. See: "Google Deal in Japan Clears Bar," Daisuke Wakabayashi, December 2, 2010, *Wall Street Journal*, http://online.wsj.com/article/SB10001424052748703377504575650061848785620.html?KEYWORDS=Google

[312] "Foundem's Google Story," August 18, 2009, *Searchneutrality.org*, http://www.searchneutrality.org/foundem-google-story

[313] "Do not neutralise the web's endless search," Marissa Mayer, July 15, 2010, Google Public Policy Blog, http://googlepublicpolicy.blogspot.com/2010/07/our-op-ed-regulating-what-is-best-in.html

[314] "Google should be watched carefully," editorial, July 15, 2010, *Financial Times*, http://www.ft.com/cms/s/0/a84e8438-9049-11df-ad26-00144feab49a.html

[315] "The Google Algorithm," editorial, July 14, 2010, *New York Times*, http://www.nytimes.com/2010/07/15/opinion/15thu3.html?_r=1

[316] Or as CEO Eric Schmidt put it, "We are one click away from losing you as a customer, so it is very difficult for us to lock you in as a customer in a way that traditional companies have."
"How Good (or Not Evil) Is Google?," David Carr, June 21, 2009, *New York Times*, http://www.nytimes.com/2009/06/22/business/media/22carr.html?pagewanted=2

[317] "Google: we're not evil and we're no monopoly, either," Omar El Akkad, October 16, 2009, *Globe and Mail*, http://www.theglobeandmail.com/news/technology/google-were-not-evil-and-were-no-monopoly-either/article1327442/page1/

[318] http://precursorblog.com/content/goobris-alert-we-want-be-santa-claus

[319] http://whatifgoogledoesit.com/

[320] http://googleopoly.net/Googleopoly_VI_Presentation.pdf

[321] "List of acquisitions by Google," Wikipedia, http://en.wikipedia.org/wiki/List_of_acquisitions_by_Google

[322] http://googleopoly.net/Googleopoly_VI_Presentation.pdf See Slide 8.

[323] "Google competition, and openness," Google presentation, Slide 26 says "Google welcomes competition because it stimulates innovation, makes us all work harder, and provides users with more choice." The slide revealingly quotes search engine analyst Gord Hotchkiss: "I think Google's competition will come from the same place Google did. It will sneak out of nowhere. ...It will come from someone small enough, visionary enough, obsessive enough and ballsy enough to still do great things, without those great things being picked to death at the boardroom table." http://www.consumerwatchdog.org/resources/Googlepresentation.pdf

[324] "Schmidt says he didn't grasp the power of Google at first," interview with Eric Schmidt, May 16, 2007, *USA Today*, http://www.usatoday.com/tech/techinvestor/corporatenews/2007-05-15-google-schmidt-qa_N.htm

[325] Speech by Eric Schmidt to the Newspaper Association, April 9, 2009, http://www.youtube.com/watch?v=orAJ-YD9FhA

[326] "How Good (or Not Evil) Is Google?" David Carr, June 21, 2009, *New York Times*, http://www.nytimes.com/2009/06/22/business/media/22carr.html?pagewanted=2

[327] "Secret of Googlenomics: Data-Fueled Recipe Brews Profitability," Steven Levy, May 22, 2009, *Wired*, http://www.wired.com/culture/culturereviews/magazine/17-06/nep_googlenomics?currentPage=all

[328] "Secret of Googlenomics: Data-Fueled Recipe Brews Profitability," Steven Levy, May 22, 2009, *Wired*, http://www.wired.com/culture/culturereviews/magazine/17-06/nep_googlenomics?currentPage=all

[329] "Secret of Googlenomics: Data-Fueled Recipe Brews Profitability," Steven Levy, May 22, 2009, *Wired*, http://www.wired.com/culture/culturereviews/magazine/17-06/nep_googlenomics?currentPage=all

[330] "Schmidt says he didn't grasp the power of Google at first," interview with Eric Schmidt, May 16, 2007, *USA Today*, http://www.usatoday.com/tech/techinvestor/corporatenews/2007-05-15-google-schmidt-qa_N.htm

[331] "Inside the Googleplex," August 30, 2007, *The Economist*, http://www.economist.com/opinion/displaystory.cfm?story_id=9719610

[332] "CEO Eric Schmidt wishes he could rescue newspapers," Adam Lashinsky, January 7, 2009, *Fortune*, http://money.cnn.com/2009/01/07/technology/lashinsky_google.fortune/

[333] "How Can You Compete With Google?" Jesse Noller, October 14, 2010, *JesseNoller.com*, http://jessenoller.com/2010/10/14/how-can-you-compete-with-google/

[334] Janet Lowe. *Google Speaks: Secrets of the World's Greatest Billionaire Entrepreneurs, Sergey Brin and Larry Page*. (New Jersey: Wiley Press, 2009) p. 132.

[335] "Inside Google: Eric Schmidt, the man with all the answers," David Rowan, June 30, 2009, *Wired*, http://www.wired.co.uk/wired-magazine/archive/2009/08/features/the-unstoppable-google?page=all

[336] "Google's new paradigm 'cloud computing and advertising go hand in hand,'" Donna Bogatin, August 23, 2006, *ZDNet*, http://blogs.zdnet.com/micro-markets/?p=369

[337] "Is Google a Media Company?," Miguel Helft, August 10, 2008, *New York Times*, http://www.nytimes.com/2008/08/11/technology/11google.html?_r=1&oref=slogin&partner=rssnyt&emc=rss&pagewanted=all

[338] "Our Philosophy: Ten Things we Know to be True," http://www.google.com/corporate/tenthings.html

[339] "Google's Goal: to organise your life," Caroline Daniel and Maija Palmer, *Financial Times*, May 22 2007, http://www.ft.com/cms/s/2/c3e49548-088e-11dc-b11e-000b5df10621.html

[340] "Secret of Googlenomics: Data-Fueled Recipe Brews Profitability, Steven Levy, May 22, 2009, *Wired*, http://www.wired.com/culture/culturereviews/magazine/17-06/nep_googlenomics?currentPage=1

[341] (Auletta, 2009) p. 282

[342] Note that when Eric Schmidt was at Novell he saw how Microsoft bought control of the distribution channels. Schmidt joined Google in March of 2001.

[343] See http://googleopoly.net/Googleopoly_VI_Presentation.pdf for my analysis of Google's "reinforcing spheres of monopoly influence."

[344] http://googleopoly.net/Googleopoly_VI_Presentation.pdf, Slide: "How Googleopoly's Core Virtuous Circle and Perpetual Feedback Loop Works."

[345] "Inside the Black Box Technology and Innovation at Google," Speech by Jonathan Rosenberg, February 27, 2008, http://static.googleusercontent.com/external_content/untrusted_dlcp/www.googl e.com/en/us/press/podium/pdf/20080227_Jonathan_Rosenberg_Technology_Inno vation.pdf

[346] http://googleopoly.net/Googleopoly_VI_Presentation.pdf, Slide: "How Google's Acquisitions Have Substantially Lessened Competition."

[347] http://googleopoly.net/Googleopoly_VI_Presentation.pdf, Slide: "How YouTube Acquisition Helped Tip Google to Monopoly."

[348] Ibid.

[349] http://googleopoly.net/Googleopoly_VI_Presentation.pdf, Slide: "How DoubleClick Acquisition Tipped Google to Monopoly."

[350] "Extending your AdWords Campaigns to the G1 and iPhone," Amanda Kelly, December 08, 2008, Google Inside AdWords, http://adwords.blogspot.com/2008/12/extending-your-adwords-campaigns-to-g1.html

[351] http://googleopoly.net/Googleopoly_VI_Presentation.pdf, Slide: "How FTC Approval of AdMob Ceded Google a Mobile Ad Monopoly."

[352] "Google Set to Acquire AdMob for $750 Million," Miguel Helft, November 9, 2009, The New York Times, http://www.nytimes.com/2009/11/10/technology/companies/10google.html

[353] http://googleopoly.net/Googleopoly_VI_Presentation.pdf, Slide: "What's one result of lax antitrust enforcement?"

[354] http://googleopoly.net/Googleopoly_VI_Presentation.pdf, Slide: "How did lax antitrust enforcement create a monocaster?"

[355] "Committed to competing fairly," Julia Holtz, Senior Competition Counsel, February 23, 2010, Google Public Policy Blog, http://googlepublicpolicy.blogspot.com/2010/02/committed-to-competing-fairly.html

[356] "Committed to competing fairly," Julia Holtz, Senior Competition Counsel, February 23, 2010, Google Public Policy Blog, http://googlepublicpolicy.blogspot.com/2010/02/committed-to-competing-fairly.html

[357] "New Complaints Filed Against Google in Europe," James Kanter, February 24, 2010, New York Times, http://www.nytimes.com/2010/02/24/technology/24google.html?ref=suitsandlitig ation

[358] "This stuff is tough," Amit Singhal, Google Fellow, February 25, 2010, http://googlepolicyeurope.blogspot.com/2010/02/this-stuff-is-tough.html

[359] "This stuff is tough," Amit Singhal, Google Fellow, February 25, 2010, http://googlepolicyeurope.blogspot.com/2010/02/this-stuff-is-tough.html

[360] "This stuff is tough," Amit Singhal, Google Fellow, February 25, 2010, http://googlepolicyeurope.blogspot.com/2010/02/this-stuff-is-tough.html

[361] "This stuff is tough," Amit Singhal, Google Fellow, February 25, 2010, http://googlepolicyeurope.blogspot.com/2010/02/this-stuff-is-tough.html

[362] "Rivals Say Google Plays Favorites: Search Giant Displays Its Own Health, Shopping, Local Content Ahead of Links to Competing Sites," Amir Efrati, December 12, 2010, *Wall Street Journal*, http://online.wsj.com/article/SB10001424052748704058704576015630188568972.html?mod=WSJ_hp_MIDDLENexttoWhatsNewsSecond

[363] http://googleopoly.net/Googleopoly_VI_Presentation.pdf Slide: "How Google rigs their info-casino game—so they can't lose."

[364] "Eric Schmidt: "We Know Where You Are, We Know What You Like," Alexia Tsotsis, September 7, 2010, *Tech Crunch*, http://techcrunch.com/2010/09/07/eric-schmidt-ifa/

[365] "Eric Schmidt: Welcome to "Age of Augmented Humanity" Liz Gannes September 7, 2010, *GigaOM*, http://gigaom.com/2010/09/07/eric-schmidt-welcome-to-the-age-of-augmented-humanity/

[366] http://googleopoly.net/Googleopoly_VI_Presentation.pdf, Slide: "Googleopoly's secret weapon."

[367] http://googleopoly.net/Googleopoly_VI_Presentation.pdf

[368] "Investigation: Google, "The Rise Of DSPs," And What's Really Fueling Its Display Ad Growth," Erick Schonfeld, November 24, 2010, *TechCrunch*, http://techcrunch.com/2010/11/24/oogle-publicis-display-dsp/

[369] "We're Google. So Sue Us." Katie Hafner, October 23, 2006, *New York Times*, "Last spring, KinderStart, a small search engine in Southern California that focuses on information for parents of young children, sued Google after it noticed that its site had been removed from Google's search results — leading to a loss of traffic and revenue for the company. …Google said in court filings that an area of the site that permitted visitors to add links had been full of pointers to low-quality or pornographic sites, indicating that it was poorly maintained or was an effort to manipulate Google's search results. KinderStart said the removal was unfair and unjustified and that Google's guidelines on ways to avoid such punishment were too vague." http://select.nytimes.com/gst/abstract.html?res=F10E11FE3C5B0C708EDDA90994DE404482

[370] "I Let Google Change My Ad Campaign and It Nearly Killed My Company," Ethan Siegel, CEO, Orb Audio, August 11, 2010, *CBS Business Network*, http://www.bnet.com/blog/smb/i-let-google-change-my-ad-campaign-and-it-nearly-killed-my-company/1785

[371] "Another Antitrust Lawsuit Against Google (myTrigger) -- Google's proliferating antitrust liabilities Part II," Scott Cleland, February 22, 2010, *Precursor blog*, http://precursorblog.com/content/another-antitrust-lawsuit-against-google-mytrigger-googles-proliferating-antitrust-liabilities-part-ii

[372] "Insurance Claim Undermines myTriggers Lawsuit Against Google," Wendy Davis, June 2, 2010, *Online Media Daily*, http://www.mediapost.com/publications/?fa=Articles.showArticle&art_aid=129395

[373] "Totlol: The New Saturday Morning Cartoons," Erick Schonfeld, November 1, 2008, *TechCrunch*, http://techcrunch.com/2008/11/01/totlol-the-new-saturday-morning-cartoons/

[374] "The Sad Tale Of Totlol And How YouTube's Changing TOS Made It Hard To Make A Buck," Erick Schonfeld, December 29, 2009, *TechCrunch*, http://techcrunch.com/2009/12/29/totlol-youtube/

[375] "Totlol Developer Forced To Shut Down Video Service For Kids," Robin Wauters, June 5, 2009, *TechCrunch*, http://techcrunch.com/2009/06/05/totlol-developer-forced-to-shut-down-kids-video-service/

[376] "The Sad Tale Of Totlol And How YouTube's Changing TOS Made It Hard To Make A Buck," Erick Schonfeld, December 29, 2009, *TechCrunch*, http://techcrunch.com/2009/12/29/totlol-youtube/

[377] "The poison of arrogance," Frédéric Filloux, July 4, 2010, *Monday Note.com*, http://www.mondaynote.com/2010/07/04/the-poison-of-arrogance/

[378] "Navx Won Lawsuit against Google," Ludovic Privat, June 30, 2010, *GPS Business News*, http://www.gpsbusinessnews.com/Navx-Won-Lawsuit-against-Google_a2333.html

[379] "Skyhook sues Google amid greater federal antitrust scrutiny," Cecilia Kang, September 16, 2010, *The Washington Post*, http://voices.washingtonpost.com/posttech/2010/09/skyhook_sues_google_for_anti-c.html

[380] "Eric Schmidt on Google's Next Tricks," Amir Efrati, July 28, 2010, *Wall Street Journal*, http://blogs.wsj.com/digits/2010/07/28/eric-schmidt-on-google%E2%80%99s-next-tricks/

[381] "Facebook Now More Popular than Google,' Ed Oswald, September 10, 2010, *PC World*, http://www.pcworld.com/article/205263/facebook_now_more_popular_than_google.html

[382] "Facebook grabs bigger slice of display ad pie," Alexei Oreskovic, November 8, 2010, Reuters, http://www.reuters.com/article/idUSTRE6A74NE20101108?utm_source=feedburner&utm_medium=feed&utm_campaign=Feed:+reuters/technologyNews+%28News+/+US+/+Technology%29

[383] http://en.wikipedia.org/wiki/Facebook

[384] "More Than 250 Million People Use Facebook on a Daily Basis," Jennifer Van Grove, November 17, 2010, *Mashable*, http://mashable.com/2010/11/16/facebook-social/?utm_source=feedburner&utm_medium=feed&utm_campaign=Feed:+Mashable/SocialMedia+%28Mashable+%BB+Social+Media+Feed%29

[385] "Google Conducting Focus Group Research Into Social Networking," Leena Rao,

July 12, 2010, *TechCrunch*, http://techcrunch.com/2010/07/12/google-social-networking-focus-group/

[386] "Encouraging people to contribute knowledge," Udi Manber, VP Engineering, December 13, 2007, *Official Google Blog*, http://googleblog.blogspot.com/2007/12/encouraging-people-to-contribute.html

[387] "Google: we're not evil and we're no monopoly, either," Omar El Akkad, October 16, 2009, *Globe and Mail*, http://www.theglobeandmail.com/news/technology/google-were-not-evil-and-were-no-monopoly-either/article1327442/page1/

[388] "Our Philosophy," Google corporate information, Ten things we know to be true, "1. Focus on the user and all else will follow.
Since the beginning, we've focused on providing the best user experience possible. Whether we're designing a new Internet browser or a new tweak to the look of the homepage, we take great care to ensure that they will ultimately serve you, rather than our own internal goal or bottom line. Our homepage interface is clear and simple, and pages load instantly. Placement in search results is never sold to anyone, and advertising is not only clearly marked as such, it offers relevant content and is not distracting. And when we build new tools and applications, we believe they should work so well you don't have to consider how they might have been designed differently." http://www.google.com/intl/en/corporate/tenthings.html

[389] "The meaning of open," Jonathan Rosenberg, Senior Vice President, December 21, 2009, *Official Google Blog*, http://googleblog.blogspot.com/2009/12/meaning-of-open.html

[390] "The meaning of open," Jonathan Rosenberg, Senior Vice President, December 21,
2009, *Official Google Blog*, http://googleblog.blogspot.com/2009/12/meaning-of-open.html

[391] "Greater transparency around government requests," David Drummond, SVP, Corporate Development and Chief Legal Officer, April 20, 2010, *Official Google Blog*, http://googleblog.blogspot.com/2010/04/greater-transparency-around-government.html

[392] "Google CEO Schmidt: "People Aren't Ready for the Technology Revolution","
Marshall Kirkpatrick, August 4, 2010, *ReadWriteWeb.com*, http://www.readwriteweb.com/archives/google_ceo_schmidt_people_arent_ready_for_the_tech.php

[393] "Google chief prizes creativity," Lionel Barber and Maija Palmer, June 3 2010, *Financial Times*, http://www.ft.com/cms/s/2/bdec0ee8-6f4f-11df-9f43-00144feabdc0.html

[394] "Google's Eric Schmidt: You can trust us with your data," Shane Richmond, July 1, 2010, *UK Telegraph*, http://www.telegraph.co.uk/technology/google/7864223/Googles-Eric-Schmidt-You-can-trust-us-with-your-data.html

[395] "Google and the Search for the Future," Holman W. Jenkins, Jr. August 14, 2010, *Wall Street Journal*, http://online.wsj.com/article/SB10001424052748704901104575423294099527212.html

[396] "2007 Global Accountability Report," One World Trust, "Google's overall accountability score is significantly lower than the average accountability scores of any of the three sectors." http://www.oneworldtrust.org/index.php?option=com_content&view=article&id=77:2007-gar&catid=48:global-accountability-report-gar&Itemid=62

[397] "The meaning of open," Jonathan Rosenberg, Senior Vice President, December 21, 2009, *Official Google Blog*, http://googleblog.blogspot.com/2009/12/meaning-of-open.html

[398] "Our op-ed: Regulating what is "best" in search?" Adam Kovacevich, Senior Manager, Public Policy Communications, July 15, 2010, *Google Public Policy Blog*, http://googlepublicpolicy.blogspot.com/2010/07/our-op-ed-regulating-what-is-best-in.html

[399] "2004 Founders' IPO Letter," From the S-1 Registration Statement "An Owner's Manual" for Google's Shareholders, Google investor relations, http://investor.google.com/corporate/2004/ipo-founders-letter.html

[400] "Hogan's Litvack Discusses Google/Yahoo," Nate Raymond, December 2, 2008, *The AM Law Daily*, http://amlawdaily.typepad.com/amlawdaily/2008/12/hogans-litvack.html

[401] "Yahoo! Inc. and Google Inc. Abandon Their Advertising Agreement," Department of Justice press release, November 5, 2008, http://www.justice.gov/opa/pr/2008/November/08-at-981.html

[402] "Google's Schmidt resigns from Apple board," Caroline McCarthy, August 3, 2009 *CNET News*, http://news.cnet.com/8301-13579_3-10301612-37.html

[403] "Antitrust: Commission probes allegations of antitrust violations by Google," European Union press release, November 30, 2010, *Europa.eu*, http://europa.eu/rapid/pressReleasesAction.do?reference=IP/10/1624&format=HTML&aged=0&language=EN&guiLanguage=en

[404] "EU Opens Google Antitrust Inquiry," Thomas Catan, Jessica E. Vascellaro and Charles Forelle, February 25, 2010, *Wall Street Journal*, http://online.wsj.com/article/SB10001424052748704188104575084062149453280.html

[405] "Controversial content and free expression on the web: a refresher," April 19, 2010, *Official Google Blog*, "We see these attempts at control in many ways. China is the most polarizing example, but it is not the only one. Google products -- from search and Blogger to YouTube and Google Docs -- have been blocked in 25 of the 100 countries where we offer our services. In addition, we regularly receive government requests to restrict or remove content from our properties." http://googleblog.blogspot.com/2010/04/controversial-content-and-free.html

[406] http://www.priv.gc.ca/media/nr-c/2010/let_100420_e.cfm

[407] "US Deputy CTO gets reprimand for Google lobbying contacts," Nate Anderson, May 2010, *ARS Technica*, http://arstechnica.com/tech-policy/news/2010/05/us-deputy-cto-reprimanded-for-google-lobbying-contacts.ars

[408] "Privacy Groups Push FTC For National Privacy Plan," John Eggerton, July 14, 2010, *Broadcasting & Cable*, http://www.broadcastingcable.com/article/454761-Privacy_Groups_Push_FTC_For_National_Privacy_Plan.php?rssid=20065

[409] ""Do Not Track" movement gaining traction in DC," David Kirkpatrick, September 7, 2010, *David Kirkpatrick blog*, http://davidkirkpatrick.wordpress.com/2010/09/07/do-not-track-movement-gaining-traction-in-dc/

[410] "FTC Staff Issues Privacy Report, Offers Framework for Consumers, Businesses, and Policymakers," December 1, 2010, press release, *Federal Trade Commission*, http://www.ftc.gov/opa/2010/12/privacyreport.shtm

[411] "Viacom Files Appeal in YouTube Case," John Letzing, December 3, 2010, *Wall Street Journal*, http://online.wsj.com/article/SB10001424052748703989004575653082185175478.html?mod=WSJ_Tech_LEFTTopNews

[412] "Why Google Ditched the Name 'Sponsored Links'," Joe Mullin, November 5, 2010, *PaidContent.Org*, http://paidcontent.org/article/419-why-google-ditched-the-name-sponsored-links/

[413] "Auction," Merriam-Webster's Dictionary of Law. Merriam-Webster, Inc., August 26, 2010. *Dictionary.com*, http://dictionary.reference.com/browse/auction

[414] "The Humans Behind the Google Money Machine," Miguel Helft, June 2, 2008, *New York Times*, http://www.nytimes.com/2008/06/02/technology/02google.html?_r=2&ref=technology&oref=slogin

[415] "The Humans Behind the Google Money Machine," Miguel Helft, June 2, 2008, *New York Times*, http://www.nytimes.com/2008/06/02/technology/02google.html?_r=2&ref=technology&oref=slogin

[416] "Screwgle™ - Google's new ad revenue model," Cade Metz, July 28, 2008, *The Register*, http://www.theregister.co.uk/2008/07/28/google_expands_automatic_matching/

[417] "Google's riches rely on ads, algorithms, and worldwide confusion," Cade Metz, March 18, 2008, *The Register*, http://www.theregister.co.uk/2008/03/18/when_google_does_evil/

[418] "Google-Yahoo Ad Deal is Bad for Online Advertising," Benjamin G. Edelman, August 12, 2008, *Harvard Business School Working Knowledge*, http://hbswk.hbs.edu/item/5995.html

[419] "Google - the world's first firewalled monopoly: Pricing power goes virtual," Cade Metz, November 20, 2008, *UK Register*, http://m.theregister.co.uk/2008/11/20/the_google_monopoly/

[420] "The SearchIgnite study on ad prices and the Yahoo-Google deal," Hal Varian, September 16, 2008, *Google Public Policy Blog*, http://googlepublicpolicy.blogspot.com/2008/09/searchignite-study-on-ad-prices-and.html

[421] "Google AdWords "Automatic Matching" Beta To Expand Tomorrow," May 19, 2008, *Search Engine Roundtable*, http://www.seroundtable.com/archives/017163.html

[422] "Google Allows Itself a Special Ad," Philipp Lenssen, August 6, 2008, *Google Blogoscoped*, http://blogoscoped.com/archive/2008-08-06-n64.html

[423] "Google AdWords Quality Score : Affiliates Worst Nightmare?," Pablo Palatnik, June 20, 2007, *Search Engine Journal*, http://www.searchenginejournal.com/google-adwords-quality-score-affiliates-worst-nightmare/5150/

[424] "Large Brands Double Dipping in Google's Organic Search Results," June 18, 2007, *SEOBook*, http://www.seobook.com/archives/002305.shtml

[425] "Click Fraud Rate Rises Slightly in Q2 2010 to 18.6 Percent," July 21, 2010, *ClickForensics.com*, http://www.clickforensics.com/newsroom/press-releases/165-click-fraud-rate-rises-slightly-in-q2-2010-to-186-percent.html

[426] (Vise and Malseed, 2005)

[427] (Vise and Malseed, 2005) p.248

[428] Ibid. Stricchiola characterizes Google's response as "Thank you for your inquiry. We see no problem."

[429] (Battelle, 2005) Battelle cites reports from Mamma.com and FindWhat.com.

[430] "The Value of Google Result Positioning," May 25, 2010, *ChitikaInsights.com*, http://chitika.com/research/2010/the-value-of-google-result-positioning/

[431] "20 (Rare) Questions for Google Search Guru Udi Manber," Glenn Derene, April 16, 2008, *Popular Mechanics*, http://www.popularmechanics.com/technology/gadgets/news/4259137

[432] "Introduction to Google Ranking," Amit Singhal, Google Fellow in Charge of the Ranking Team, July 9, 2008, *The Official Google Blog*, http://googleblog.blogspot.com/2008/07/introduction-to-google-ranking.html

[433] "Google caught in anti-Semitism flap," David Becker, April 7, 2004, *CNET News*, "Google spokesman David Krane said the company's search results are determined by a complex set of algorithms that measure factors such as how many sites link to a given page. The company can't and won't change the ranking for Jew Watch, regardless of how many signatures the petition attracts, he said." http://news.cnet.com/2100-1038_3-5186012.html

[434] "Google Usually Promises Unbiased Results, but Occasionally Admits Otherwise," comments by Google's Marissa Mayer, Seattle Conference on Scalability, 2007, http://www.benedelman.org/hardcoding/

[435] http://www.searchneutrality.org/

[436] "Google's Schmidt Says Internet 'Cesspool' Needs Brands," Nat Ives, October 8, 2008, *Advertising Age*, ""We don't actually want you to be successful," he said. The

company's algorithms are trying to find the most relevant search results, after all, not the sites that best game the system. "The fundamental way to increase your rank is to increase your relevance," he added."
http://adage.com/mediaworks/article?article_id=131569

[437] "The Anatomy of a Large-Scale Hypertextual Web Search Engine," Sergey Brin and Lawrence Page, 1998, "Currently, the predominant business model for commercial search engines is advertising. The goals of the advertising business model do not always correspond to providing quality search to users. For example, in our prototype search engine one of the top results for cellular phone is "The Effect of Cellular Phone Use Upon Driver Attention", a study which explains in great detail the distractions and risk associated with conversing on a cell phone while driving. This search result came up first because of its high importance as judged by the PageRank algorithm, an approximation of citation importance on the web [Page, 98]. It is clear that a search engine which was taking money for showing cellular phone ads would have difficulty justifying the page that our system returned to its paying advertisers. For this type of reason and historical experience with other media [Bagdikian 83], we expect that advertising funded search engines will be inherently biased towards the advertisers and away from the needs of the consumers. ...Since it is very difficult even for experts to evaluate search engines, search engine bias is particularly insidious. A good example was OpenText, which was reported to be selling companies the right to be listed at the top of the search results for particular queries [Marchiori 97]. This type of bias is much more insidious than advertising, because it is not clear who "deserves" to be there, and who is willing to pay money to be listed. This business model resulted in an uproar, and OpenText has ceased to be a viable search engine. But less blatant bias are likely to be tolerated by the market. For example, a search engine could add a small factor to search results from "friendly" companies, and subtract a factor from results from competitors. This type of bias is very difficult to detect but could still have a significant effect on the market. Furthermore, advertising income often provides an incentive to provide poor quality search results. For example, we noticed a major search engine would not return a large airline's homepage when the airline's name was given as a query. It so happened that the airline had placed an expensive ad, linked to the query that was its name. A better search engine would not have required this ad, and possibly resulted in the loss of the revenue from the airline to the search engine. In general, it could be argued from the consumer point of view that the better the search engine is, the fewer advertisements will be needed for the consumer to find what they want. This of course erodes the advertising supported business model of the existing search engines. However, there will always be money from advertisers who want a customer to switch products, or have something that is genuinely new. But we believe the issue of advertising causes enough mixed incentives that it is crucial to have a competitive search engine that is transparent and in the academic realm."
http://infolab.stanford.edu/~backrub/google.html

[438] "Students Found To Blindly Follow Google," Doug Caverly , July 27, 2010, *WebProNews*, http://www.webpronews.com/topnews/2010/07/27/students-found-to-blindly-follow-google

[439] "Google admits that employees change index rankings," Tom Foremski, July 13, 2010, *ZDNet*, http://www.zdnet.com/blog/foremski/google-admits-that-employees-change-index-rankings/1420

[440] "In Google's Opinion...." John Battelle, December 1, 2010, *Searchblog*, http://battellemedia.com/archives/2010/12/in_googles_opinion

[441] "Google should be watched carefully," July 15 2010, Editorial, *Financial Times*, http://www.ft.com/cms/s/0/a84e8438-9049-11df-ad26-00144feab49a.html

[442] "Using site speed in web search ranking," Amit Singhal, Google Fellow and Matt Cutts, Principal Engineer, Google Search Quality Team, April 09, 2010, *Google Webmaster Central Blog*, http://googlewebmastercentral.blogspot.com/2010/04/using-site-speed-in-web-search-ranking.html

[443] "Google tweaks search results with mystery site speedometer," Cade Metz, April 9, 2010, *The UK Register*, "But as you might expect, some webmasters aren't happy. "I do not think that this is a solid idea," reads one response to Google's post. "What about sites that post lots of photos on their pages or use complex services that take longer to load? What about all the sites that use advertisement[s]? They obviously load slower than a plain HTML site."" http://www.theregister.co.uk/2010/04/09/google_adds_site_speed_to_search_ranking/

[444] "Google Suggest Has a Branded Commerce Bias," Greg Battle, July 19, 2010, *LeftoverTakeout.com*, http://leftovertakeout.com/post/831944097/google-suggest-has-a-branded-commerce-bias

[445] "TradeComet.com Files Federal Antitrust Lawsuit against Google," TradeComet press release, February 17, 2009, *BusinessWire.com*, http://www.businesswire.com/news/home/20090217006644/en/TradeComet.com-Files-Federal-Antitrust-Lawsuit-Google

[446] "TradeComet.com Files Federal Antitrust Lawsuit against Google," TradeComet press release, February 17, 2009, *BusinessWire.com*, http://www.businesswire.com/portal/site/home/permalink/?ndmViewId=news_view&newsId=20090217006644&newsLang=en

[447] "Stuck in Google's Doghouse," Joe Nocera, September 12, 2008, *New York Times*, http://www.nytimes.com/2008/09/13/technology/13nocera.html?pagewanted=1&_r=2&ref=business

[448] "TradeComet's AntiTrust Complaint Against Google is Dismissed," Geoffrey Manne, March 9, 2010, *Forbes.com*, http://blogs.forbes.com/streettalk/2010/03/09/tradecomets-antitrust-complaint-against-google-is-dismissed/?partner=contextstory

[449] "Google destroys longest-running showbiz news site in Net history, won't explain why," John Brownlee, November 30, 2009, *Geek.com*,

http://www.geek.com/articles/news/google-destroys-longest-running-showbiz-news-site-in-net-history-wont-explain-why-20091130/

[450] "G-Railed: Why Did Google Bury the Web's Oldest Entertainment Publication?" Dan Macsai, December 2, 2009, *Fast Company*, http://www.fastcompany.com/blog/dan-macsai/popwise/why-did-neutral-google-de-list-webs-oldest-entertainment-publication

[451] "Europe Zeroes In on Google," Charles Forelle and Thomas Catan, December 1, 2010, *Wall Street Journal*, http://online.wsj.com/article/SB10001424052748704679204575646233474884868.html?ru=yahoo

[452] "A New Tool From Google Alarms Sites," Bob Tedeschi, March 24, 2008, *New York Times*, http://www.nytimes.com/2008/03/24/business/media/24ecom.html?pagewanted=1&_r=2&ref=business

[453] "Bringing federal IT into the cloud," Harry Wingo, Policy Counsel, July 1, 2010, *Google Public Policy Blog*, "First, cloud computing can provide improved security. Under legacy computing models, data is stored on local computers – this is the equivalent of keeping cash under your mattress. Storing data securely in the cloud is like keeping cash in a bank." http://googlepublicpolicy.blogspot.com/2010/07/bringing-federal-it-into-cloud.html

[454] "Google Trada Investment Smells of Interest Conflict," Clint Boulton, July 21, 2010, *eWeek Google Watch*, http://googlewatch.eweek.com/content/google_advertising/google_trada_investment_sparks_conflict_of_interest_concern.html?kc=rss

[455] "How Google Is Screwing Its Own Advertisers with Comparison Ads," John Hargrave, October 19, 2010, *Search Engine Journal*, http://www.searchenginejournal.com/how-google-is-screwing-its-own-advertisers-with-comparison-ads/25008/#ixzz12ucNmMRJ

[456] http://www.google.com/googlebooks/chrome/big_18.html

[457] "Yahoo! 'owns several patents' on Google Instant," Cade Metz, September 20, 2010, *The UK Register*, http://www.theregister.co.uk/2010/09/20/yahoo_owns_several_patents_on_google_instant/

[458] "Google chief warns politicians," Jean Eaglesham, October 3, 2006, *Financial Times*, http://www.ft.com/cms/s/0/c09fc2d6-5308-11db-99c5-0000779e2340.html

[459] "The Google Algorithm," Editorial, July 14, 2010, *New York Times*, http://www.nytimes.com/2010/07/15/opinion/15thu3.html?_r=2

[460] "Unrest over Google's secret formula," Richard Waters, July 11 2010, *Financial Times*, http://www.ft.com/cms/s/0/1a5596c2-8d0f-11df-bad7-00144feab49a.html

[461] "Diller calls Google travel deal 'disturbing'," Richard Waters, July 11, 2010, *Financial Times*, www.ft.com/cms/s/0/2f582730-8d1c-11df-bad7-00144feab49a.html

[462] "Do not neutralise the web's endless search," Marissa Mayer, Google VP of search product and user experience, July 14 2010, *Financial Times*, http://www.ft.com/cms/s/0/0458b1a4-8f78-11df-8df0-00144feab49a.html

[463] http://www.brainyquote.com/quotes/quotes/m/miltonfrie153358.html

[464] "comScore Reports Global Search Market Growth of 46 Percent in 2009," Google sites performed 87 billion searches in December 2009—nearly 3 billion per day. January 22, 2010, *comScore.com*, http://www.comscore.com/Press_Events/Press_Releases/2010/1/Global_Search_Market_Grows_46_Percent_in_2009

[465] "We knew the web was big...," Jesse Alpert and Nissan Hajaj, July 25, 2008, *Official Google Blog*, http://googleblog.blogspot.com/2008/07/we-knew-web-was-big.html

[466] "Google by the Numbers Infographic," October 5, 2010, *InfoGraphicsShowcase.com*, http://www.infographicsshowcase.com/google-by-the-numbers-infographic/

[467] "Google Has Well Over A Million Advertisers," Barry Schwartz, January 9, 2009, *Search Engine Land*, http://searchengineland.com/google-has-well-over-a-million-advertisers-16068

[468] http://spreadsheets.google.com/pub?key=ty_BGDs9hnuBMRvj3AFeB2g&output=html

[469] "Google chief Eric Schmidt on the data explosion," Kenny MacIver, August 4, 2010, *Global Intelligence for the CIO*, http://www.i-cio.com/blog/august-2010/eric-schmidt-exabytes-of-data

[470] "Google chief Eric Schmidt on the data explosion," Kenny MacIver, August 4, 2010, *Global Intelligence for the CIO*, http://www.i-cio.com/blog/august-2010/eric-schmidt-exabytes-of-data

[471] "Google chief Eric Schmidt on the data explosion," Kenny MacIver, August 4, 2010, *Global Intelligence for the CIO*, http://www.i-cio.com/blog/august-2010/eric-schmidt-exabytes-of-data

[472] "The Search Party: Google squares off with its Capitol Hill critics," Ken Auletta, January 14, 2008, *New Yorker*, http://www.newyorker.com/reporting/2008/01/14/080114fa_fact_auletta?printable=true#ixzz0xBIDXTjd

[473] http://googleopoly.net/googleopoly.pdf, pp. 13-19

[474] http://googleopoly.net/googleopoly_2.pdf pp. 3-4

[475] http://googleopoly.net/googleopoly.pdf, pp. 13-19

[476] "Google is watching you: 'Big Brother' row over plans for personal database," Robert Verkaik, May 24, 2007, *The Independent*, http://www.independent.co.uk/news/science/google-is-watching-you-450084.html

[477] http://googlemonitor.com/wp-content/uploads/2010/06/Google's_Total_Information_Awareness.pdf

[478] http://googlemonitor.com/wp-content/uploads/2010/06/Google's_Total_Information_Awareness.pdf

[479] "Too Powerful? Us? Surely You Jest," Interview with Eric Schmidt, April 9, 2007, *BussinessWeek*, http://www.businessweek.com/magazine/content/07_15/b4029007.htm

[480] "Google Already Making Microsoft Mistakes It Wants To Avoid," Erik Sherman, November 6, 2009, *CBS Interactive Business Network*, http://www.bnet.com/blog/technology-business/google-already-making-microsoft-mistakes-it-wants-to-avoid/1843

[481] "Top 5 moments from Eric Schmidt's talk in Abu Dhabi," Jon Fortt, March 11, 2010, *Fortune*, http://tech.fortune.cnn.com/2010/03/11/top-five-moments-from-eric-schmidts-talk-in-abu-dhabi/

[482] "Google, Caffeine and the future of search," Matt Warman, June 17, 2010, *UK Telegraph*, http://www.telegraph.co.uk/technology/google/7833590/Google-Caffeine-and-the-future-of-search.html

[483] "Google, Caffeine and the future of search," Matt Warman, June 17, 2010, *UK Telegraph*, http://www.telegraph.co.uk/technology/google/7833590/Google-Caffeine-and-the-future-of-search.html

[484] "From the height of this place," Jonathan Rosenberg, February 16, 2009, *The Official Google Blog*, http://googleblog.blogspot.com/2009/02/from-height-of-this-place.html

[485] "Schmidt says he didn't grasp the power of Google at first," Interview, Isaac Brekken, May 16, 2007, *USA Today*, http://www.usatoday.com/tech/techinvestor/corporatenews/2007-05-15-google-schmidt-qa_N.htm

[486] "Users' complaints to FTC show another side of Google," Verne Kopytoff, October 8, 2007, *San Francisco Chronicle*, http://www.sfgate.com/cgi-bin/article.cgi?f=/c/a/2007/10/08/MN5JSA9MV.DTL&hw=user+complaints&sn=002&sc=954

[487] "The day the music blogs died: behind Google's musicblogocide," Nate Anderson, February 15, 2010, *ARS Technica*, http://arstechnica.com/tech-policy/news/2010/02/the-day-the-music-blogs-died-behind-googles-musicblogocide.ars

[488] "J. Edgar Hoover," http://en.wikipedia.org/wiki/J._Edgar_Hoover

[489] "Google, 10 years in: big, friendly giant or a greedy Goliath?" David Smith, August 17, 2008, *UK Guardian*, http://www.guardian.co.uk/media/2008/aug/17/googlethemedia.google

[490] "The Evil Side of Google? Exploring Google's User Data Collection," Danny Dover, June 24, 2008, *The Daily SEO Blog*, http://www.seomoz.org/blog/the-evil-side-of-google-exploring-googles-user-data-collection#list

[491] http://www.seomoz.org/team/danny

[492] http://precursorblog.com/content/j-edgar-google-information-is-power-no-accountability

[493] "Governments, Competitors Afraid of Google's "Disruptive" Business Model, Says CEO," Jason Mick, April 13, 2010, *DailyTech*, http://www.dailytech.com/Governments+Competitors+Afraid+of+Googles+Disruptive+Business+Model+Says+CEO/article18117.htm

[494] "EU group criticizes Google-DoubleClick deal," Aoife White, Associated Press, July 5, 2007, *USA Today*, http://www.usatoday.com/tech/news/internetprivacy/2007-07-05-eu-google-doubleclick_N.htm

[495] "Stopping Google: With one company now the world's chief gateway to information, some critics are hatching ways to fight its influence," Drake Bennett, June 22, 2008, *Boston Globe*, http://www.boston.com/bostonglobe/ideas/articles/2008/06/22/stopping_google/

[496] "The Search Party: Google squares off with its Capitol Hill critics," Ken Auletta, January 14, 2008, *New Yorker*, http://www.newyorker.com/reporting/2008/01/14/080114fa_fact_auletta?printable=true#ixzz0xBIDXTjd

[497] "Data Mining You to Death: Does Google Know Too Much?" Julia Bonstein, Marcel Rosenbach and Hilmar Schmundt, October 30, 2008, *Der Spiegel*, http://www.spiegel.de/international/germany/0,1518,587546,00.html

[498] "Google-Yahoo Poses Ad-Rate Worries," Jessica E. Vascellaro and Emily Steel, June 14, 2008, *Wall Street Journal*, http://resources.alibaba.com/topic/306416/Google_Yahoo_Poses_Ad_Rate_Worries.htm

[499] "Is Google Too Powerful?" Rob Hof, April 9, 2007, *BusinessWeek*, http://www.businessweek.com/magazine/content/07_15/b4029001.htm

[500] http://precursorblog.com/node/339

[501] http://precursorblog.com/node/435

[502] http://precursorblog.com/node/402

[503] "Firefox and the Anxiety of Growing Pains," Noam Cohen, May 21, 2007, *New York Times*, http://www.nytimes.com/2007/05/21/technology/21link.html?_r=2&adxnnl=1&oref=slogin&adxnnlx=1179768947-//kApQQMtN3Ic89ss7aAJg&pagewanted=print

[504] http://investor.google.com/corporate/2004/ipo-founders-letter.html

[505] "Lieberman: YouTube Not Doing Enough to Remove Terrorist Content," Jack Date, May 19, 2008, *ABC News*, http://abcnews.go.com/TheLaw/LawPolitics/story?id=4889745&page=1

[506] http://precursorblog.com/node/769

[507] "Google's Chrome now silently auto-updates Flash Player," Gregg Keizer, April 1, 2010, *Computerworld*, http://www.computerworld.com/s/article/9174581/Google_s_Chrome_now_silently_auto_updates_Flash_Player

[508] http://precursorblog.com/content/googles-default-opt-all-appitalism-investigation-uncovers-massive-google-advertising-overcharges

[509] "Google chief prizes creativity," Lionel Barber and Maija Palmer, June 3, 2010, *Financial Times*, "Eric Schmidt veers between the defensive and the philosophical when describing how Google is coping with the constant eruption of controversy over its handling of privacy, copyright and other tricky public policy issues."Whack-a-mole is our life," says the youthful-looking 55-year-old chief executive of the world's most powerful and profitable internet company, based in Mountain View, California. "We are simply the symbol of the question of public and private behaviour, and special interests and narrow interests." http://www.ft.com/cms/s/2/bdec0ee8-6f4f-11df-9f43-00144feabdc0.html?ftcamp=rss#axzz1DTVQT8Ar

[510] "Google chief prizes creativity," Lionel Barber and Maija Palmer, June 3 2010, *Financial Times*, http://www.ft.com/cms/s/2/bdec0ee8-6f4f-11df-9f43-00144feabdc0,dwp_uuid=adc119e2-003b-11df-8626-00144feabdc0.html

[511] "Google Buzz's open approach leads to stalking threat," Charles Arthur, February 12, 2010, *Technology Blog, UK Guardian*, http://www.guardian.co.uk/technology/blog/2010/feb/12/google-buzz-stalker-privacy-problems

[512] "Google launches Buzz teen safety video," April 6th, 2010, *SafeKids.com*, http://www.safekids.com/tag/google-buzz/

[513] "Google's Eric Schmidt: You can trust us with your data," Shane Richmond, July 1, 2010, *UK Telegraph*, http://www.telegraph.co.uk/technology/google/7864223/Googles-Eric-Schmidt-You-can-trust-us-with-your-data.html

[514] http://www.precursorblog.com/content/google-ceo-the-one-sentence-manager-accountability-system

[515] "The Search Party: Google squares off with its Capitol Hill critics," Ken Auletta, January 14, 2008, *New Yorker*, http://www.newyorker.com/reporting/2008/01/14/080114fa_fact_auletta?printable=true#ixzz0xBIDXTjd

[516] "Google chief prizes creativity," Lionel Barber and Maija Palmer, June 3, 2010, *Financial Times*, http://www.ft.com/cms/s/2/bdec0ee8-6f4f-11df-9f43-00144feabdc0,dwp_uuid=adc119e2-003b-11df-8626-00144feabdc0.html

[517] "Google CEO talks of good, evil and monopoly fears," Eric Auchard, June 12, 2008, *Reuters*, http://www.reuters.com/article/idUSN1119985120080612

[518] "Google Trends Adds Another Way to Inaccurately Track Website Traffic," Adam Ostrow, June 20, 2008, *Mashable*, http://mashable.com/2008/06/20/google-trends-website-tracking/

[519] "Google to Offer a Tool To Measure Web Hits," Emily Steel, June 24, 2008, *Wall Street Journal*, http://online.wsj.com/article/SB121425232721997689.html?mod=2_1571_leftbox

[520] http://precursorblog.com/content/conflicted-google-crushing-its-third-party-accountability-comscore-payback

[521] "Microsoft buster Gary Reback goes after Google on books," Cecilia Kang, November 6, 2009, *Washington Post*, http://voices.washingtonpost.com/posttech/2009/11/gary_reback_the_microsoft_bust.html

[522] http://precursorblog.com/content/more-evidence-googles-not-neutral-and-seeks-be-supreme-arbiter-truth-internet

[523] http://en.wikipedia.org/wiki/Google_Book_Search_Settlement_Agreement

[524] "Google & the Future of Books," Robert Darnton, February 12, 2009, *The New York Review of Books*, http://www.nybooks.com/articles/archives/2009/feb/12/google-the-future-of-books/?page=1

[525] "Googleopoly," Grace Westcott, February 20, 2009, *Globe and Mail*, http://www.theglobeandmail.com/news/arts/books/article972380.ece

[526] "The Internet's Librarian," Andy Potts, March 5th, 2009 , *The Economist*, http://www.economist.com/science/tq/displaystory.cfm?story_id=13174399&fsrc=rss

[527] "Google patents search that tracks your mouse moves," Cade Metz, July 27, 2010, *The UK Register*, http://www.theregister.co.uk/2010/07/27/google_patents_mouse_movement_search_tweaks/

[528] "Google developing eavesdropping software," Faultline (Rethink Research Associates), September 3, 2006, *The UK Register*, http://www.theregister.co.uk/2006/09/03/google_eavesdropping_software/

[529] "The Search Party," Ken Auletta, January 14, 2008, *The New Yorker*, http://www.newyorker.com/reporting/2008/01/14/080114fa_fact_auletta?printable=true#ixzz0xBKcNu3t

[530] "The Brain at Google: How Google makes smart employees even smarter," Dr. David Rock, December 6, 2009, *Psychology Today*, http://www.psychologytoday.com/blog/your-brain-work/200912/the-brain-google

[531] "Google Street View accused of Congress 'snooping'," Maggie Shiels, July 9, 2010, *BBC News*, http://news.bbc.co.uk/2/hi/technology/8802741.stm

[532] "Google Seduces With Utility," David Carr, November 23, 2008, *New York Times*, http://www.nytimes.com/2008/11/24/business/media/24carr.html?_r=1

[533] "Top 5 moments from Eric Schmidt's talk in Abu Dhabi," Jon Fortt, March 11, 2010, *Fortune*, http://tech.fortune.cnn.com/2010/03/11/top-five-moments-from-eric-schmidts-talk-in-abu-dhabi/

[534] "Google's Business Model: YOU Are the Product," Mike Elgan, February 5, 2009, *Internet.com*, http://itmanagement.earthweb.com/article.php/3801006/Googles-Business-Model-YOU-Are-the-Product.htm

[535] "Writer finds public wary of Google," Devon Haynie, October 8, 2010, *The Journal Gazette*, http://www.journalgazette.net/article/20101008/LOCAL04/310089940/1002/LOCAL

[536] "100 Best Companies to Work For," February 2, 2009, *Fortune*, http://money.cnn.com/magazines/fortune/bestcompanies/2009/snapshots/4.html

[537] "Five Silicon Valley companies fought release of employment data, and won," Mike Swift, February 14, 2010, *San Jose Mercury News*, http://www.mercurynews.com/news/ci_14382477?nclick_check=1

[538] "Google at 12: A company navigating the conflicts that come with age," Mike Swift, September 26, 2010, *SiliconValley.com*, http://www.peakpositions.com/seonews/google-at-twelve.htm

[539] (Vise & Malseed, 2005), Appendix II

[540] "Google at 12: A company navigating the conflicts that come with age," Mike Swift, September 26, 2010, *SiliconValley.com*, http://www.peakpositions.com/seonews/google-at-twelve.htm

[541] "The Google Culture," Google corporate website, http://www.google.com/corporate/culture.html

[542] "Google's Computing Power Refines Translation Tool," Miguel Helft, March 8, 2010, *New York Times*, http://www.nytimes.com/2010/03/09/technology/09translate.html?_r=1

[543] The author thanks the individual who coined the term "goobris" and wishes to remain anonymous.

[544] "The Value of Vision Michael Saylor wants MicroStrategy to last as long as the Roman Empire and be as important as GE. Hubris? Sure, but his ambition infects employees and fires up customers," Daniel Roth, May 24, 1999, *Fortune*, http://money.cnn.com/magazines/fortune/fortune_archive/1999/05/24/260289/index.htm

[545] "The Value of Vision," Daniel Roth, May 24, 1999, *Fortune* magazine, http://money.cnn.com/magazines/fortune/fortune_archive/1999/05/24/260289/index.htm

[546] (Battelle, 2005) p. 55

[547] "Michael J. Saylor," http://en.wikipedia.org/wiki/Michael_J._Saylor

[548] "Eric Schmidt: Welcome to "Age of Augmented Humanity"," Liz Gannes September 7, 2010, *GigaOM*, http://gigaom.com/2010/09/07/eric-schmidt-welcome-to-the-age-of-augmented-humanity/

[549] "Google's goal: to organise your daily life," Caroline Daniel and Maija Palmer, May 22, 2007, *Financial Times*, http://www.ft.com/cms/s/2/c3e49548-088e-11dc-b11e-000b5df10621.html

[550] "Sergey Brin: "We Want Google To Be The Third Half Of Your Brain." Jay Yarow, September 8, 2010, *Business Insider*, http://www.businessinsider.com/sergey-brin-we-want-google-to-be-the-third-half-of-your-brain-2010-9

[551] "Six Delusions of Google's Arrogant Leaders," Ryan Tate, March 12, 2010, *Gawker.com*, http://gawker.com/5491756/six-delusions-of-googles-arrogant-leaders

[552] "What we're driving at," Sebastian Thrun, October 9, 2010, *The Official Google Blog*, http://googleblog.blogspot.com/2010/10/what-were-driving-at.html

[553] "Google Plans Alternative Inflation Index Using Web Data," Robin Harding, October 12, 2010, *Financial Times*, http://www.cnbc.com/id/39626164

[554] "Google CEO Schmidt: "People Aren't Ready for the Technology Revolution"," Marshall Kirkpatrick, August 4, 2010, *ReadWriteWeb*, http://www.readwriteweb.com/archives/google_ceo_schmidt_people_arent_ready_for_the_tech.php?utm_source=feedburner&utm_medium=feed&utm_campaign=Feed:+readwriteweb+%28ReadWriteWeb%29

[555] "The Search Party," Ken Auletta, January 14, 2008, *The New Yorker*, http://www.newyorker.com/reporting/2008/01/14/080114fa_fact_auletta?printable=true#ixzz0xBKcNu3t

[556] "The Search Party," Ken Auletta, January 14, 2008, *The New Yorker*, http://www.newyorker.com/reporting/2008/01/14/080114fa_fact_auletta?printable=true#ixzz0xBKcNu3t

[557] "Senkaku, Diaoyu and Google Maps," Yoree Koh, October 14, 2010, *Wall Street Journal*, http://blogs.wsj.com/japanrealtime/2010/10/14/senkaku-diaoyu-and-google-maps/?KEYWORDS=Google

[558] "How long will Google's magic last?" December 2, 2010, *Economist*, http://www.economist.com/node/17633138

[559] (Auletta, 2009) p. 137, "Like Microsoft in the late nineties, the Google leadership, "composed of ideological technologists," as [Elliot] Schrage put it in 2007, was slow to appreciate the political and the human dimensions of the technical decisions it made."

[560] (Stross, 2008) p.58, describes how Google got two local officials to sign confidentiality agreements as part of a deal to build a data center in Dalles, Oregon.

[561] Eric Schmidt, Chairman, *NewAmerica.net*, http://newamerica.net/user/181

[562] "HHS buys 'ObamaCare'," Ben Smith, December 17, 2010, *Politico.com*, Google often displays two sets of ads on search results pages. One set is displayed in a separate column on the right side of the page; these ads are clearly distinguished from organic search results. Another set of ads are displayed above and resemble organic search results in format; these ads are only distinguished by a low contrast violet background that may be difficult to discern under certain ambient light or viewing angle conditions. http://www.politico.com/blogs/bensmith/1210/HHS_buys_ObamaCare.html

[563] "2004 Founders' IPO Letter," From the S-1 Registration Statement "An Owner's Manual" for Google's Shareholders, *Google investor relations*, http://investor.google.com/corporate/2004/ipo-founders-letter.html

[564] "2004 Founders' IPO Letter," From the S-1 Registration Statement "An Owner's Manual" for Google's Shareholders, *Google investor relations*, http://investor.google.com/corporate/2004/ipo-founders-letter.html

[565] "The Anatomy of a Large-Scale Hypertextual Web Search Engine," Sergey Brin and Lawrence Page, 1998, http://infolab.stanford.edu/~backrub/google.html

[566] "2004 Founders' IPO Letter," From the S-1 Registration Statement "An Owner's Manual" for Google's Shareholders, *Google investor relations*; http://investor.google.com/corporate/2004/ipo-founders-letter.html

[567] "Al Gore's $100 Million Makeover," Ellen McGirt, July 1, 2007, *Fast Company*, http://www.fastcompany.com/magazine/117/features-gore.html

[568] (Vise & Malseed, 2005) p. 218

[569] (Vise & Malseed, 2005) p. 218

[570] "Al Gore Advised Google About 'Search Quality'," Noel Sheppard, October 15, 2009, *NewsBusters*, http://newsbusters.org/blogs/noel-sheppard/2009/10/15/al-gore-advised-google-about-its-search-quality

[571] "Google's givers go Democratic," Jim Hopkins, February 13, 2005, *USA Today*, http://www.usatoday.com/money/industries/technology/2005-02-13-google-give-usat_x.htm

[572] http://www.whitehouse.gov/the-press-office/president-obama-announces-members-science-and-technology-advisory-council

[573] "President-elect Obama meets with economic advisers, calls for "swift action" on the economy," Macon Phillips, November 7, 2008, *Change.gov*, http://change.gov/newsroom/entry/president_elect_obama_meets_with_economic_advisers_calls_for_swift_action_o/

[574] "Google Execs Pay $150,000 for Obama Bash," Owen Thomas, December 27, 2008, *ValleyWag.com*, http://valleywag.gawker.com/5119039/google-execs-pay-150000-for-obama-bash

[575] http://en.wikipedia.org/wiki/George_Lakoff

[576] George Lakoff, *Don't Think of an Elephant!: Know Your Values and Frame the Debate--The Essential Guide for Progressives* (White River Junction, VT: Chelsea Green Publishing, 2004) p. 94.

[577] http://www.youtube.com/watch?v=jNLP88aTg_8

[578] "Our philosophy," Google corporate website, No. 6 of "Ten things we know to be true." The complete text of No. 6 reads "You can make money without doing evil. Google is a business. The revenue we generate is derived from offering search technology to companies and from the sale of advertising displayed on our site and on other sites across the web. Hundreds of thousands of advertisers worldwide use AdWords to promote their products; hundreds of thousands of publishers take advantage of our AdSense program to deliver ads relevant to their site content. To ensure that we're ultimately serving all our users (whether they are advertisers or not), we have a set of guiding principles for our advertising programs and practices:
* We don't allow ads to be displayed on our results pages unless they are relevant where they are shown. And we firmly believe that ads can provide useful information if, and only if, they are relevant to what you wish to find – so it's possible that certain searches won't lead to any ads at all. * We believe that advertising can be effective without being flashy. We don't accept pop–up advertising, which interferes with your ability to see the content you've requested. We've found that text ads that are relevant to the person reading them draw much

higher clickthrough rates than ads appearing randomly. Any advertiser, whether small or large, can take advantage of this highly targeted medium. * Advertising on Google is always clearly identified as a "Sponsored Link," so it does not compromise the integrity of our search results. We never manipulate rankings to put our partners higher in our search results and no one can buy better PageRank. Our users trust our objectivity and no short-term gain could ever justify breaching that trust."
http://www.google.com/corporate/tenthings.html

[579] "Playboy Interview: Google Guys," David Sheff, September 2004, *Playboy Magazine*, http://www.google-watch.org/playboy.html

[580] "Philanthropy Google's Way: Not the Usual," Katie Hafner, September 14, 2006, *New York Times*,
http://www.nytimes.com/2006/09/14/technology/14google.html?_r=1

[581] "Google v the world," Lex column, December 29, 2010, *Financial Times*, The column's concluding paragraph reads: "Meanwhile the company can afford to experiment and disrupt freely, because it is largely in charge of providing access to information. The world has every reason to applaud Google, but few reasons to trust it. http://www.ft.com/cms/s/3/c9a01f52-1361-11e0-a367-00144feabdc0.html#axzz1AI16nrPU

[582] http://www.google.com/corporate/ux.html "7. Plan for today's and tomorrow's business. - Those Google products that make money strive to do so in a way that is helpful to users. To reach that lofty goal, designers work with product teams to ensure that business considerations integrate seamlessly with the goals of users. Teams work to make sure ads are relevant, useful, and clearly identifiable as ads."

[583] "Eric Schmidt: Google Mission Is to 'Change the World'," Betsy Schiffman, June 11, 2008, *Wired*, http://www.wired.com/epicenter/2008/06/live-blogging-e/

[584] Code of Conduct, http://investor.google.com/corporate/code-of-conduct.html#VIII

[585] "Growing Google searches for the right balance," Richard Waters, September 21 2007, *Financial Times*, http://www.ft.com/cms/s/0/80f23636-67da-11dc-8906-0000779fd2ac.html

[586] "Google Violates Its Own Don't Be Evil Motto," Intelligence Squared debate, November 18, 2008, http://intelligencesquaredus.org/index.php/past-debates/google-violates-its-dont-be-evil-motto/

[587] "Google's unhappy twelfth birthday," Tim Black, September 29, 2010, *SpikedOnline.com*, http://www.spiked-online.com/index.php/site/article/9711/

[588] "Google Shows Thin Skin, Pushes Back on Criticism," Liz Gannes, October 14, 2010, *GigaOM*, http://gigaom.com/2010/10/14/google-shows-thin-skin-pushes-back-on-criticism/

[589] "DOJ settles no-recruit claims against tech companies," Tom Krazit, September 24, 2010, *CNET News*, http://news.cnet.com/8301-30684_3-20017617-265.html

[590] "Did Google misuse non-compete agreements of DoubleClick employees?" Toni Bowers, April 14, 2008, *TechRepublic*, http://blogs.techrepublic.com.com/career/?p=295

[591] "Five Silicon Valley companies fought release of employment data, and won," Mike Swift, February 14, 2010, *San Jose Mercury News*, http://www.mercurynews.com/news/ci_14382477?nclick_check=1

[592] "Rosetta Stone Sues Google Over Trademarks in Searches," Cecilia Kang, July 11, 2009, *The Washington Post*, http://www.washingtonpost.com/wp-dyn/content/article/2009/07/10/AR2009071003526.html

[593] "FTC probe may force Apple/Google board members to part ways," Jacqui Cheng, May 5, 2009, *ARS Technica*, http://arstechnica.com/apple/news/2009/05/ftc-probe-could-force-applegoogle-board-members-to-part-ways.ars

[594] "Dr. Eric Schmidt Resigns from Apple's Board of Directors, August 3, 2009, *Apple press release*, http://www.apple.com/pr/library/2009/08/03bod.html

[595] "Google execs take off with landing privileges at Moffett Field," Verne Kopytoff, September 8, 2007, *San Francisco Chronicle*, http://www.sfgate.com/cgi-bin/article.cgi?file=/c/a/2007/09/08/BUSNS0G94.DTL

[596] "Google Founders' Ultimate Perk: A NASA Runway," Miguel Helft, September 13, 2007, *New York Times*, http://www.nytimes.com/2007/09/13/technology/13google.html?_r=2&oref=slogin

[597] (Vise and Malseed, 2005) Google negotiated prices based on the amount of square footage leased. Presumably, warehouse owners were unprepared for the power and cooling requirements of data centers using stacked PCs.

[598] (Stross, 2008)

[599] "The high cost of wooing Google," July 23, 2007, *BusinessWeek*, http://www.businessweek.com/magazine/content/07_30/b4043066.htm?chan=search

[600] "Were we Googled or Gouged?" Tommy Tomlinson, February 11, 2007, *Charlotte.com*, http://www2.nccommerce.com/eclipsfiles/16056.pdf

[601] Ibid. "Local and state officials -- including Lenoir Mayor David Barlow -- held secret talks with Google for more than a year."

[602] (Stross, 2008) p.59

[603] "The Business of Restoring Trust," L. Gordon Crovitz, January 30, 2011, *Wall Street Journal*, http://online.wsj.com/article/SB10001424052748703956604576110393691348706.html

[604] http://www.brainyquote.com/quotes/quotes/m/miltonfrie412624.html

[605] "Why Google won't turn off location customization," Chris Matyszczyk, October 31, 2010, *CNET News*, http://news.cnet.com/8301-17852_3-20021289-71.html

[606] http://www.brainyquote.com/quotes/quotes/m/miltonfrie412622.html

[607] "Comments of Google, Inc.," GN Docket No. 10-127, July 15, 2010, Federal Communications Commission, http://www.scribd.com/mobile/documents/34400479

[608] "Comments to California Public Utilities Commission," submitted by Google October 26, 2009, California Public Utilities Commission, Proceeding R08-12-009, "At Google, we believe that the smart grid is as much about defining new ways to generate and exchange useful information as it is about finding smarter ways to deliver and use energy." http://www.google.com/powermeter/about/cpuc.html

[609] http://www.google.com/intl/en-US/health/about/index.html

[610] "All-Access Pass," Karen Sommer Shalett, November 14, 2009, *Modern Luxury*, http://dc.modernluxury.com/style/all-access-pass

[611] "The Code Is the Law," Lawrence Lessig, April 9, 1999, *The Industry Standard*, http://www.lessig.org/content/standard/0,1902,4165,00.html

[612] http://creativecommons.org/

[613] "Creative Humbug," Péter Benjamin Tóth, June 24, 2005, *The INDICARE Project*, http://www.indicare.org/tiki-read_article.php?articleId=118

[614] "Web 2.0: It's worse than you think," Andrew Keen, February 14, 2006, *The Weekly Standard* Blog, http://www.weeklystandard.com/Content/Public/Articles/000/000/006/714fjczq.asp

[615] "Google's Earth," William Gibson, August 31, 2010, *New York Times*, http://www.nytimes.com/2010/09/01/opinion/01gibson.html?_r=1

[616] (Jarvis, 2009)

[617] "Eric Schmidt: Google Mission Is to 'Change the World'," Betsy Schiffman, June 11, 2008, *Wired*, http://www.wired.com/epicenter/2008/06/live-blogging-e/#ixzz11mLmwOOF

[618] "Come to Google "and change the world"," Marc Chacksfield, October 9, 2009, *TechRadar.com*, http://www.techradar.com/news/internet/come-to-google-and-change-the-world--641785?src=rss#ixzz11mMwBzEg

[619] http://investor.google.com/corporate/2004/ipo-founders-letter.html

[620] "Google's Schmidt: 'You don't change the world incrementally'," John Cook, July 16, 2009, *TechFlash.com*, http://www.techflash.com/seattle/2009/07/Googles_Schmidt_You_dont_change_the_world_incrementally_50968072.html

[621] "Schmidt on Rose on Search," John Battelle, June 6, 2005, *Searchblog.com*, http://battellemedia.com/archives/2005/06/schmidt_on_rose_on_search#ixzz16zHlUoXM

[622] "Schmidt: Google gets 'right up to the creepy line'," Sara Jerome, October 1, 2010, *The Hill's Technology Blog*, http://thehill.com/blogs/hillicon-valley/technology/122121-schmidt-google-gets-right-up-to-the-creepy-line

[623] "Google dubs Oracle suit 'attack on Java community'," Cade Metz, August 16, 2010, *UK Register*, http://www.theregister.co.uk/2010/08/16/google_oracle_android_lawsuit/

[624] "Google's Schmidt: The Device Is Not Magical, It's The Servers Behind Them," Tricia Duryee, September 28, 2010, *UK Guardian*, http://paidcontent.org/article/419-googles-schmidt-the-device-is-not-magical-its-the-servers-behind-them/

[625] *Don't Think of an Elephant!: Know Your Values and Frame the Debate--The Essential Guide for Progressives* (White River Junction, VT: Chelsea Green Publishing, 2004)

[626] "If Google Is the Inverse of Apple, Then is Eric Schmidt the Inverse of Steve Jobs?"
John Paczkowski, September 29, 2010, *Digital Daily*, http://digitaldaily.allthingsd.com/20100929/google-the-inverse-of-apple/

[627] "Schmidt: Google is the 'inverse' of Apple," Cade Metz, September 28, 2010, *UK Register*, http://www.theregister.co.uk/2010/09/28/schmidt_calls_google_the_inverse_of_a pple/

[628] "Android Apps More Open Than Users Know," Tony Bradley, September 30, 2010, *PCWorld*, http://www.pcworld.com/businesscenter/article/206644/android_apps_more_ope n_than_users_know.html

[629] "Cyberattack on Google Said to Hit Password System," John Markoff, April 19, 2010, *New York Times*, http://www.nytimes.com/2010/04/20/technology/20google.html?_r=3&ref=techn ology

[630] http://www.google.com/transparencyreport/

[631] http://www.google.com/ads/politicaltoolkit/

[632] "Google Goes to Washington With Own Brand of Lobbying," Kevin J. Delaney and Amy Schatz, July 20, 2007, *Wall Street Journal*, http://online.wsj.com/article/SB118489524982572543.html

[633] http://www.youtube.com/whitehouse

[634] "White House exempts YouTube from privacy rules," Chris Soghoian, January 22, 2009, *CNET News*, http://news.cnet.com/8301-13739_3-10147726-46.html

[635] "Is the White House changing its YouTube tune?"Chris Soghoian, March 2, 2009, *CNET News*, http://news.cnet.com/8301-13739_3-10184578-46.html

[636] "On YouTube, Lawmakers Have Sites to Behold," Kim Hart, January 13, 2009, *Washington Post*, http://www.washingtonpost.com/wp-dyn/content/article/2009/01/12/AR2009011203049.html

[637] "Congress comes to YouTube," Steve Grove, January 12, 2009, *Google Public Policy Blog*, http://googlepublicpolicy.blogspot.com/2009/01/congress-comes-to-youtube.html

[638] "Google's Top Policy Executive to Join Obama Administration," Miguel Helft, May 29, 2009, *New York Times*, http://bits.blogs.nytimes.com/2009/05/29/googles-top-policy-exec-to-join-obama-administration/

639 "Consumer Groups to Obama: Google Lobbyist's Appointment to Technology Post Raises Ethics Rules Questions for White House," June 3, 2009, *Center for Digital Democracy*, http://www.democraticmedia.org/node/404

640 "US Deputy CTO gets reprimand for Google lobbying contacts," Nate Anderson, May 2010, *ARS Technica*, http://arstechnica.com/tech-policy/news/2010/05/us-deputy-cto-reprimanded-for-google-lobbying-contacts.ars

641 "White House Reprimands Ex-Googler After Consumer Watchdog FOIA Request; Group Says Deputy Chief Technology Officer Andrew McLaughlin Should Resign," Consumer Watchdog press release, May 18, 2010, *PRNewswire.com*, http://www.prnewswire.com/news-releases/white-house-reprimands-ex-googler-after-consumer-watchdog-foia-request-group-says-deputy-chief-technology-officer-andrew-mclaughlin-should-resign-94194679.html

642 "HHS is Paying Google with Taxpayer Money to Alter 'Obamacare' Search Results (Updated)," Jeffrey H. Anderson, January 3, 2011, *The Weekly Standard blog*, http://www.weeklystandard.com/blogs/hhs-paying-google-taxpayer-money-alter-obamacare-search-results_525959.html

643 "Google Grants Turns 5," Google Grants Team, April 2, 2008, *Google Grants Blog*, http://googlegrants.blogspot.com/2008/04/google-grants-turns-5.html

644 http://www.movements.org/pages/about/

645 "Jared Cohen starts Google Ideas," Seth Weintraub, September 7, 2010, *Fortune*, http://tech.fortune.cnn.com/2010/09/07/jared-cohen-starts-google-ideas/?utm_source=twitterfeed&utm_medium=twitter

646 "Eric Schmidt Warns Politicians That Elections Will Forever Change," Barry Schwartz, October 4, 2006, *Search Engine Watch*, http://blog.searchenginewatch.com/061004-091035

647 "Politicians yet to realise impact of internet, warns Google chief," Jean Eaglesham, October 4 2006, *Financial Times*, http://www.ft.com/cms/s/0/06adcbce-5345-11db-99c5-0000779e2340.html

648 "Google: political system "shocking," we want to change the game," Matthew Lasar, October 5, 2010, *ARS Technica*, http://arstechnica.com/telecom/news/2010/10/does-google-still-qualify-for-sainthood.ars?old=mobile

649 http://www.2600.com/googleblacklist/

650 Adams has since taken a job at Facebook. "Google Social Researcher Jumps Ship for Facebook," Liz Gannes, December 20, 2010, *All Things Digital*, http://networkeffect.allthingsd.com/20101220/google-social-researcher-jumps-ship-for-facebook/

651 "The Real Life Social Network Slideshow," Paul Adams, July 16, 2010, *Dan London*, http://www.dan-london.com/2010/the-real-life-social-network-slideshow/

652 "Facebook Groups Launch To Bridge Online, Real-Life Gap," Craig Kanalley, October 6, 2010, *The Huffington Post*, http://www.huffingtonpost.com/2010/10/06/facebook-groups-launch-to_n_752918.html?ref=twitter

[653] "The Real Life Social Network Slideshow," Slide 170, Paul Adams, July 16, 2010, *Dan London*, http://www.dan-london.com/2010/the-real-life-social-network-slideshow/

[654] "Internet, Google will Sway 2008 Elections: Company Executive," page 4, March 16, 2007, *Communications Daily*, http://www.warren-news.com/

[655] http://precursorblog.com/node/326

[656] "Google: political system "shocking," we want to change the game," Matthew Lasar, October 5, 2010, *ARS Technica*, http://arstechnica.com/telecom/news/2010/10/does-google-still-qualify-for-sainthood.ars?old=mobile

[657] http://www.youtube.com/watch?v=cl2uctN7doA

[658] "Sen. Susan Collins' Web Ads Run Up Against Google, MoveOn.org," William LaJeunesse and Ron Ralston, October 12, 2007, *Fox News*, http://www.foxnews.com/story/0,2933,301267,00.html

[659] "Google is latest weapon against Republicans," Sarah Lai Stirland, October 18, 2010, *Politico.com*, http://www.politico.com/news/stories/1010/43767.html

[660] "A different way to make a big difference in 2010," Chris Bowers, October 8, 2010, *Daily Kos*, http://www.dailykos.com/story/2010/10/8/1202/96710

[661] "Google Intensity Map Tracks Political Prognostications," E.B. Boyd, October 29, 2010, *Fast Company*, http://www.fastcompany.com/1698876/googles-creates-intensity-map-to-track-political-prognostications?partner=rss&utm_source=feedburner&utm_medium=feed&utm_campaign=Feed%3A+fastcompany%2Fheadlines+%28Fast+Company+Headlines%29&utm_content=Google+Reader

[662]

http://www.pewcenteronthestates.org/uploadedFiles/Voting_Information_Project_brief.pdf

[663] "Google polling app misleads voters," Tony Romm, November 2, 2010, *Politico.com*, http://www.politico.com/news/stories/1110/44571.html

[664] Brave New Google," Nicholas Carr, August 14, 2010, *Rough Type Blog*, http://www.roughtype.com/archives/2010/08/brave_new_googl.php

[665] http://yalepress.yale.edu/book.asp?isbn=9780300122237

[666] Richard H. Thaler and Cass R. Sunstein, *Nudge: Improving Decisions About Health, Wealth, and Happiness* (Connecticut: Yale University Press, 2008) p. 90. "While working on this book, Thaler sent an email to his economist friend Hal Varian, who is affiliated with Google." http://books.google.com/books?id=dSJQn8egXvUC&printsec=frontcover&dq=nudge&hl=en&ei=bH63TNyDPMH58Ab_mdCeCQ&sa=X&oi=book_result&ct=result&resnum=1&ved=0CCoQ6AEwAA#v=onepage&q&f=false

[667] "Finding common ground on an open Internet," Eric Schmidt, Chairman and CEO of Google, and Lowell McAdam, President and CEO of Verizon Wireless, October 21, 2009, *Google Public Policy Blog*,

http://googlepublicpolicy.blogspot.com/2009/10/finding-common-ground-on-open-internet.html

[668] "FCC announces plan to protect access to an open Internet," Vint Cerf, Vice President and Chief Internet Evangelist, September 21, 2009, *Google Public Policy Blog*, http://googlepublicpolicy.blogspot.com/2009/09/fcc-announces-plan-to-protect-access-to.html

[669] "Testimony of Mr. Vinton G. Cerf, Vice President & Chief Internet Evangelist, Google, Inc.," June 14, 2006, *United States Senate Committee on the Judiciary*, http://judiciary.senate.gov/hearings/testimony.cfm?id=1937&wit_id=5416

[670] "Embracing disruption," Rian Liebenberg, Engineering Director, March 15, 2010, *Google European Public Policy Blog*, http://googlepolicyeurope.blogspot.com/2010/03/embracing-disruption.html

[671] "FSF responds to Oracle v. Google and the threat of software patents," Brett Smith September 8, 2010, Free Software Foundation press release, http://www.fsf.org/news/oracle-v-google

[672] "The Free Software Definition," *GNU Operating System*, http://www.gnu.org/philosophy/free-sw.html

[673] "Free Software, Free Society: Selected Essays of Richard M. Stallman, GNU Press, 2002, http://www.gnu.org/philosophy/fsfs/rms-essays.pdf

[674] "Free Software, Free Society: Selected Essays of Richard M. Stallman, GNU Press, 2002, p. 128, http://www.gnu.org/philosophy/fsfs/rms-essays.pdf

[675] "Free Software, Free Society: Selected Essays of Richard M. Stallman, GNU Press, 2002, p. 133, http://www.gnu.org/philosophy/fsfs/rms-essays.pdf

[676] "Free Software, Free Society: Selected Essays of Richard M. Stallman, GNU Press, 2002, pp. 133-4, http://www.gnu.org/philosophy/fsfs/rms-essays.pdf

[677] "Free Software, Free Society: Selected Essays of Richard M. Stallman, GNU Press, 2002, p. 134, http://www.gnu.org/philosophy/fsfs/rms-essays.pdf

[678] "The dotCommunist Manifesto," Eben Moglen, January 2003, p. 3, http://emoglen.law.columbia.edu/publications/dcm.pdf

[679] "The dotCommunist Manifesto," Eben Moglen, January 2003, p. 6, http://emoglen.law.columbia.edu/publications/dcm.pdf

[680] "The dotCommunist Manifesto," Eben Moglen, January 2003, p. 7, http://emoglen.law.columbia.edu/publications/dcm.pdf

[681] The Future of Ideas: the Fate of the Commons in the Connected World (2001); Free Culture: the Nature and Future of Creativity (2004); and Code Version 2.0 (2006) an update of Lessig's first book, Code and Other Laws of Cyberspace (1999).

[682] http://www.youtube.com/watch?v=JL1Z7_IMFs4

[683] The Future of Ideas – the Fate of the Commons in a Connected World, P. 85, Lawrence, Lessig, http://thefutureofideas.s3.amazonaws.com/lessig_FOI.pdf

[684] http://www.kith-kin.co.uk/shop/free-culture/

[685] "What Is Web 2.0: Design Patterns and Business Models for the Next Generation of Software," Tim O'Reilly, September 30, 2005, *O'Reilly Media*, http://oreilly.com/web2/archive/what-is-web-20.html

[686] "The Fuss About Gmail and Privacy: Nine Reasons Why It's Bogus," Tim O'Reilly, April 16, 2004, http://www.oreillynet.com/pub/wlg/4707

[687] "Watch our new Times Square video: Don't Be Evil?" Jamie Court, August 30, 2010, *Inside Google*, http://insidegoogle.com/2010/08/do-not-track-me/

[688] "Tim O'Reilly sticks up for Google's Eric Schmidt after icecream truck driver ad," Sara Jerome, September 7, 2010, *The Hill*, http://thehill.com/blogs/hillicon-valley/technology/117477-tim-oreilly-sticks-up-for-googles-eric-schmidt-after-icecream-truck-driver-ad

[689] http://en.wikipedia.org/wiki/Burning_Man

[690] http://www.burningman.com/whatisburningman/about_burningman/principles.html

[691] "Oodles of doodles," Dennis Hwang, June 8, 2004, *Official Google Blog*, http://googleblog.blogspot.com/2004/06/oodles-of-doodles.html

[692] http://www.google.com/logos/logos98-3.html

[693] Carl Shapiro and Hal R. Varian, *Information Rules: a Strategic Guide to the Network Economy*, (Boston: Harvard Business Press, 1998)

[694] Yochai Benkler, *The Wealth of Networks: How Social Production Transforms Markets and Freedom*, (Connecticut: Yale University Press, 2006)

[695] Yochai Benkler, *The Wealth of Networks: How Social Production Transforms Markets and Freedom*, (Connecticut: Yale University Press, 2006), p. 23

[696] Yochai Benkler, *The Wealth of Networks: How Social Production Transforms Markets and Freedom*, (Connecticut: Yale University Press, 2006), p. 468

[697] Yochai Benkler, *The Wealth of Networks: How Social Production Transforms Markets and Freedom*, (Connecticut: Yale University Press, 2006), p. 473

[698] Chris Anderson, *The Long Tail: Why the Future of Business is Selling Less of More*, (New York: Hyperion, 2006)

[699] Chris Anderson, *Free: the Future of a Radical Price*, (New York: Hyperion, 2009)

[700] "Chris Anderson on Free," interview with Alistair Croll, May 5, 2009, *Human 2.0*, http://www.human20.com/chris-anderson-on-free/

[701] http://googleopoly.net/Googleopoly_IV_The_Googleopsony_Case.pdf

[702] "Race Is On to 'Fingerprint' Phones, PCs," Julia Angwin and Jennifer Valentino-Devries, November 30, 2010, *Wall Street Journal*, http://online.wsj.com/article/SB10001424052748704679204575646704100959546.html

[703] "Supreme Court Rules in MGM v. Grokster," June 27, 2005, *United States Copyright Office*, http://www.copyright.gov/docs/mgm/index.html

[704] "Marissa Mayer's Next Big Thing: "Contextual Discovery" — Google Results Without Search," MG Siegler, December 8, 2010, *TechCrunch*, http://techcrunch.com/2010/12/08/googles-next-big-thing/

[705] ""Do Not Track" Explained," Arvind Narayanan, September 20, 2010, *33 Bits of Entropy*, http://33bits.org/2010/09/20/do-not-track-explained

[706] http://precursorblog.com/content/my-house-internet-privacy-testimony-a-consumer-driven-technologycompetition-neutral-privacy-framework

[707] Google's Company Overview, http://www.google.com/intl/en/corporate/

[708] And Sergey Brin once told Technology Review's editor in chief, "The perfect search engine would be like the mind of God," What's Next for Google, Charles H. Ferguson, January 2005, *Technology Review*, http://signallake.com/innovation/FergusonWhatsNextForGoogle010105.pdf

[709] "When Google Runs Your Life" Quentin Hardy, December 28, 2009, *Forbes*, http://www.forbes.com/forbes/2009/1228/technology-google-apps-gmail-bing.html

[710] "Google, Caffeine and the Future of Search," Matt Warman, June 17, 2010, *The Telegraph*, http://www.telegraph.co.uk/technology/google/7833590/Google-Caffeine-and-the-future-of-search.html

[711] "Marissa Mayer's Next Big Thing: 'Contextual Discovery' – Google Results without Search," MG Seigler, December 8, 2010, *Techcrunch*, http://techcrunch.com/2010/12/08/googles-next-big-thing/

[712] Google.com, Google's 2004 IPO Founders Letter, http://investor.google.com/corporate/2004/ipo-founders-letter.html

[713] "The Google Hive Mind," Danny Sullivan, September 27, 2008, *Search Engine Land*, http://searchengineland.com/the-google-hive-mind-14832

[714] ClaytonChristensen.com, http://www.claytonchristensen.com/disruptive_innovation.html

[715] "Zero Day Threat: The Shocking Truth about How Banks and Credit Bureaus Help Cyber Crooks Steal Your Money and Identity," Byron Acohido and Jon Swartz, (New York: Union Square Press, 2008), http://zerodaythreat.com/

[716] "Eric Schmidt expects another 10 years at Google," Georgina Prodhan, January 25, 2011, *Reuters*, http://www.reuters.com/article/2011/01/25/us-google-schmidt-idUSTRE70O2TE20110125

[717] George Orwell, *Nineteen Eighty-Four*, (London: Secker and Warburg, 1949)

[718] George Lakoff, *The Political Mind: A Cognitive Scientist's Guide to Your Brain and Its Politics*, (New York: Penguin, 2009)

[719] George Orwell, *Animal Farm*, (London: Secker and Warburg, 1945)

[720] "7 Creepy Faux Pas of Google CEO Eric Schmidt," Austin Carr, October 6, 2010, *Fast Company*, http://www.fastcompany.com/1693384/google-ceo-eric-schmidt-gaffes-creepy-privacy-faux-pas

[721] "7 Creepy Faux Pas of Google CEO Eric Schmidt," Austin Carr, October 6, 2010, *Fast Company*, http://www.fastcompany.com/1693384/google-ceo-eric-schmidt-gaffes-creepy-privacy-faux-pas

[722] "7 Creepy Faux Pas of Google CEO Eric Schmidt," Austin Carr, October 6, 2010, *Fast Company*, http://www.fastcompany.com/1693384/google-ceo-eric-schmidt-gaffes-creepy-privacy-faux-pas

[723] "Google CEO: Change Names to Avoid Social Networking Past," Brian Heater, August 18, 2010, *PC Magazine*,
http://www.pcmag.com/article2/0,2817,2367961,00.asp
[724] "Google: political system "shocking," we want to change the game," Matthew Lasar, October 6, 2010, *ARS Technica*,
http://arstechnica.com/telecom/news/2010/10/does-google-still-qualify-for-sainthood.ars?old=mobile
[725] "Marissa Mayer's Next big Thing: 'Contextual Discovery' Google Results without Search," MG Seigler, December 8, 2010, *Techcrunch*,
http://techcrunch.com/2010/12/08/googles-next-big-thing/
[726] "Google's Priority Mailbox and the Future of the Web," Stacey Higginbotham, January 12, 2011, *GigaOm.com*, http://gigaom.com/collaboration/googles-priority-mailbox-and-the-future-of-the-web/

Index